Abortion Bibliography

for 1977

Abortion Bibliography

for 1977

Compiled by

Mary K. Floyd

The Whitston Publishing Company
Troy, New York
1979

PREFACE

Abortion Bibliography for 1977 is the seventh annual
list of books and articles surrounding the subject of abortion
in the preceeding year. It appears serially each fall as a contribution toward documenting in one place as comprehensively as
possible the literature of one of our central social issues. It is
an attempt at a comprehensive world bibliography.

Searches in compiling this material have covered the following sources: *Applied Science and Technology Index; Bibliogra-
phic Index; Biological Abstracts; British Books in Print; British
Humanities Index; Business Periodicals Index; Canadian Periodi-
cal Index; Catholic Periodicals and Literature Index; Cumulative
Book Index; Current Index to Journals in Education; Education
Index; Guide to Social Science and Religion in Periodical Litera-
ture; Hospital Literature Index; Human Resources Abstracts;
Humanities Index; Index to Legal Periodicals; Index Medicus;
Index to Periodical Articles Related to Law; International Nurs-
ing Index; Library of Congress Catalog: Books: Subjects; The
New York Times Index; Nursing Literature Index; Nursing
Management and Allied Health Literature; Philosophers Index;
Psychological Abstracts; Public Affairs Information Service;
Readers Guide to Periodical Literature; Social Sciences Index;
Sociological Abstracts; Subject Guide to Books in Print; U.S.
Superintendent of Documents: Monthly Catalog of U.S. Govern-
ment Publications; Whitaker's Cumulative Book Index.*

The bibliography is divided into two sections: a title section
in alphabetical order; and a subject section. Thus, if the research-
er does not wish to observe the subject heads of the compiler,
he can use the title section exclusively. The 234 subject heads
have been allowed to issue from the nature of the material

indexed rather than being imposed from Library of Congress subject heads of other standard lists.

Countries are listed alphabetically under subjects: "Abortion: Africa," etc.; with states listed alphabetically under "Abortion: United States:" Arkansas, California, etc.; drugs are listed under the specific drug involved; entries evolving from Biological, Psychological or Sociological Abstracts are so indicated with abstract number cited; and all abstracts of news stories appearing in The New York Times Index include story length indicators: (L) long, (M) medium and (S) short. Editorials, editorial page columns and reviews will not include this indicator. In addition, each Times entry concludes with date, page, column, (e.g., May 1, 1:8 means story was published on May 1, page 1, column 8). Sunday sections, other than the main news section, are identified by Roman numerals following the date (e.g., May 6, IV, 3:4 means the numeral IV indicates the News of the Week in Review section).

The Book section has been expanded to include Government Publications and Monographs.

The Subject Heading Index has been expanded to include page numbers.

Mary K. Floyd
Troy, New York

LIST OF PERIODICALS

AORN Journal. Association of Operating Room Nurses, Inc.
Acta Anaesthesiologica Belgica
Acta Biologica et Medica Germanica
Acta Europaea Fertilitatis
Acta Medica Scandinavica
Acta Obstetrica y Ginecologica Hispana-Lusitana
Acta Obstetrica et Gynaecologica Japonica
Acta Obstetricia et Gynecologica Scandinavica
Acta Obstetricia et Gynecologica Scandinavica. Supplement
Acta Sociologica
Acta Veterinaria Scandinavica
Advances in Prostaglandin and Thromboxane Research
Akron Law Review
Akusherstvo i Ginekologiia (Moscow)
Akusherstvo i Ginekologiia (Sofia)
America
American Academy of Religion Journal
American Heart Journal
American Journal of Comparative Law
American Journal of Diseases of Children
American Journal of Nursing
American Journal of Obstetrics and Gynecology
American Journal of Orthopsychiatry
American Journal of Psychotherapy
American Journal of Public Health
Analysis
Anglican Theological Review
The Anglo-American Law Review
Annales de Biologie Animale Biochimie Biophysique
Annales Chirurgiae et Gynaecologiae Fenniae
Annales de Genetique

Annales de Recherches Veterinares
Annali di Ostetricia, Ginecologia, Medicina Perinatale
Annali Sclavo
Annals of Clinical Research
Archiv fur Gynaekologie
Archives d'Anatomie et de Cytologie Pathologique
Archives of Sexual Behavior
Arizona State Law Review
Arkansas Law Review
Australasian Nurses Journal
Australian Veterinary Journal

Bangladesh Medical Research Council Bulletin
Berliner und Munchener Tierarztliche Wochenschrift
Biology of the Neonate
Biology of Reproduction
Bratislauske Lekarske Listy
Brigham Young University Law Review
British Journal of Cancer
British Journal of Criminology
British Journal of Obstetrics and Gynaecology
British Medical Journal
British Veterinary Journal
Bulletin de l'Association des Anatomistes (Nancy)

C.I.C.I.A.M.S. Nouvelles; Bulletin d'Information du Comite
    International Catholique des Infirmieres et Assistantes Medico-
    Sociales
Canadian Medical Association Journal
Canadian Nurse
Canadian Psychiatric Association Journal
Canadian Veterinary Journal
Catholic Digest
Catholic Lawyer
Catholic Mind
Central States Speech Journal
Ceskoslovenska Gynekologie
Ceskoslovenska Pediatrie
Chatelaine
Chelsea Journal

East African Medical Journal
Economist
Emory Law Journal
Encounter (Christian Theological Seminary)
Ethics
European Journal of Intensive Care
Experientia

Faith for the Family
Family Planning Perspectives
Federal Register
Fel'dsker i Akusherka
Fertility and Sterility
Fortschritte du Medizin
The Forum
Fracastoro

Geburtshilfe und Frauenheilkunde
Genetika
Ginecologia y Obstetricia de Mexico
Ginekologia Polaska
Giornale Italiano di Psicologia
Good Housekeeping
Guardian
Gynaekologische Rundschau

Haemostasis
Harvard Theological Review
Hastings Center Report
Hastings Law Journal
Health and Social Work
Health Education Monographs
Health Journal
Hospital Law
Hospital Progress
Hospitals; Journal of the American Hospital Association
Human Genetics
The Humanist

Indian Journal of Medical Research
Infirmière Canadienne
L'Infirmiere Francais
International Journal for Vitamin and Nutrition Research
International Journal of Bio-Medical Computing
International Journal of Gynaecology and Obstetrics
International Surgery
Irish Medical Journal
Israel Annals of Psychiatry and Related Disciplines
Israel Journal of Medical Sciences

JAMA; Journal of the American Medical Association
JOGN; Journal of Obstetric, Gynecologic and Neonatal Nursing
Japanese Journal for Midwives
Japanese Journal of Human Genetics
Journal of the American Osteopathic Association
Journal of the American Veterinary Medical Association
Journal of the Arkansas Medical Society
Journal of Biosocial Science
Journal of Clinical Endocrinology and Metabolism
Journal of Comparative Pathology
Journal of Consulting and Clinical Psychology
Journal of Criminal Law and Criminology
Journal of Cross-Cultural Psychology
Journal of Endocrinology
Journal of Family Law
Journal du Gynecologie, Obstetrique et Biologie de la Reproduction
Journal of Health Politics, Policy and Law
Journal of Hygiene
Journal of the Indian Medical Association
Journal of Infectious Diseases
Journal of International Medical Research
Journal of the Kansas Medical Society
Journal of Legal Medicine
Journal of Marriage and Family Counceling
Journal of Medical Entomology
Journal of Medical Ethics
Journal of Medical Genetics
Journal of the Medical Society of New Jersey
Journal of Occupational Medicine

Journal of Pediatric Psychology
Journal of Philosophy
Journal of Psychiatric Nursing and Mental Health Services
The Journal of Religious Ethics
Journal of Reproduction and Fertility
Journal of Reproductive Medicine
Journal of the Royal College of General Practitioners
Journal of School Health
The Journal of Sex Research
Journal of the South Carolina Medical Association
Journal of the Tennessee Medical Association
Journal of Urology
Judaism
Jugoslovenska Ginekologiya i Opstetricija

Kansas Law Review
Korean Central Journal of Medicine
Korean Nurse
Krankenpflege

Labour Research Bulletin
Lakartidningen
Lancet
Last Post
Linacre Quarterly
Listener
Louisiana Law Review

Maclean's
Marketing
Maternal-Child Nursing Journal
Medical Care
Medical Journal of Australia
Medical Letter on Drugs and Therapeutics
Medical Research
Medical Times
Medico-Legal Bulletin
Meditsinskaia Sestra
Medizinische Monatsschrift

Medizinische Welt
Midwife, Health Visitor and Community Nurse
Mikrobiyoloji Bulteni
Minerva Ginecologia
Minnesota Medicine
Missouri Law Review
Modern Healthcare, Short-Term Care Edition
Modern Veterinary Practice
Montana Law Review
Moody Monthly
Mother Jones
Ms Magazine

National Catholic Reporter
National Journal
National Review
Native People
Nederlands Tijdschrift voor Geneeskunde
Neurologia, Neurocirugia, Psiquratria
New England Journal of Medicine
New Humanist
New Scholasticism
New Society
New Statesman
New York Law School Law Review
New York State Journal of Medicine
The New York Times
New Zealand Psychologist
New Zealand Veterinary Journal
Newsweek
Nigerian Nurse
North Carolina Medical Journal
Northwestern University Law Review
Nouvelle Presse Medicale
Nursing Forum (Auckland)
The Nursing Journal of Singapore
Nursing Mirror and Midwives' Journal
Nursing Research
Nursing Times

Observer
Obstetrics and Gynecology
Occupational Health (London)
Oeffentliche Gesundheitswesen
Ohio Northern University Law Review
Operation Research
Origins
Orvosi Hetilap
Osgoode Hall Law Journal
L'Osservatore Romano
Osterreichische Krankenpflegezeitschrift
Our Sunday Visitor
Our Sunday Visitor Magazine

Pediatriia Akusherstvo i Ginekologiia
Perkins School of Theology Journal
Personalist
Perspectives in Nephrology and Hypertension
Philosophy and Public Affairs
Philosophy Research Archives
Phylon
Polski Tygodnik Lekarski
The Pope Speaks
Population and Development Review
Population Review
Population Studies
Postgraduate Medical Journal
Practitioner
Praxis
Proceedings of the American Catholic Philosophical Association
Proceedings—Annual Meeting of the United States Animal Health
    Association
Proceedings of the Royal Society of London; B: Biological
    Sciences
Prostaglandins
Psychiatric Nursing
Psychiatry
Psychological Reports
Psychology of Women Quarterly
Psychology Today
Psychotherapy and Medical Psychology

Public Opinion Quarterly

Quill and Quire

RN; National Magazine for Nurses
Reproduccion
Review of Religious Research
Revista Chilena de Obstetricia y Ginecologia
Revista Enfermagem em Novas Dimensoes
Revista da Escola de Enfermagen da Universidade de Sao Paulo
Risk
Roentgenblaetter

St. John's Law Review
Sairaanhoitaja
Saskatchewan Law Review
School Counselor
Schweizer Archiv fur Tierheilkunde
Schweizerische Medizinische Wochenschrift
Scientia Sinica
Scientific American
Semaine des Hopitaux de Paris
Sign
Singapore Medical Journal
Social Behavior and Personality
Social Psychiatry
Social Science and Medicine
Social Science Quarterly
Social Studies
Social Theory and Practice
Social Work
Socialist Revolution
Sociological Review: Monographs
South African Medical Journal
Southern Medical Journal
Sovetskae Zdravookhranenie
Srpski Arhiv za Celokupno Lekarstvo
Stimezo-Research
Studies in Family Planning

Supervisor Nurse
Sygeplejersken

Teratology; Journal of Abnormal Development
Texas Tech Law Review
Thai Journal of Nursing
Theology Today
Therapeutische Umschaw
Tidsskrift for den Norske Laegeforening
Time
Times
Transactions of the Pacific Coast Obstetrical and Gynecological
    Society
Transfusion
Trial
Tropical Animal Health and Production
Tsitologiia i Genetika

Ugeskrift for Laeger
University of British Columbia Law Review
University of Detroit Journal of Urban Law
University of Florida Law Review
U.S. News and World Report

Veterinariia
Veterinarno-Meditsinski Nauki
Veterinary Record
Viata Medicala; Revista de Informore Profesionala si Stüntifica
    a Codrelor Medii Sanitare
Victorian Studies
Virus (Tokyo)
Voprosy Okhrany Materinstva i Detstva

Washburn Law Journal
West Indian Medical Journal
Wiadomosci Lekarskie
Wiener Medizinische Wochenschrift
World of Irish Nursing

World Medical Journal
Worldview

Zdravookhranenie Rossiiskoi Federatsii
Zeitschrift fur Geburtschilfe und Perinatologie
Zeitschrift fur Parasitenkunde
Zeitschrift fuer Tierzuechtung und Zuechtungsbiologie
Zentralblatt fur Bakteriologie Parasitenkunde, Infektionskrank-
    heiten und Hygiene; Erste Abteilung: Originale, Reihe B: Hy-
    giene, Praeventive Medizin
Zentralblatt fur Gynaekologie

SUBJECT HEADING INDEX

TABLE OF CONTENTS

BOOKS, GOVERNMENT PUBLICATIONS, AND MONOGRAPHS

Archiprete, Kaye, et al. THE ABORTION BUSINESS: A Report on Free-Standing Abortion Clinics. Cambridge, Massachusetts: Women's Research Action Project, 1975.

Atkinson, ed. ABORTION RECONSIDERED: Methodist Statement and its Background. Epworth Press, 1977.

Blandau, R. J., ed. AGING GAMETES. Basel, Karger, 1975.

Brown, Harold O. DEATH BEFORE BIRTH Nelson, 1977.

Canada. COMMITTEE ON THE OPERATION OF THE ABORTION LAW. Report. Ottawa: Printing and publishing, Supply and services, 1977

Connery, John. ABORTION: The Development of the Roman Catholic Perspective. Chicago: Loyola University Press, 1977.

Cook, Rebecca J. TEN YEARS OF CHANGE IN ABORTION LAW, 1967-1976. London: Internat planned parenthood fed Published by People, 1977.

Floyd, Mary K., compiler. ABORTION BIBLIOGRAPHY FOR 1976. Troy, New York: Whitston Publishing Company, 1976.

Gordon, Sol, and Roger W. Libby, editors. SEXUALITY TODAY AND TOMORROW: Contemporary Issues in Human Sexuality. North Scrituate, Massachusetts: Duxbury Press, 1976.

Greenwood, et al. ABORTION IN DEMAND. London: Pluto Press, 1976.

Hook, E. G., et al, editors. POPULATION CYTOGENETICS. New York: Academic Press, 1977. QH 455 S989P 1975.

Kalmar, R., ed. ABORTION: The emotional implications. Dubuque, Iowa: Kendall/Hunt Publishing Company, 1977.

Karmin, S. M., ed. OBSTETRIC AND GYNAECOGICAL USES OF PROSTAGLANDINS. Lancaster, England: MPT Press, 1976. QU 90 S990 1976.

Manier, Edward, and William T. Liu, editors. ABORTION, NEW DIRECTIONS FOR POLICY STUDIES. Notre Dame: University of Notre Dame Press, 1977.

NATIONAL ABORTION RIGHTS ACTION LEAGUE AND ANTIOCH SCHOOL OF LAW. Washington: Women's Rights Clinic, 1976.

Oldershaw, K. L. CONTRACEPTION, ABORTION & STERILIZATION IN GENERAL PRACTICE. Chicago: Year Book Medical Publishers, 1976.

Omran, Abdel R., ed. LIBERALIZATION OF ABORTION LAWS: Implications. Chapel Hill: University of North Carolina, Carolina Population Center, 1976.

Pelrine, Eleanor Wright. MORGENTALER: The Doctor who Couldn't Turn Away. Agincourt, Ontario: Gage, 1975.

PSYCHOSOCIAL ASPECTS OF ABORTION IN ASIA: Proceedings of the Asian Regional Research Seminar on Psychosocial Aspects of Abortion, Kathmandu, Nepal, 26-29 November, 1974. Kathmandu: Family Planning Association of Nepal: Washington: Transnational Family Research Program, American Institutes for Research, 1975.

Right to Life Association. South Australia Division. Research Committee. RESEARCH LIBRARY BIBLIOGRAPHY, Summer 1974-75. Everard Park: The Committee, 1975.

Steinhoff, Patricia G., et al. ABORTION POLITICS: The Hawaii Experience. Honolulu: University Press of Hawaii, 1977.

Tietze, Christopher, et al. ABORTION 1974-1975: Need and Services in the United States, Each State and Metropolitan Area: A Report by the Alan Guttmacher Institute. New York: The Institute, 1976.

United States. Bureau of Epidemiology. Family Planning Evaluation Division. ABORTION SURVEILLANCE, Annual Summary, 1975. Atlanta, Georgia: Center for Disease Control, 1977.

United States. Commission on Civil Rights. Wyoming Advisory Committee. ABORTION SERVICES IN WYOMING: A Report. Washington: Commission on Civil Rights, 1977.

United States. Congress. House. Committee on the Judiciary. Subcommittee on Civil and Constitutional Rights. PROPOSED CONSTITUTIONAL AMENDMENTS ON ABORTION: Hearings: Pts. 1-2, February 4-March 26, 1976. Washington: G.P.O., 1976.

United States. Congress. Senate. Committee on the Judiciary. Subcommittee on Constitutional Amendments. ABORTION: Hearings Before the Subcommittee on Constitutional Amendments of the Committee on the Judiciary, United States Senate, Ninety-third Congress, second session. Washington: G.P.O., 1976.

Washington (state). Department of Social and Health Services. Special Services Section. ABORTIONS: Report for Calendar Year 1975 by Linda M. Sipes. Olympia: The Department, 1976.

Weisheit, Eldon. SHOULD I HAVE AN ABORTION? St. Louis: Concordia Publishing House, 1976.

WHO (World Health Organization). HEALTH ASPECTS OF HUMAN RIGHTS. WITH SPECIAL REFERENCE TO DEVELOPMENTS IN BIOLOGY AND MEDICINE. Geneva:

WHO, 1976.

—. PREGNANCY AND ABORTION IN ADOLESCENCE.
London: HSMO, 1976.

WORKING OF THE ABORTION ACT: Committee Report.
London: HSMO, 1974.

PERIODICAL LITERATURE

TITLE INDEX

Abdominal pain in early pregnancy and its treatment, by C. Yi. KOREAN CENTRAL JOURNAL OF MEDICINE 29(6): 543-545, 1976. (Bio. Abstrs. Apr., 1977, 47773)

Abdominal wall endometriosis following hypertonic saline abortion, by B. T. Ferrari, et al. JOURNAL OF THE AMERICAN MEDICAL ASSOCIATION 238(1):56-57, July 4, 1977.

The abortifacient and oxytocic effects of an intravaginal silicone rubber device containing a 0.5% concentration of 15(S)-15-methyl-prostaglandin F2alpha methyl ester, by N. H. Lauersen, et al. AMERICAN JOURNAL OF OBSTETRICS AND GYNECOLOGY 127(7):784-787, April 1, 1977.

The abortifacient effectiveness and plasma prostaglandin concentrations with 15(S)-15-methyl prostaglandin F2alpha methyl ester-containing vaginal silastic devices, by N. H. Lauersen, et al. FERTILITY AND STERILITY 27(12):1366-1373, December, 1976.

Abortion, abstract norms, and social control: the decision of the West German federal constitutional court, by H. Gerstein, et al. EMORY LAW JOURNAL 25:849-878, Fall, 1976.

Abortion [letter]. LANCET 2(8031):247, July 30, 1977.

Abortion—action by nineteen year-old unmarried female against the Arizona board of regents to determine the constitutionality of a state statute prohibiting nontherapeutic abortions at the university hospital. JOURNAL OF FAMILY LAW 15:113-118, 1976-1977.

Abortion and the autonomous womens movement, by S. Chelnov. SOCIALIST REVOLUTION 7(1):79-95, 1977. (Soc. Abstrs. 1977, 77I9912)

Abortion and Catholic public officials: statement, by J. Marshall, et al. ORIGINS 7:136-138, August 11, 1977.

Abortion and child abuse; excerpt from Death before birth, by H. O. J. Brown. CHRISTIANITY TODAY 22:34, October 7, 1977.

Abortion and constitution: United States and West Germany, by D. P. Kommers. AMERICAN JOURNAL OF COMPARATIVE LAW 25:255-286, Spring, 1977.

Abortion and the court, by J. Kennedy. SIGN 57:22, September, 1977.

Abortion and democratic politics, by M. Simms. NEW HUMANIST 93:15-17, May-August, 1977.

Abortion and euthanasia: recent developments of the law, by D. J. Horan. FORUM 12:960-979, Summer, 1977.

Abortion and family-building models: fertility limitation in Hungary, by K. Ford. DEMOGRAPHY 13:495-505, November, 1976.

Abortion and the golden rule, by R. M. Hare. PHILOSOPHY AND PUBLIC AFFAIRS 4:201-222, Spring, 1975; Reply by G. Sher, 6:185-199, Winter, 1977

Abortion and human rights, by N. C. Gillespie. ETHICS 98:237-243, April, 1977.

Abortion and the husband's rights: a reply to Wesley Teo, by L. M. Purdy. ETHICS 86(3):247-251, 1976. (Soc. Abstrs.

1977, 77I9710)

Abortion and the law: the impact on hospital policy of the Roe and Doe decisions, by K. A. Kemp, et al. JOURNAL OF HEALTH POLITICS, POLICY AND LAW 1(3):319-337, Fall, 1976.

Abortion and maternal deaths [letter]. BRITISH MEDICAL JOURNAL 2(6029):232, July 24, 1976.

—, by A. Cartwright. BRITISH MEDICAL JOURNAL 2(6039): 813, October 2, 1976.

—, by I. Chalmers. BRITISH MEDICAL JOURNAL 2(6037): 698, September 18, 1976.

Abortion and other signs of disease in cows experimentally infected with Sarcocystis fusiformis from dogs, by R. Fayer, et al. JOURNAL OF INFECTIOUS DISEASES 134(6):624-628, December, 1976.

Abortion and reproductive performance of cattle in northern Nigeria: a questionnaire survey, by S. Nuru, et al. TROPICAL ANIMAL HEALTH AND PRODUCTION 8(4):213-219, November, 1976.

Abortion and the right to life, by L. S. Carrier. SOCIAL THEORY AND PRACTICE 3(4):381-401, 1975. (Soc. Abstrs. 1977, 77I8239)

Abortion and the sanctity of life, by W. D. Cobb. ENCOUNTER (CHRISTIAN THEOLOGICAL SEMINARY) 38:273-287, Summer, 1977.

Abortion and simple consciousness, by W. S. Pluhar. THE JOURNAL OF PHILOSOPHY 74:159-172, March, 1977.

Abortion and the Supreme Court: some are more equal than others, by M. C. Segers. HASTINGS CENTER REPORT 7(4):5-6, August, 1977.

Abortion aid barrred by Bell in rape cases, by A. Clymer. THE

NEW YORK TIMES (M) August 2, 1:3, 1977.

Abortion aid gets a vote, by S. Cloud, Jr. THE NEW YORK TIMES (M) August 7, XXIII, 20:5, 1977.

Abortion alert, by G. Steinem. MS MAGAZINE 6:118, November, 1977.

Abortion; almost legal. ECONOMIST 262:42+, January 29, 1977.

Abortion (amendment) bill [letter]. LANCET 1(8011):606, March 12, 1977.

Abortion, analogies and the emergence of value, by P. F. Camenisch. THE JOURNAL OF RELIGIOUS ETHICS 4:131-158, Spring, 1976.

Abortion—the anti-life decision, by C. Koop. CHRISTIAN READER p. 82, September-October, 1976.

Abortion applicants: characteristics distinguishing dropouts remaining pregnant and those having abortion, by M. E. Swigar, et al. AMERICAN JOURNAL OF PUBLIC HEALTH 67: 142-150, February, 1977.

Abortion as a public health argument, by G. Ciasca. MINERVA GINECOLOGIA 28(9):719-721, September, 1976.

Abortion as a reality, by H. Schmidt-Matthiesen. THERAPEUTISCHE UMSCHAW 33(4):289-293, April, 1976.

Abortion at the Felix Bulnes Hospital. Sociodemographic and medical data, by R. Viada, et al. REVISTA CHILENA DE OBSTETRICIA Y GINECOLOGIA 40(5):235-241, 1975.

Abortion: back to square one [effect of anti-abortion movement], by L. Shapiro. MOTHER JONES 2:13-14, September-October, 1977.

Abortion: beyond rhetoric to access, by E. W. Freeman. SOCIAL WORK 21:483-487, November, 1976.

Abortion: a challenge to Halakhak, by B. Greenberg. JUDAISM p. 201, Spring, 1976.

Abortion clinic damaged by fire. THE NEW YORK TIMES (S) February 25, D, 14:3, 1977.

Abortion counselling: a new role for nurses, by B. Easterbrook, et al. CANADIAN NURSE 73:28-30, January, 1977.

Abortion cutoff causing hardship for poor women around country, by S. V. Roberts. THE NEW YORK TIMES (M) December 25, 20:1, 1977.

Abortion deaths associated with the use of prostaglandin F2a, by W. Cates, Jr., et al. AMERICAN JOURNAL OF OB-STETRICS AND GYNECOLOGY 127(3):219-222, 1977. (Bio. Abstrs. June, 1977, 65533)

Abortion: a dyadic perspective, by A. Rothstein. AMERICAN JOURNAL OF ORTHOPSYCHIATRY 47:111-118, January, 1977.

Abortion: the fall, by C. Francome. NEW SOCIETY pp. 234-235, February 3, 1977.

Abortion, fetal research, and the law, by J. M. Humber. SOCIAL THEORY AND PRACTICE 4:127-147, Spring, 1977.

Abortion foes gain support as they intensify campaign, by L. Johnstoix. THE NEW YORK TIMES (M) October 23, 1:1, 1977.

Abortion foes look to ultimate victory, by W. Robbins. THE NEW YORK TIMES (M) June 19, 24:1, 1977.

Abortion foes urged to join new causes. THE NEW YORK TIMES (M) March 28, 63:4, 1977.

Abortion for poor: legal confusion, by D. Henry. THE NEW YORK TIMES (M) July 24, XXIII, 1:1, 1977.

Abortion: from the perspective of responsibility, by E. C. Gardner. PERKINS SCHOOL OF THEOLOGY JOURNAL 30:10-28, Spring, 1977.

Abortion-fund fight expected in Albany, by R. J. Meislin. THE NEW YORK TIMES (M) December 9, 16:4, 1977.

Abortion hazards, by D. Lahiri, et al. JOURNAL OF THE INDIAN MEDICAL ASSOCIATION 66(11):288-294, June 1, 1976.

Abortion: the husband's constitutional rights, by W. D. H. Teo. ETHICS 85(4):337-342, 1975. (Soc. Abstr. 1977, 7717168)

Abortion in Bangkok, by S. Kaedsawang. THAI JOURNAL OF NURSING 25(3):209-217, July, 1976.

Abortion in Chinese law, by B. H.-k Luk. AMERICAN JOURNAL OF COMPARATIVE LAW 25:372-392, Spring, 1977.

Abortion in England, 1890-1914, by A. McLaren. VICTORIAN STUDIES 20:379-400, Summer, 1977.

Abortion in the law: an essay on absurdity, by L. H. Newton. ETHICS 87:244-250, April, 1977.

Abortion in a mare due to coccidioidomycosis, by R. F. Langham, et al. JOURNAL OF THE AMERICAN VETERINARY MEDICAL ASSOCIATION 170(2):178-180, January 15, 1977.

Abortion in the moral reflections of the Catholic physician, by N. Miccolis. MINERVA GINECOLOGIA 28(9):742-746, September, 1976.

Abortion in Mulago Hospital, Kampala, by C. Lwanga. EAST AFRICAN MEDICAL JOURNAL 54(3):142-148, March, 1977.

Abortion in sheep and goats in Cyprus [letter], by P. Fiset. VETERINARY RECORD 99(16):323, October 16, 1976.

Abortion in South Carolina, by D. N. Bishop, et al. JOURNAL

OF THE SOUTH CAROLINA MEDICAL ASSOCIATION 72(12):455-459, December, 1976.

Abortion induced through massage, by F. Havranek. CESKO-SLOVENSKA GYNEKOLOGIE 42(7):532, August, 1977.

Abortion information: a guidance viewpoint, by P. L. Wolleat. SCHOOL COUNSELOR 22(5):338-341, 1975. (Psycho. Abstrs. 1977, 14033)

Abortion is a hotly debated issue in many lands, by W. Safon. THE NEW YORK TIMES (M) January 22, 26:4, 1977.

The abortion issue and Secretary Califano [letter], by S. J. La Guimina. THE NEW YORK TIMES February 18, 26:6, 1977.

Abortion issue: a case against a constitutional amendment [letter], by R. L. Diyack. THE NEW YORK TIMES March 14, 28:4, 1977.

The abortion issue: past, present and future, by K. W. Green, et al. CURRENT PROBLEMS IN PEDIATRICS 7:1-44, August, 1977.

Abortion: an issue that won't go away, by P. Ferris. OBSERVER p. 13, January 30, 1977.

Abortion issues flares anew, by M. Waldron. THE NEW YORK TIMES (M) January 30, XI, 4:1, 1977.

Abortion; it will not go away [Britain]. ECONOMIST 262:26, February 5, 1977.

Abortion: the last resort, by M. Segers. AMERICA p. 456, December 27, 1975.

Abortion law is approved in Israel, by W. Farrell. THE NEW YORK TIMES (M) February 1, 11:1, 1977.

Abortion law: a study of R. v. Morgentaler [(1975) 53 D L R (3d) 161]. SASKATCHEWAN LAW REVIEW 39:259-284,

1974-1975.

Abortion: let the silent majority prevail [editorial] , by D. Anderson. CHATELAINE 50:2, January, 1977.

Abortion on demand [letters] . THE NEW YORK TIMES May 15, VI, 62, 1977.

—, by J. Bury. BRITISH MEDICAL JOURNAL 1(6066):975, April 9, 1977.

Abortion on request [letter] , by M. Simms. LANCET 1(8008): 423, February 19, 1977.

Abortion—one mother's view, by M. DuVal. THE NEW YORK TIMES (M) October 2, XI, 24:5, 1977.

Abortion or contraception? by C. Giannice. MINERVA GINE-COLOGIA 28(7-8):671-675, July-August, 1976.

Abortion or the unwanted child: a choice for a humanistic society. JOURNAL OF PEDIATRIC PSYCHOLOGY 1(2): 62-67, Spring, 1976.

Abortion—Pennsylvania Medicaid regulations and procedures denying non-therapeutic abortions to indigent women held inconsistent with title XIX of the social security act. JOUR-NAL OF FAMILY LAW 15:587-592, 1976-1977.

Abortion: a philosophical and historical analysis, by J. R. Connery. HOSPITAL PROGRESS 58(4):49-50, April, 1977.

Abortion practice in NZ public hospitals. NURSING FORUM (Auckland) 3(4):5-7, November-December, 1975.

Abortion—a positive experience [letter] ? by R. L. Matthews. CANADIAN MEDICAL ASSOCIATION JOURNAL 116(8): 836-837, April 23, 1977.

Abortion—possible alternatives to unconstitutional spousal and parental consent provisions of Missouri's abortion law.

MISSOURI LAW REVIEW 42:291-297, Spring, 1977.

Abortion: a problem-solving approach. SOCIAL STUDIES 68(3):120-123, May-June, 1977.

Abortion, property rights, and the right to life, by L. H. O'Driscoll. PERSONALIST 58:99-114, April, 1977.

Abortion—the question is whether the government should pay, by S. Jacobs. NATIONAL JOURNAL 9:713-715, May 7, 1977.

Abortion rate is rising for girls age 14 and under, 1975 data show. THE NEW YORK TIMES (M) October 26, 22:1, 1977.

Abortion recordkeeping and right of privacy, by A. S. Kramer. JOURNAL OF CRIMINAL LAW AND CRIMINOLOGY 68:74-77, March, 1977.

Abortion. Report of a commission of the Paris Academy of Medicine, by M. R. Merger. GYNAEKOLOGISCHE RUNDSCHAU 16(3):185-191, 1976.

Abortion: the risk, by C. Brewer. NEW SOCIETY p. 281, February 10, 1977.

Abortion statistics for the Federal Republic of Germany— notification requirements for the physician performing the abortion, by W. Christian. OEFFENTLICHE GESUND-HEITSWESEN 38(11):676-680, November, 1976.

Abortion statutes after Danforth (Planned Parenthood of Cent. Mo. v. Danforth, 96 Sup. Ct. 2831): an examination. JOURNAL OF FAMILY LAW 15:537-567, 1976-1977.

An abortion stick in the duodenum and gallbladder, by G. M. Gandhi, et al. INTERNATIONAL SURGERY 61(11-12): 594-595, November-December, 1976.

Abortion study with names. THE NEW YORK TIMES (M) May 15, IV, 1:5, 1977.

Abortion trail, by J. Turner. NEW SOCIETY p. 123, October 20, 1977.

Abortion utilization: does travel distance matter? by J. D. Shelton, et al. FAMILY PLANNING PERSPECTIVES 8(6):260-262, November-December, 1976.

Abortion views and practices among Danish family physicians, by M. Gammeltoft, et al. JOURNAL OF BIOSOCIAL SCIENCE 8(3):287-292, 1976. (Socio. Abstrs. 1977, 7713508)

Abortion vs. human rights, by J. Campbell. CHELSEA JOURNAL p. 226, September-October, 1976.

Abortion: waging war on the poor; reprint from Forum Letter, September 16, 1977, by R. Weuhaus. OUR SUNDAY VISITOR MAGAZINE 66:11, November 13, 1977.

Abortion: who pays? by S. Fraker, et al. NEWSWEEK 90:12-13, July 4, 1977.

Abortion: why the doctors are closing ranks against new curbs, by P. Healy. TIMES p. 14, July 8, 1977.

Abortions and public policy [editorial], by A. Yankauer. AMERICAN JOURNAL OF PUBLIC HEALTH 67(7):604-605, July, 1977.

—. II. [editorial], by A. Yankauer. AMERICAN JOURNAL OF PUBLIC HEALTH 67(9):817-818, September, 1977.

Abortions at Nacka Hospital, 1975—somatic complications and preventive technics, by K. Sigurdsson. LAKARTIDNINGEN 74(5):318-321, February, 1977.

Abortions in sheep and goats in Cyprus [letter], by R. W. Crowther. VETERINARY RECORD 99(23):466, December 4, 1976.

Abortions in Singapore, by C. S. Chai. THE NURSING JOURNAL OF SINGAPORE 17(1):18-19, May, 1977.

Abortions in Tennessee—1975, by A. R. Hinman. JOURNAL OF THE TENNESSEE MEDICAL ASSOCIATION 70(3):163-167, March, 1977.

Abortions on teenagers are estimated at 275,000. THE NEW YORK TIMES (S) March 9, 14:3, 1977.

Abortions: public and private facilities [Great Britain]. LABOUR RESEARCH 66:106-107, May, 1977.

Abortive infection of mice inoculated intraperitoneally with chlamydia ovis, by A. Rodolakis. ANNALES DE RECHERCHES VETERINARES 7(2):195-205, 1976.

Abruptio placentae and perinatal death: a prospective study, by R. L. Naeye, et al. AMERICAN JOURNAL OF OBSTETRICS AND GYNECOLOGY 128(7):740-746, August 1, 1977.

Abruptio placentae in rhesus monkey causing brain damage to the fetus [letter], by R. E. Myers, et al. AMERICAN JOURNAL OF OBSTETRICS AND GYNECOLOGY 126(8):1048-1049, December 15, 1976.

Absence of chronoperiodic response following intra-amniotic instillation of hypertonic saline, by D. A. Edelman, et al. AMERICAN JOURNAL OF OBSTETRICS AND GYNECOLOGY 127(4):446-447, February 15, 1977.

Accord is emerging in congress on bar to medicaid abortion, by M. Tolchin. THE NEW YORK TIMES (M) September 28, 1:6, 1977.

Accord on abortion collapses again, by M. Tolchin. THE NEW YORK TIMES (M) November 2, 19:5, 1977.

Accord on abortion seems to be distant, by M. Tolchin. THE NEW YORK TIMES (M) October 6, 21:1, 1977.

Action of prostaglandin F2 alpha on pregnancy in mice. Prevention of its abortive property by progesterone, by L. Mercier-Parot, et al. COMPTES RENDUS DES SEANCES

DE LA SOCIETE DE BIOLOGIE ET DE SES FILIALES 170(3):529-532, October, 1976.

Actions taken by the Supreme Court: abortion. THE NEW YORK TIMES (S) January 26, 14:1, 1977.

Acute renal failure of obstetric origin, by K. S. Chugh, et al. OBSTETRICS AND GYNECOLOGY 48(6):642-646, December, 1976.

Advances in the diagnosis of bovine abortion, by H. W. Dunne, et al. PROCEEDINGS—ANNUAL MEETING OF THE UNITED STATES ANIMAL HEALTH ASSOCIATION (77):515-523, 1974.

Aetiology of spontaneous abortion: a cytogenetic and epidemiological study of 288 abortuses and their parents, by J. G. Lauritsen. ACTA OBSTETRICIA ET GYNECOLOGICA SCANDINAVICA. SUPPLEMENT 52:1-29, 1976. (Bio. Abstrs. March, 1977, 26402)

After Edelin: little guidance, by J. A. Robertson. HASTINGS CENTER REPORT 7(3):15-17, 45, June, 1977.

Again, back-alley and self-induced abortions, by Y. B. Burke. THE NEW YORK TIMES (M) August 22, 23:1, 1977.

Agonizing decisions in mental retardation, by R. C. Yeaworth. AMERICAN JOURNAL OF NURSING 77:864-867, May, 1977.

Albany bars a halt in abortions study, by R. J. Meislin. THE NEW YORK TIMES (S) May 24, 39:6, 1977.

Albany Senate passes court bill but its enactment is still distant: Anti-Abortion Amendment, by R. J. Meislin. THE NEW YORK TIMES (S) May 25, II, 2:2, 1977.

Almost legal. ECONOMIST 262:42, 44, January 29, 1977.

The American way of death, by H. Brown. MOODY MONTHLY p. 32, December, 1976.

Amidation of proteins of different placental tissues in miscarriage, by T. S. Dluxhevskaia, et al. VOPROSY OKHRANY MATERINSTVA I DETSTVA 21(8):71-75, August, 1976.

Amikacin for treatment of septic abortions: summary, by J. Bravo-Scandoval, et al. JOURNAL OF INFECTIOUS DISEASES 134(Suppl):S380, November, 1976.

Amniotic fluid adenosine 3' 5'—monophosphate in prostaglandin-induced midtrimester abortions, by R. R. Weiss, et al. OBSTETRICS AND GYNECOLOGY 49(2):223-226, 1977. (Bio. Abstrs. July, 1977, 4344)

Amniotic fluid removal prior to saline abortion, by A. C. Mehta, et al. ANNALES CHIRURGIAE ET GYNAECOLOGIAE FENNIAE 65(1):68-71, 1976. (Bio. Abstrs. February, 1977, 23550)

Anaesthetics as an occupational hazard [editorial]. MEDICAL JOURNAL OF AUSTRALIA 1(13):427-428, March 26, 1977.

Analysis of the abortive action induced by prostaglandin F2 alpha in the mouse. Study of ova and their transplantation, by L. Mercier-Parot. COMPTES RENDUS DES SEANCES DE LA SOCIETE DE BIOLOGIE ET DE SES FILIALES 170(3):532-536, October, 1976.

An analysis of clergymen's attitude toward abortion, by S. Price-Bonham, et al. REVIEW OF RELIGIOUS RESEARCH 17(1):15-27, 1975. (Socio. Abstrs. 1977, 7715263)

Analysis of statistical data concerning artifical abortions in a number of foreign countries, by I. P. Katkova. SOVETSKAE ZDRAVOOKHRANENIE (7):30-34, 1976.

And the poor get buried [letter], by W. Cates, Jr., et al. FAMILY PLANNING PERSPECTIVES 9(1):2, January-February, 1977.

Anesthesia for elective termination of pregnancy [letter], by J. P. Annis. JAMA; JOURNAL OF THE AMERICAN MEDI-

CAL ASSOCIATION 236(23):2941-2943, December 27, 1976.

Another double standard; call to concern campaign. AMERICA 137:274, October 29, 1977.

Another opinion on abortion. SYGEPLEJERSKEN 75(33):13-14, August 20, 1975.

Anti-abortion Bill stirs new debate, by M. Waldron. THE NEW YORK TIMES (M) February 27, XI, 1:1, 1977.

Anti-abortion forces gain. THE NEW YORK TIMES (M) June 26, IV, 1:1, 1977.

Anti-abortion myths. NEW HUMANIST 92:175-178, January-February, 1977.

Anti-abortion petition. THE NEW YORK TIMES (S) April 21, 18:6, 1977.

Antibiotic therapy of septic puerperal and postabortion diseases, by V. K. Prorokova, et al. PEDIATRIIA AKUSHERSTVO I GINEKOLOGIIA (3):33-36, May-June, 1977.

The antiemetic effect of dixyrazine in postoperative patients: a double-blind study, by I. Kivalo, et al. ANNALES CHIRURGIAE ET GYNAECOLOGIAE FENNIAE 65(4):295-299, 1976. (Bio. Abstrs. May, 1977, 53319)

Application of physiotherapy in threatened spontaneous abortion, by V. M. Strugatskif, et al. MEDITSINSKAIA SESTRA 35(11):27-32, November, 1976.

Are there too many advantages already for the wealthy woman? by G. Hill. TIMES p. 16, February 25, 1977.

Are you sorry you had an abortion? Interviews, by M. Rockmore. GOOD HOUSEKEEPING 185:120-121+, July, 1977.

Assessment of the structure and function of the therapeutic abortion committee, by M. E. Krass. CANADIAN MEDICAL

ASSOCIATION JOURNAL 116(7):786+, April 9, 1977.

The association of maternal lymphocytotoxic antibodies with obstetric complications, by R. E. Harris, et al. OBSTETRICS AND GYNECOLOGY 48(3):302-304, 1976. (Bio. Abstrs. February, 1977, 20979)

The association of multiple induced abortions with subsequent prematurity and spontaneous abortion, by L. H. Roht, et al. ACTA OBSTETRICA ET GYNAECOLOGICA JAPONIA 23(2):140-145, 1976.

Attempt at handling the new legal regulation to paragraph 218, by P. Stoll, et al. FORTSCHRITTE DU MEDIZIN 94(33): 1893-1894, November 18, 1976.

An attempt to evaluate the risk of death in utero, by C. Huraux-Rendu, et al. JOURNAL DE GYNECOLOGIE, OBSTE-TRIQUE ET BIOLOGIE DE REPRODUCTION 5(5):675-680, 1976. (Bio. Abstrs. April, 1977, 37255)

Attention may have shifted from it, but abortion remains a major issue, by C. Hawkes. MACLEAN'S 90:80, November 14, 1977.

Attitudes of American teenagers toward abortion, by M. Zelnik, et al. FAMILY PLANNING PERSPECTIVES 7(2):89-91, 1975. (Socio. Abstrs. 1977, 7717096)

Attitudes of rural Thai women towards induced abortion, by R. G. Burnight, et al. JOURNAL OF BIOSOCIAL SCIENCE 9(1):61-72, January, 1977.

Attitudes of women who have had abortion, by I. Bogen. THE JOURNAL OF SEX RESEARCH 10(2):97-109, 1974. (Socio. Abstrs. 1977, 7714333)

Attitudes related to the number of children wanted and expected by college students in three countries, by H. G. Gough, et al. JOURNAL OF CROSS-CULTURAL PSYCHOLOGY 7(4): 413-424, 1976. (Psycho. Abstrs. 1977, 12581)

Attitudes toward abortion: a pilot crosscultural comparison, by
V. L. Zammuner. GIORNALE ITALIANO DI PSICOLOGIA
3(1):75-116, 1976. (Psycho. Abstrs. 1977, 5750)

Avulsion of the ureter from both ends as a complication of
interruption of pregnancy with vacuum aspirator, by C.
Dimopoulos, et al. JOURNAL OF UROLOGY 118(1 Pt. 1):
108, July, 1977.

Bacterial infection in cows associated with abortion, endometritis
and sterility, by I. Gelev. VETERINARNO-MEDITSINSKI
NAUKI 13(6):15-23, 1976.

Badgley committee: abortion law retained, by E. Le Bourdais.
DIMENSIONS IN HEALTH SERVICE 54(4):34-35, April,
1977.

The Badgley report on the abortion law [editorial], by W. D.
Thomas. CANADIAN MEDICAL ASSOCIATION JOUR-
NAL 116(9):966, May 7, 1977.

Balanced translocation t (3; 21) (q 11; q 21) as a cause of habitual abortions, by N. I. Smirnova, et al. TSITOLOGIIA I
GENETIKA 11(1):74-76, January-February, 1977.

A ban on abortions paid for by medicaid criticized as unfair, by
M. Tolchin. THE NEW YORK TIMES (S) June 2, II, 5:1,
1977.

Basal body temperature recordings in spontaneous abortion, by
J. Cohen. INTERNATIONAL JOURNAL OF GYNAECOL-
OGY AND OBSTETRICS 14(2):117-122, 1976. (Bio.
Abstrs. June, 1977, 61966)

Benyon's progress [editorial]. LANCET 2(8029):120-121, July
16, 1977.

Bernardin finds gain in esteem for Catholics of U.S., by K. A.
Briggs. THE NEW YORK TIMES (M) March 3, 16:2, 1977.

Between guilt and gratification, by N. Rosen. THE NEW YORK
TIMES (L) April 17, VI, 70, 1977.

Bill would restrict abortions on young, by L. Greenhouse. THE NEW YORK TIMES (M) June 10, IV, 15:4, 1977.

Biochemical indices in infectious diseases following labor and abortion, by N. N. Kulikova, et al. AKUSHERSTVO I GINEKOLOGIIA (4):35-39, April, 1976.

Bioethics and health education: some issues of the biological revolution, by G. B. Fulton. JOURNAL OF SCHOOL HEALTH 47:205-211, April, 1977.

Birth control: contraception, abortion, sterilization, by Ferraris. MINERVA GINECOLOGIA 29(4):249-252, April, 1977.

Birth despite vasectomy and abortion held not a "wrong", by S. Gursky. JOURNAL OF LEGAL MEDICINE 5(7):29-31, July, 1977.

The birth of a bill restricting a women's rights, by J. Turner. GUARDIAN p. 11, February 17, 1977.

Births aborted among the users of the voluntary family planning program of the Instituto Mexicano del Seguro Social, by J. E. Garcia de Alba, et al. GINECOLOGIA Y OBSTETRICIA DE MEXICO 41(245)235-242, March, 1977.

Born and the unborn alike; position of the Catholic Church, by A. Bernard. AMERICA 136:270-272, March 26, 1977.

Bovine abortion [letter], by J. G. Maddox. VETERINARY RECORD 99(25-26):517+, December 25, 1976.

Bovine leptospirosis: demonstration of leptospires of the Hebdomadis serogroup in aborted fetuses and a premature calf, by W. A. Ellis, et al. VETERINARY RECORD 99(22):430-432, November 27, 1976.

Bovine leptospirosis: infection by the Hebdomadis serogroup and abortion—a herd study, by W. A. Ellis, et al. VETERINARY RECORD 99(21):409-412, November 20, 1976.

Bovine mycotic abortion: some epidemiological aspects, by B.

M. Williams, et al. VETERINARY RECORD 100(18):382-385, April 30, 1977.

Brucella abortus in the bitch, by S. R. Bicknell, et al. VETERI-NARY RECORD 99(5):85-86, July 31, 1976.

Caffeine and pregnancy. A retrospective survey, by P. S. Weathersbee, et al. POSTGRADUATE MEDICAL JOUR-NAL 62(3):64-69, September, 1977.

Califano declares dispute on abortion is unfair to poor. THE NEW YORK TIMES (M) October 12, 13:1, 1977.

Califano makes plans for abortion alternatives. OUR SUNDAY VISITOR 66:1, September 4, 1977.

Califano would bar U.S. aid to abortion, by N. Hicks. THE NEW YORK TIMES (M) January 14, 14:1, 1977.

Califano's appearance is picketed. THE NEW YORK TIMES (M) November 13, 42:1, 1977.

Can technology solve the abortion dilemma, by M. Maguire. CHRISTIAN CENTURY p. 918, October 27, 1976.

The Canadian abortion law [letter]. CANADIAN MEDICAL ASSOCIATION JOURNAL 116(3):238+, February 5, 1977.

Carey appoints panel on abortion consent. THE NEW YORK TIMES (S) January 9, 42:3, 1977.

Carter asks Congress to disregard Ford proposals to cut funds for social programs, by D. E. Rosenbaum. THE NEW YORK TIMES (M) February 23, B, 5:5, 1977.

Carter staff prepares memo on abortion. THE NEW YORK TIMES (M) July 29, 16:1, 1977.

Case against abortion [review article], by R. Case. CHRISTIAN-ITY TODAY 21:45-46, March 18, 1977.

Case of convulsions with late onset after ketalar anesthesia, by

A. Dimitrov, et al. AKUSHERSTVO I GINEKOLOGIIA (Sofia) 15(3):229-230, 1976.

A case of toxoplasmosis detected by the Sabin-Feldman test, by K. Altintas. MIKROBIYOLOJI BULTENI 11(1):113-115, January, 1977.

Case reports: unrecognized, oviduct pregnancy and therapeutic abortion by uterine aspiration, by C. Villaneueva. JOURNAL OF THE KANSAS MEDICAL SOCIETY 77(10):448-449, October, 1976.

Case study: the unwanted child: caring for a fetus born alive after an abortion, by Bok, et al. HASTINGS CENTER REPORT 6:10-15, October, 1976.

Catholic Hospital Association criticizes HEW's "cost-cutting" proposals for abortion and living wills. HOSPITAL PROGRESS 58:20-21, August, 1977.

Catholic prelates organizing a drive against abortions, by K. A. Briggs. THE NEW YORK TIMES (M) August 17, 1:4, 1977.

Causes of abortions, by S. Chang. KOREAN CENTRAL JOURNAL OF MEDICINE 29(2):123-124, 1975. (Bio. Abstrs. April, 1977, 43617)

Causes of late abortion [letter], by C. Brewer. LANCET 1(8008):422-423, February 19, 1977.

Causes of spontaneous abortions and their microscopic aspects, by Z. Szczurek, et al. GINEKOLOGIA POLOSKA 48(5): 451-458, May, 1977.

C&C symposium, paying for abortion: is the court wrong? CHRISTIANITY AND CRISIS 37:202-207, September 19, 1977.

Cellular and humoral immune aspects in mixed wife-husband leukocyte cultures in spontaneous abortions, by I. Halbrecht, et al. ACTA EUROPAEA FERTILITATIS 7(3):249-255, September, 1976.

23

Cervical dilatation with 16,16 dimethyl PGE2 p-benzaldehyde semicarbazone ester prior to vacuum aspiration in first trimester nulliparae, by S. M. Karim, et al. PROSTAGLANDINS 13(2):333-338, February, 1977.

Cervical pregnancy: report of three cases and a review of the literature, by H. Khosravi, et al. INTERNATIONAL JOURNAL OF GYNAECOLOGY AND OBSTETRICS 14(3):237-240, 1976. (Bio. Abstrs. June, 1977, 71947)

Cervico-vaginal injuries in cases of second trimester termination of pregnancy, by V. N. Purandare, et al. PROSTAGLANDINS 13(2):349-354, February, 1977.

Changes in the concentration of cortisol in amniotic fluid after intra-amniotic prostaglandin for midtrimester abortion, by I. Z. MacKenzie, et al. BRITISH JOURNAL OF OBSTETRICS AND GYNAECOLOGY 84(8):608-612, August, 1977.

Changes in congenital oral cleft incidence in relation to induced abortions, by A. P. Polednak, et al. AMERICAN JOURNAL OF OBSTETRICS AND GYNECOLOGY 126(6):734-735, November 15, 1976.

Changing abortion debate, by R. N. Ostling. THEOLOGY TODAY 34:161-166, July, 1977.

The characteristics of uterine contracile function in pregnant women in threatened abortion, by G. P. Kravets. PEDIATRIIA AKUSHERSTVO I GINEKOLOGIIA (4):39-41, July-August, 1976.

Charges sisters' statement undermines bishops' stand, by T. Barbarie. OUR SUNDAY VISITOR 66:2, November 6, 1977.

Child support: implications of abortion on the relative parental duties. UNIVERSITY OF FLORIDA LAW REVIEW 28: 988-989, Summer, 1976.

Children born to women denied abortion, by Z. Dytrych, et al.

FAMILY PLANNING PERSPECTIVES 7(4):165-171, 1975. (Socio. Abstrs. 1977, 7717333)

Choice of analgesia or anesthesia for pain relief in suction curettage, by J. A. Rock, et al. OBSTETRICS AND GYNECOLOGY 49(6):721-723, June, 1977.

Choose life: promoting the value and quality of life; LCWR Task Force report, August 28, 1977. ORIGINS 7:161+, September 1, 1977.

The Christian and abortion, by M. Leggett. CHRISTIAN STANDARD p. 7, December 5, 1976.

Chromosomal anomalies in early spontaneous abortion. (Their consequences on early embryogenesis and in vitro growth of embryonic cells), by J. G. Boué, et al. CURRENT TOPICS IN PATHOLOGY 62:193-208, 1976.

Chromosome anomalies and miscarriage, by Iu. I. Novikov, et al. AKUSHERSTVO I GINEKOLOGIIA (Moscow) (12):32-35, December, 1976.

Civil law and Christian morality: abortion and the churches, by C. Curran. CLERGY REVIEW 62:227-242, June, 1977.

Clinic and client: an investigation into the experiences of Dutch women in outpatient abortion clinics, by A. Schroeder. STIMEZO-RESEARCH 1:85, 1975. (Psycho. Abstrs. 1977, 8832)

The clinic over the sea, by A. McHardy. GUARDIAN p. 9, October 31, 1977.

Clinical and pathomorphological study on placentae during abortions in the second trimester, by A. Sed'ova, et al. CESKOSLOVENSKA GYNEKOLOGIE 41(8):569-571, October, 1976.

Clinical and x-ray studies on the relationship between interruption of pregnancy and premature labor, by R. Voigt, et al. ZENTRALBLATT FUR GYNAEKOLOGIE 98(25):1589-

1593, 1976.

Clinical application of prostaglandins in obstetrics and gynecology, by F. J. Brunnberg. ACTA BIOLOGICA ET MEDICA GERMANICA 35(8-9):1243-1247, 1976.

Clinical aspects of premature detachment of normally functioning placentas, by Z. N. Zaidieva. AKUSHERSTVO I GINEKOLOGIIA (Moscow) (1):56-59, 1977.

Clinical comparison of abortifacient activity of vaginally administered prostaglandin E2 in two dosage forms, by T. J. Roseman, et al. AMERICAN JOURNAL OF OBSTETRICS AND GYNECOLOGY 129(2):225-227, September 15, 1977.

A clinical comparison of prostaglandin F2alpha and intra-amniotic saline for induction of midtrimester abortion, by G. S. Berger, et al. ANNALES CHIRURGIAE ET GYNAECOLOGIAE FENNIAE 66(1):55-58, 1977.

Clinical details, cytogenic studies, and cellular physiology of a 69, XXX fetus, with comments on the biological effect of triploidy in man, by C. M. Gosden, et al. JOURNAL OF MEDICAL GENETICS 13(5):371-380, October, 1976.

Clinical experiences with the gestagen. Turinal in treating threatened and habitual abortions, by A. Pociatek, et al. BRATISLAUSKE LEKARSKE LISTY 67(1):87-91, January, 1977.

Clinical experiences with prostaglandin E2 and F2 alpha in the termination of pregnancy and labor induction in intrauterine fetal death, by J. Kunz, et al. SCHWEIZERISCHE MEDIZINISCHE WOCHENSCHRIFT 107(22):757-763, June 4, 1977.

Clinical problems of ovulation defects, by A. Grant. INTERNATIONAL JOURNAL OF GYNECOLOGY AND OBSTETRICS 14(2):123-128, 1976. (Bio. Abstrs. April, 1977, 44075)

Clinical results of two-time abortion technics with special regard to ascending genital infections, by H. Kreibich, et al. ZEN-TRALBLATT FUR GYNAEKOLOGIE 99(12):755-762, 1977.

Coagulopathy with midtrimester induced abortion: association with hyperosmolar urea administration, by R. T. Burkman, et al. AMERICAN JOURNAL OF OBSTETRICS AND GYNECOLOGY 127(5):533-536, 1977. (Bio. Abstrs. August, 1977, 23526)

Combined outpatient laparoscopic sterilization with therapeutic abortion, by C. E. Powe, Jr., et al. AMERICAN JOURNAL OF OBSTETRICS AND GYNECOLOGY 126(5):565-567, November 1, 1976.

Comments on Cameron and Tichenon's remarks on our 1966 paper, by H. Forssman, et al. PSYCHOLOGICAL REPORTS 39(2):400, 1976. (Psycho. Abstrs. 1977, 8100)

Common HLA antigens in couples with repeated abortions, by L. Komlos, et al. CLINICAL IMMUNOLOGY AND IMMUNO-PATHOLOGY 7(3):330-335, May, 1977.

Comparison between intra-amniotic administration of prostaglandin F2a and its 15-methyl derivative for induction of second trimester abortion, by O. Ylikorkala. ANNALS OF CLINI-CAL RESEARCH 9(2):58-61, 1977. (Bio. Abstrs. November, 1977, 52789)

A comparison of flexible and nonflexible plastic cannulae for performing first trimester abortion, by L. Andolsek, et al. INTERNATIONAL JOURNAL OF GYNAECOLOGY AND OBSTETRICS 14(3):199-204, 1976.

Comparison of vaginal cytology with plasma progesterone levels in early human pregnancy, by I. Khanna, et al. INDIAN JOURNAL OF MEDICAL RESEARCH 64(9):1267-1271, 1976. (Bio. Abstrs. May, 1977, 50500)

Comparative characteristics of the water-soluble afterbirth tissue proteins in normal and incomplete pregnancy, by T. S.

Dluzhevskaia, et al. AKUSHERSTVO I GINEKOLOGIIA (Moscow) (3):37-41, March, 1977.

Comparative evaluation of different methods of general anesthesia during surgical termination of early pregnancy, by V. A. Glotova. VOPROSY OKHRANY MATERINSTVA I DETSTVA 21(4):81-84, April, 1976.

Comparative-obstetrical views and experimental investigations concerning psychosomatic disorders during pregnancy and parturition, by C. Naaktgeboren, et al. ZEITSCHRIFT FUER TIERZUECHTUNG UND ZUECHTUNGSBIOLOGIE 93(3/4):264-320, 1976. (Bio. Abstrs. October, 1977, 41331)

Comparative study of the causes of induced abortion and the knowledge of family planning, by M. D. Ramos Netto. REVISTA ENFERMAGEM EM NOVAS DIMENSOES 1(4): 172, September-October, 1975.

A comparative study of plasma 17beta-oestradiol, progesterone, placental lactogen and chorionic gonadotrophin in abortion induced with intra-amniotic prostaglandin F2alpha, by R. H. Ward, et al. BRITISH JOURNAL OF OBSTETRICS AND GYNAECOLOGY 84(5):363-369, May, 1977.

Complications following induced abortion by vacuum aspiration: patient characteristics and procedures, by M. Cheng, et al. STUDIES IN FAMILY PLANNING 8(5):125-129, May, 1977.

Complications in induced abortions, by H. Kirchhoff. WIENER MEDIZINISCHE WOCHENSCHRIFT 126(49-50):696-699, December 3, 1976.

Compromise is voted by house and senate in abortion dispute, by M. Tolchin. THE NEW YORK TIMES (M) December 8, 1:6, 1977; December 8, 14:4, 1977.

Compromise nearer on medicaid abortion, by M. Tolchin. THE NEW YORK TIMES (M) September 30, 20:1, 1977.

Concepts and limits of therapeutic abortion, by N. Ragucci.

MINERVA GINECOLOGIA 28(9):697-699, Setepmber, 1976.

Conferees ease the deadlock on medicaid abortions, by M. Tolchin. THE NEW YORK TIMES (M) November 1, 29:1, 1977.

Conferees on medicaid abortions deadlocked after a futile session, by M. Tolchin. THE NEW YORK TIMES (M) September 13, 14:3, 1977.

Conferees still fail to agree on abortion, by M. Tolchin. THE NEW YORK TIMES (M) November 28, 19:1, 1977.

Congress returning from recess faces vital issues at years end, by M. Tolchin. THE NEW YORK TIMES (M) November 29, 18:1, 1977.

Congressmen offer new abortion plan, by M. Tolchin. THE NEW YORK TIMES (M) October 1, 8:1, 1977.

Conservative treatment of women in perforations of the uterus in legal abortions, by D. Mladenovic, et al. SRPSKI ACHIV ZA CELOJUPNO LEKARSTVO 104(2):119-127, February, 1976.

Conspiracy of silence facilitates abortion in Brazil, by M. Galanternick. THE NEW YORK TIMES (M) May 28, 46:1, 1977.

A constitutional amendment to restrict abortion, by D. Louisell. CATHOLIC MIND p. 25, December, 1976.

Constitutional law: abortion, parental and spousal consent requirements, right to privacy. AKRON LAW REVIEW 10: 367-382, Fall, 1976.

Constitutional law: abortion, parental consent, minors' right to due process, equal protection and privacy. AKRON LAW REVIEW 9(1):158-165, Summer, 1975.

Constitutional law—abortion—statute requiring spousal and parental consent declared unconstitutional. CUMBERLAND

LAW REVIEW 7:539-550, Winter, 1977.

Constitutional law—blanket parental consent requirement for minor's abortion decision is unconstitutional. TEXAS TECH LAW REVIEW 8:394-402, Fall, 1976.

Constitutional law: elimination of spousal and parental consent requirements for abortion. WASHBURN LAW JOURNAL 16:462-468, Winter, 1977.

Constitutional law—a state may constitutionally regulate the abortion decision during the first trimester of pregnancy if it can show that the regulation is necessary to protect a compelling state interest and the regulation, as applied, does not unnecessarily burden the woman's right to privacy. DRAKE LAW REVIEW 26:716-727, 1976-1977.

Constitutional law—substantive due process—abortion—reasonable statutory recordkeeping and reporting requirements upheld. BRIGHAM YOUNG UNIVERSITY LAW REVIEW 1976:977-999, 1976.

Constitutional protection for the unborn, by J. L. Bernardin. THE NEW YORK TIMES (M) February 26, 19:3, 1977.

Consultation, when abortion is demanded, by W. Greve, et al. PSYCHOTHERAPY AND MEDICAL PSYCHOLOGY 27(2): 58-63, March, 1977.

Contraception, abortion and veneral disease: teenagers knowledge and the effect of education, by P. A. Reichelt, et al. FAMILY PLANNING PERSPECTIVE 7(2):83-88, 1975. (Socio. Abstrs. 1977, 7717089)

Contraceptive practice by women presenting to a free-standing abortion clinic, by S. Treloar, et al. MEDICAL JOURNAL OF AUSTRALIA 1(15):527-532, April 9, 1977.

Contraceptive practice in the context of a nonrestrictive abortion law: age-specific pregnancy rates in New York City, 1971-1973, by C. Tietze. FAMILY PLANNING PERSPECTIVES 7(5):192-202, 1975. (Socio. Abstrs. 1977, 7717046)

Contraceptive risk taking and abortion: results and implications of a San Francisco Bay Area study, by K. Luker. STUDIES IN FAMILY PLANNING 8(8):190-196, August, 1977.

Contraceptive use and subsequent fertility, by G. R. Huggins. FERTILITY AND STERILITY 28(6):603-612, 1977. (Bio. Abstrs. December, 1977, 71780)

Contribution to the treatment of threatened abortion, by J. Kunz, et al. SCHWEIZERISCHE MEDIZINISCHE WOCHENSCHRIFT 106(42):1429-1435, October 16, 1976.

Cooke, at reception on the East Side, assails abortion, by G. Dugan. THE NEW YORK TIMES (M) January 22, 25:3, 1977.

Cooperation of a gynecologist and pathologist in the study and evaluation of the chorion during early abortion, by P. Drac, et al. CESKOSLOVENSKA GYNEKOLOGIE 41(8):571-572, October, 1976.

Correlation of sex hormone levels with target tissue reaction in deficiency of the lutein phase of the menstrual cycle, by O. N. Savchenko, et al. VOPROSKY OKHRANY MATERINSTVA I DETSTVA 21(10):68-72, October, 1976.

Cortisol levels in amniotic fluid in prostaglandin F2a-induced midtrimester abortion, by Z. Koren, et al. AMERICAN JOURNAL OF OBSTETRICS AND GYNECOLOGY 127 (6):639-642, 1977. (Bio. Abstrs. July, 1977, 10540)

Counselling for abortion, by M. Blair. MIDWIFE HEALTH VISITOR AND COMMUNITY NURSE 11(11):355-356, November, 1975.

Countdown to an abortion, by T. Ashford. AMERICA 136: 128-130, February 12, 1977.

The course of pregnancy and outcome of labor in women with chronic pyelonephritis, by L. S. Koval'chuk. AKUSHERSTVO I GINEKOLOGIIA (Moscow) (10):47-50, October, 1976.

The court and a conflict of principles, by S. Callahan. HAST-
INGS CENTER REPORT 7(4):7-8, August, 1977.

Court blocks abortion curb. THE NEW YORK TIMES (S)
February 13, 36:1, 1977.

Court blocks on abortion for teen-aged student on male friend's
plea. THE NEW YORK TIMES (S) April 22, 28:1, 1977.

The court, the Congress and the president: turning back the
clock on the pregnant [laws prohibiting use of federal funds
to pay for abortions, and Supreme Court rulings]. FAMILY
PLANNING PERSPECTIVES 9:207-214, September-October, 1977.

Court hearing set on abortion funding, by M. Waldron. THE
NEW YORK TIMES (M) July 10, XI, 1:5, 1977.

Court may OK government funding of abortions, by P. L. Geary.
HOSPITAL PROGRESS 58(1):10+, January, 1977.

Court rules states may deny medicaid for some abortions, by L.
Oelsner. THE NEW YORK TIMES (M) June 21, 1:6, 1977.

Court to hear plea to bar abortions under medicaid, by W. H.
Waggoner. THE NEW YORK TIMES (S) June 25, 49:2,
1977.

Courts rule on constitutionality of hospital bans on elective
abortions. HOSPITAL LAW 10:3-4, January, 1977.

Criminologic considerations concerning criminal abortion, by F.
Carrieri. MINERVA GINECOLOGIA 28(9):725-729, September, 1976.

Critical evaluation of legal abortion, by M. Harry. WORLD
MEDICAL JOURNAL 23:83-85, November-December,
1976.

Culture and treatment results in endometritis following elective
abortion, by R. T. Burkman, et al. AMERICAN JOURNAL
OF OBSTETRICS AND GYNECOLOGY 128(5):556-559,

1977. (Bio. Abstrs. November, 1977, 57802)

Curb on medicaid funds for abortions defended. THE NEW
YORK TIMES (S) February 15, 49:4, 1977.

Curbs on medicaid abortions posing perils and problems for the
poor, by L. Oelsner. THE NEW YORK TIMES (M) December 19, 35:3, 1977.

Cutoffs on medicaid prompt shift in thinking on abortion, by L.
Oelsner. THE NEW YORK TIMES (M) December 11,
82:3, 1977.

Cytogenetic findings in fifty-five couples with recurrent fetal
wastage, by J. R. Byrd, et al. FERTILITY AND STERILITY
28(3):246-250, March, 1977.

Cytogenetic studies in families with habitual abortions, by G.
Bulkova, et al. AKUSHERSTVO I GINEKOLOGIIA (Sofia)
15(4):265-268, 1976.

Cytogenetic studies in spontaneous abortions, by S. Gilgenkrantz,
et al. BULLETIN DE L'ASSOCIATION DES ANATO-
MISTES 60(169):357-365, 1976. (Bio. Abstrs. September,
1977, 26622)

Cytogenetic studies in sterility and miscarriage, by V. I. Kucharenko, et al. AKUSHERSTVO I GINEKOLOGIIA (Moscow)
(5):1-4, May, 1977.

Cytogenetics of habitual abortion and other reproductive wastage,
by M. A. Stenchever, et al. AMERICAN JOURNAL OF OB-
STETRICS AND GYNECOLOGY 127(2):143-150, January
15, 1977.

Danger: constitutional convention ahead, by E. Doerr.
HUMANIST 37:50-51, March, 1977.

Death after legal abortion by catheter placement, by D. A.
Grimes, et al. AMERICAN JOURNAL OF OBSTETRICS
AND GYNECOLOGY 129(1):107-108, September 1, 1977.

Death after paracervical block [letter] , by J. Slome. LANCET 1(8005):260, January 29, 1977.

Deaths from paracervical anesthesia used for first-trimester abortion, 1972-1975, by D. A. Grimes, et al. NEW ENGLAND JOURNAL OF MEDICINE 295(25):1397-1399, 1976. (Bio. Abstrs. May, 1977, 54151)

Debating abortion, by J. Garn. NATIONAL REVIEW 29:1299+, November 11, 1977.

Declaration on procured abortion, by J. Hamer. C.I.C.I.A.M.S. NOUVELLES (2):7-18, 1975.

Delivery or abortion in inner-city adolescents, by S. H. Fischman. AMERICAN JOURNAL OF ORTHOPSYCHIATRY 47:127-133, January, 1977.

Demystification of life, by R. J. Henle. COMMONWEAL 104: 457-460, July 22, 1977.

Determination of prenatal sex ratio in man, by M. Yamamoto, et al. HUMAN GENETICS 36(3):265-269, 1977. (Bio. Abstrs. October, 1977, 38521)

Determination of Rh blood group of fetuses in abortions by suction curettage, by R. M. Greendyke, et al. TRANSFUSION (Phil) 16(3):267-269, 1976. (Bio. Abstrs. January, 1977, 1108)

The development of coagulopathy in missed abortion, by H. Heyes, et al. GEBURTSHILFE UND FRAUENHEILKUNDE 37(7):595-599, July, 1977.

Developmental anomalies of the umbilical vessels (arteria umbilicalis singularis) and spontaneous abortion, by E. Horak, et ael. ORVOSI HETILAP 118(29):1721-1726, July 17, 1977.

A developmental approach to post-abortion depression, by F. M. Burkle, Jr. PRACTITIONER 218(1304):217-225, February, 1977.

34

Diagnosis and treatment of abortions, by Y. Chang. KOREAN CENTRAL JOURNAL OF MEDICINE 29(2):125-127, 1976. (Bio. Abstrs. April, 1977, 43616)

The diagnosis and treatment of threatened miscarriage, by B. Faris. AUSTRALASIAN NURSES JOURNAL 4(4):7, October, 1975.

The diagnosis of salmonella abortion in cattle with particular reference to Salmonella dublin. A review, by M. Hinton. JOURNAL OF HYGIENE 79(1):25-38, August, 1977.

Diagnostic and prognostic importance of the chorionic gonadotropin test in threatened abortions, by D. I. Dimitrov. AKUSHERSTVO I GINEKOLOGIIA (Sofia) 16(3):220-221, 1977.

Dilatation and curettage for second-trimester abortions, by A. A. Hodari, et al. AMERICAN JOURNAL OF OBSTETRICS AND GYNECOLOGY 127(8):850-854, 1977. (Bio. Abstrs. September, 1977, 29734)

Dilemmas and pressures. On patients and nurses—abortion legislation. Part 2, by E. Donachie. WORLD OF IRISH NURSING 6:1+, June, 1977.

Direct evidence of luteal insufficiency in women with habitual abortion, by J. L. Horta, et al. OBSTETRICS AND GYNECOLOGY 49(6):705-708, June, 1977.

Do potential people have moral rights, by M. A. Warren. PHILOSOPHY AND PUBLIC AFFAIRS 7:275-289, June, 1977.

Doctors have varied reactions to abortion. OUR SUNDAY VISITOR 66:3, May 29, 1977.

Don't know: item ambiguity or respondent uncertainty? by C. H. Coombs, et al. PUBLIC OPINION QUARTERLY 40: 497-514, Winter, 1976-1977.

A double-blind comparison of clindamycin with penicillin plus chloramphenicol in treatment of septic abortion, by A. W.

Cow, et al. JOURNAL OF INFECTIOUS DISEASES 135 (Suppl):S35-39, March, 1977.

Dr. Mildred Jefferson speaks her mind; cond from the Boston Sunday Globe, December 5, 1976, by O. McManus. CATHOLIC DIGEST 41:63-67, June, 1977.

The Dutch on abortion: opinions on terminating life in the case of abortion, euthanasia, acts of war and punishment, by R. Veenhoven, et al. STIMEZO-RESEARCH 3:70, 1975. (Psycho. Abstrs. 1977, 10068)

Dutch tolerance of illegal abortions draws clients from all over Europe. THE NEW YORK TIMES (M) June 18, 48:4, 1977.

Early pregnancy hemorrhages and their management, by M. Shin. KOREAN CENTRAL JOURNAL OF MEDICINE 29(1):5-8, 1975. (Bio. Abstrs. April, 1977, 41853)

Early termination of pregnancy by H. Karman's method, by D. Vasileva. AKUSHERSTVO I GINEKOLOGIIA (Sofia) 16(1):74-81, 1977.

Ectopic pregnancies and the use of intrauterine device and low dose progestogen contraception, by P. Rantakyla, et al. ACTA OBSTETRICIA ET GYNECOLOGICA SCANDINAVICA 56(1):61-62, 1977. (Bio. Abstrs. July, 1977, 5564)

Ectopic pregnancy and first trimester abortion, by L. A. Schonberg. OBSTETRICS AND GYNECOLOGY 49(1 Suppl):73-75, January, 1977.

Edelin case rekindles right-to-life hopes, by R. Adams. FAITH FOR THE FAMILY p. 9, November-December, 1975.

Edelin decision revisited: a survey of the reactions of Connecticut's OB/GYNs, by G. Affleck, et al. CONNECTICUT MEDICINE 41:637-640, October, 1977.

Effect of abortion on obstetric patterns [letter], by A. F. Pentecost. BRITISH MEDICAL JOURNAL 2(6086):578, August

27, 1977.

The effect of attitude and statement favorability upon the judgment of attitude statements. SOCIAL BEHAVIOR AND PERSONALITY 4(2):249-255, 1976.

Effect of 15(s)15-methyl-PGF2alpha-methyl ester vaginal suppositories on circulating hormone levels in early pregnancy, by C. P. Puri, et al. PROSTAGLANDINS 13(2):363-373, February, 1977.

The effect of government policies on out-of-wedlock sex and pregnancy, by K. A. Moore, et al. FAMILY PLANNING PERSPECTIVES 9(4):164-169, July-August, 1977.

Effect of induced (artificial) abortion on the secondary sex ratio in man, by G. D. Golovachev, et al. AKUSHERSTVO I GINEKOLOGIIA (Moscow) (12):40-43, December, 1976.

The effect of industrialization on spontaneous abortion in Iran, by N.Kavoussi. JOURNAL OF OCCUPATIONAL MEDICINE 19(6):419-423, 1977. (Bio. Abstrs. November, 1977, 59812)

Effect of interruption on the prognosis of children from the following pregnancy, by J. Ringel, et al. CESKOSLOVENSKA PEDIATRIE 31(8):442-445, August, 1976.

Effect of L-10503 (a novel antifertility compound) on the synthesis and metabolism of prostaglandins in vivo and in vitro in the pregnant rat placenta, ovary, kidney, and lung, and in rat deciduoma, by L. J. Lerner, et al. ADVANCES IN PROSTAGLANDIN AND THROMBOXANE RESEARCH 2:645-653, 1976.

The effect of legalization of abortion on population growth and public health, by C. Tietze. FAMILY PLANNING PERSPECTIVES 7(3):123-127, 1975. (Socio. Abstrs. 1977, 77I7047)

The effect of prostaglandin F2a on endocrine parameters in early pregnancy, by M. Schmidt-Gollwitzer, et al. ARCHIV FUR

GYNAEKOLOGIE 222(2):149-157, 1977. (Bio. Abstrs. September, 1977, 28936)

The effect of prostaglandin F2alpha on pregnancy in rats and attempts to counteract its abortifacient action, by L. Mercier-Parot, et al. COMPTES RENDUS HERDOMADAIRES DES SEANCES DE L'ACADEMIE DES SCIENCES: D: SCIENCES NATURELLES 283(4):353-355, September 13, 1976.

Effect of prostaglandin PGF2a on the synthesis of placental proteins and human placental lactogen (HPL), by O. Genbacev, et al. PROSTAGLANDINS 13(4):723-733, 1977. (Bio. Abstrs. September, 1977, 28782)

Efficacy of amikacin in septic abortion: serum and urine antibiotic concentrations, by J. Bravo-Sandoval, et al. JOURNAL OF INTERNATIONAL MEDICAL RESEARCH 4(4): 223-227, 1976.

Eisenmenger's syndrome in pregnancy: does heparin prophylaxis improve the maternal mortality rate?, by J. A. Pitts, et al. AMERICAN HEART JOURNAL 93(3):321-326, 1977. (Bio. Abstrs. November, 1977, 58782)

Elective abortion: complications seen in a free-standing clinic, by G. J. L. Wulf, Jr., et al. OBSTETRICS AND GYNECOLOGY 49(3):351-357, 1977. (Bio. Abstrs. July, 1977, 5457)

An empirical argument against abortion, by J. Newman. NEW SCHOLASTICISM 60:384-395, Summer, 1977.

End to medicaid abortion funds, by R. Wilkins. THE NEW YORK TIMES (M) October 11, 24:3, 1977.

Endotoxic shock in obstetrics, by R. Valle, et al. REVISTA CHILENA DE OBSTETRICIA Y GINECOLOGIA 41(3): 158-165, 1976.

An epidemiological study of psychological correlates of delayed decisions to abort, by M. B. Bracken. DISSERTATION ABSTRACTS INTERNATIONAL 35(7-B):3425-3426, 1975. (Psycho. Abstrs. 1977, 3132)

Epidemiology of rubella during 1971-1975. Comparison with abortus cases and malformed newborn in Lombardia (Italy), by V. Carreri, et al. ANNALI SCLAVO 18(5):714-719, September-October, 1976.

Epidural analgesia in midtrimester abortion, by S. Grunstein, et al. INTERNATIONAL JOURNAL OF GYNAECOLOGY AND OBSTETRICS 14(3):257-260, 1976. (Bio. Abstrs. August, 1977, 16420)

Equal rights plan and abortion are opposed by 15,000 at rally, by J. Klemesrud. THE NEW YORK TIMES (M) November 20, 32:5, 1977.

Equine herpesviruses: type 3 as an abortigenic agent, by L. J. Gleeson, et al. AUSTRALIAN VETERINARY JOURNAL 52(8):349-354, August, 1976.

ERA, abortion attract uninvolved; women's meetings agenda items, by M. Papa. NATIONAL CATHOLIC REPORTER 13:1+, July 15, 1977.

Estrogen content in the blood in the artifical interruption of a 1st pregnancy, by G. E. Kniga, et al. AKUSHERSTVO I GINEKOLOGIIA (Moscow) (6):62-63, June, 1976.

Ethical considerations of prenatal genetic diagnosis, by J. F. Tormey. CLINICAL OBSTETRICS AND GYNECOLOGY 19(4):957-963, December, 1976.

Ethical problems in obstetrics and gynaecology, by J. Bonnar. WORLD OF IRISH NURSING 6(4):1, April, 1977.

Ethics and nurses, by C. J. Rogan. NURSING MIRROR AND MIDWIVES' JOURNAL 143:75-76, October 21, 1976.

Eugenic indications in the current status of abortion, by G. Giocoli. MINERVA GINECOLOGIA 28(9):700-703, September, 1976.

Eugenic indications; problems provoked by present-day genetics, by G. Mollica. MINERVA GINECOLOGIA 28(9):714-716,

September, 1976.

European experience with prenatal diagnosis of congenital disease: a survey of 6121 cases, by H. Galjaard. CYTO-GENETICS AND CELL GENETICS 16(6):453-467, 1976. (Bio. Abstrs. December, 1977, 65804)

Evaluation of hypercoagulability in septic abortion, by H. Graeff, et al. HAEMOSTASIS 5(5):285-294, 1976.

Evaluation of intramuscular 15(S)-15-methyl prostaglandin F2a tromethamine salt for induction of abortion, medications to attenuate side effects, and intracervical laminaria tents, by W. Gruber, et al. FERTILITY AND STERILITY 27(9): 1009-1023, 1976. (Bio. Abstrs. March, 1977, 28807)

Evaluation of two dose schedules of 15(S)15 methyl PGF2a methyl ester vaginal suppositories for dilatation of cervix prior to vacuum aspiration for late first trimester abortions, by B. Zoremthangi, et al. CONTRACEPTION 15(3):285-294, 1977. (Bio. Abstrs. August, 1977, 16522)

Evolution of a women's clinic: an alternate system of medical care, by M. J. Gray, et al. AMERICAN JOURNAL OF OBSTETRICS AND GYNECOLOGY 126(7):760-768, December 1, 1976.

Experience with legal abortion, by H. Sjövall. LAKARTIDNINGEN 73(46):3991-3995, November 10, 1976.

Experimental and epizootiologic evidence associating Ornithodoros coriaceus Koch (Acari: Argasidae) with the exposure of cattle to epizootic bovine abortion in California, by E. T. Schmidtmann, et al. JOURNAL OF MEDICAL ENTOMOLOGY 13(3):292-299, December 8, 1976.

Experimentally induced pine needle abortion in range cattle, by L. F. James, et al. CORNELL VETERINARIAN 67(2): 294-299, April, 1977.

Extra-amniotic 15(S)-15 methyl PGF2a to induce abortion: a study of three administration schedules. PROSTAGLANDINS

12(3):443-453, 1976. (Bio. Abstrs. January, 1977, 10597)

Extrauterine contraceptive device and pregnancy. Spontaneous labor. Extraction of IUD by laparoscopy, by G. Galan, et al. REVISTA CHILENA DE OBSTETRICIA Y GINECOLOGIA 41(7):237-241, 1976.

Factors influencing the state of the fetus and the course of abortion after the intra-amniotic instillation of a saline solution, by A. Atanasov, et al. AKUSHERSTVO I GINEKOLOGIIA (Sofia) 16(1):62-66, 1977.

Factors minimising mortality and morbidity from infection after intra-amniotic saline infusion for medical termination of pregnancy, by R. N. Ghosh, et al. JOURNAL OF THE INDIAN MEDICAL ASSOCIATION 66(11):283-285, June 1, 1976.

Facts about abortion for the teenager, by S. Greenhouse. SCHOOL COUNSELOR 22(5):334-337, 1975. (Psycho. Abstrs. 1977, 13407)

Facts and artifacts in the study of intra-uterine mortality: a reconsideration from pregnancy histories, by H. Leridon. POPULATION STUDIES 30(2):319-335, 1976. (Bio. Abstrs. January, 1977, 5545 and Soc. Abstrs. 1977, 77I9623)

Failed prostaglandin F2alpha-induced abortion: a case report, by R. G. Cunanan, Jr., et al. OBSTETRICS AND GYNECOLOGY 49(4):495-496, April, 1977.

Failed termination of pregnancy due to uterus bicornis unicollis with bilateral pregnancy, by M. A. Pelosi, et al. AMERICAN JOURNAL OF OBSTETRICS AND GYNECOLOGY 128(8): 919-920, August 15, 1977.

Failure to demonstrate equine rhinopneumonitis virus as a cause of abortion in mares in New Zealand, by H. G. Pearce, et al. NEW ZEALAND VETERINARY JOURNAL 24(7):127-131, July, 1976.

Failure to diagnose pregnancy as cause of the late abortion

[letter] , by C. Brewer. LANCET 1(8001):46, January 1, 1977.

Family planning. KOREAN CENTRAL JOURNAL OF MEDICINE 31(6):649-650, 1976. (Bio. Abstrs. December, 1977, 66070)

Family planning measures—their merits and demerits, by D. Roy. JOURNAL OF THE INDIAN MEDICAL ASSOCIATION 66(11):265-268, June 1, 1976.

The fate of pregnancy after a cuneiform ovarian resection performed in cases of Stein-Leventhal syndrome clinically diagnosed, by F. Divila, et al. CESKOSLOVENSKA GYNEKOLOGIE 41(9):669-671, November, 1976.

Federal employees get aid for abortion, by L. K. Altman. THE NEW YORK TIMES (M) December 12, 27:1, 1977.

Federal judge again bids H.E.W. continue medicaid for abortions, by M. H. Siegel. THE NEW YORK TIMES (M) July 29, 1:1, 1977.

Federal judge lifts order requiring U.S. to pay for abortions, by E. J. Dionne, Jr. THE NEW YORK TIMES (M) August 5, 1:1, 1977.

Fertility control—symposium on prostaglandins: comment, by W. E. Brenner. FERTILITY AND STERILITY 27(12): 1380-1386, December, 1976.

Fertility in women with gonadal dysgenesis, by F. I. Reyes, et al. AMERICAN JOURNAL OF OBSTETRICS AND GYNECOLOGY 126(6):668-670, 1976. (Bio. Abstrs. March, 1977, 32715)

Fetal loss, twinning and birth weight after oral-contraceptive use, by K. J. Rothman. NEW ENGLAND JOURNAL OF MEDICINE 297(9):468-471, September 1, 1977.

Fetal outcome in trial of antihypertensive treatment in pregnancy, by C. W. G. Redman, et al. LANCET 2(7989):753-

756, 1976. (Bio. Abstrs. February, 1977, 13896)

Fetocide for convenience [letter] , by J. J. van der Wat. SOUTH AFRICAN MEDICAL JOURNAL 52(5):165, July 23, 1977.

Fever in a 22 years old woman. PRAXIS 64(38):1155-1156, September 21, 1976.

Find D&E is safest method of midtrimester abortion, but saline is less risky than prostaglandins: JPSA. FAMILY PLANNING PERSPECTIVES 8:275, November-December, 1976.

Follow-up of 50 adolescent girls 2 years after abortion, by H. Cvejic, et al. CANADIAN MEDICAL ASSOCIATION JOURNAL 116(1):44-46, 1977. (Bio. Abstrs. November, 1977, 53455)

The frequency of uterine contractions in abruptio placentae, by H. J. Odendaal. SOUTH AFRICAN MEDICAL JOURNAL 50(54):2129-2131, December 18, 1976.

Functional state of the blood coagulation and anticoagulation systems in women in missed abortion or labor, by M. M. Kligerman, et al. PEDIATRIIA AKUSHERSTVO I GINE-KOLOGIIA (4):37-39, July-August, 1976.

A further chromosome analysis in induced abortions, by M. Yamamoto, et al. HUMAN GENETICS 34(1):69-71, 1976. (Bio. Abstrs. March, 1977, 32690)

Fusion of homologous chromosomes (15q15q) as cause of recurrent abortion [letter] , by M. Bartsch-Sandhoff. LANCET 1(8010):551, March 5, 1977.

Genetic counselling and parental diagnosis for chromosome anomalies: use of study of spontaneous abortions, by J. Boue, et al. INTERNATIONAL JOURNAL OF GYNAE-COLOGY AND OBSTETRICS 14(4):290-295, 1976. (Bio. Abstrs. September, 1977, 32528)

Genetically determined pathology of fertility in population of couples with spontaneous (habitual) abortions, by V. P.

Kulazhenko, et al. GENETIKA 13(1):138-145, 1977. (Bio. Abstrs. October, 1977, 44940)

Glutamate dehydrogenase isoenzymes of the placenta and fetal membranes in normal pregnancy and pregnancy complicated by sex gland hypofunction, by T. N. Pogorelova, et al. AKUSHERSTVO I GINEKOLOGIIA (Moscow) 5:64-66, May, 1976.

Glycosaminoglycans in the amniotic fluid in normal pregnancy and in cases of clinical signs of threatened fetus, by A. Bromboszcz, et al. GINEKOLOGIA POLASKA 47(11): 1261-1267, November, 1976.

Gov. Grasso orders a halt to payments for elective abortions, by L. Fellows. THE NEW YORK TIMES (M) June 22, 17:4, 1977.

Gravibinon "Schering" in the treatment of habitual abortion and prevention of abortion in uterus hypoplasticus, by I. Shurka-leve, et al. AKUSHERSTVO I GINEKOLOGIIA (Sofia) 15(4):255-259, 1976.

Grieving and unplanned pregnancy, by M. E. Swiger, et al. PSYCHIATRY 39(1):72-80, 1976. (Socio. Abstrs. 1977, 7715933)

Grievous moral mischief, by J. A. Tetlow. AMERICA 137:359, November 19, 1977.

The growth of the ewe abortion chlamydial agent in McCoy cell cultures, by D. Hobson, et al. JOURNAL OF COMPARA-TIVE PATHOLOGY 87(1):155-159, January, 1977.

The gynecological and endocrinological sequelae after the use of MAP during the pregnancy, by E. Padovani, et al. FRACAS-TORO 68(1-2):101-117, 1975. (Bio. Abstrs. December, 1977, 66288)

An habitual aborter's self-concept during the course of a success-ful pregnancy, by Y-M. Chao. MATERNAL-CHILD NURS-ING JOURNAL 6:165-175, Fall, 1977.

Habitual abortion in cats [letter] , by G. M. Acland, et al. AUS-
TRALIAN VETERINARY JOURNAL 50(4):179-180,
April, 1974.

Hare, abortion and the golden rule, by H. Sher. PHILOSOPHY
AND PUBLIC AFFAIRS 6:185-190, Winter, 1977.

Hare on abortion, by R. Werner. ANALYSIS 36:177-181, June,
1976.

Health education activities in the prevention of abortion, by E.
V. Smoliakova. FEL'DSKER I AKUSHERKA 42(1):35-
38, January, 1977.

Helping hand awaits unwed mothers, by A. A. Narvaez. THE
NEW YORK TIMES (M) February 13, XI, 6:5, 1977.

High court, Congress act on abortion. NATIONAL CATHOLIC
REPORTER 13:8, July 1, 1977.

High court silence, by I. Silver. THE NEW YORK TIMES (M)
August 6, 17:3, 1977.

High court's abortion rulings: what they mean. U.S. NEWS
AND WORLD REPORT 83:66, July 4, 1977.

Hip prosthesis and post-abortion streptococcal infection in lupus,
by P. Godeau, et al. SEMAINE DES HOPITAUX DE PARIS
53(10):633-635, March 9, 1977.

Hormone changes in relation to the time of fetal death after
prostaglandin-induced abortion, by I. S. Fraser, et al.
PROSTAGLANDINS 13(6):1161-1178, 1977. (Bio. Abstrs.
November, 1977, 58981)

Hormone therapy in threatened abortion and premature labor,
by G. Kikawa. JAPANESE JOURNAL FOR MIDWIVES
30(12):750-752, December, 1976.

House bars medicaid abortions and funds for enforcing quotas,
by M. Tolchin. THE NEW YORK TIMES (M) June 18,
1:13, 1977.

House leaders seek to end standoff with senate over abortion funds, by M. Tolchin. THE NEW YORK TIMES (M) September 27, 24:3, 1977.

House liberals join conservatives in rejecting a new abortion plan, by M. Tolchin. THE NEW YORK TIMES (M) December 7, 19:3, 1977.

House rejects plan on medicaid abortion voted by the senate, by M. Tolchin. THE NEW YORK TIMES (M) November 4, 1:5, 1977.

House votes change in stand on abortion, by M. Tolchin. THE NEW YORK TIMES (M) October 13, 15:1, 1977.

House votes to bar abortion aid for victims of rape and incest. THE NEW YORK TIMES (M) August 3, 11:1, 1977.

How many illegal abortions? by C. Francome. THE BRITISH JOURNAL OF CRIMINOLOGY 16(4):389-392, 1976. (Socio. Abstrs. 1977, 7718243)

How many trials will Morgentaler face? by E. Farkas. LAST POST 5:13-14, December, 1976.

How to stimulate the placental function, by A. Fanard, et al. REPRODUCTION 3(1-2):15-25, January-June, 1976.

How women feel about abortion: psychological, attitudinal and physical effects of legal abortion, by L. M. Shalaby. DISSERTATION ABSTRACTS INTERNATIONAL 36(4-A): 2035, 1975. (Psycho. Abstrs. 1977, 10191)

Human rights: do we practice what we preach; address to Knights of Columbus, August 16, 1977, by J. Bernardin. ORIGINS 7:201-204, September 15, 1977.

Human rights in relationship to induced abortion, by C. Tietze. THE JOURNAL OF SEX RESEARCH 10(2):97-109, 1974. (Socio. Abstrs. 1977, 7714024)

The humanity of the unborn; reprint from The Washington Post, by H. Hyde. L'OSSERVATORE ROMANO 37(494):15, September, 1977.

Human and persons, by L. Newton. ETHICS p. 332, July, 1975.

Husband's rights in abortion, by A. Etzioni. TRIAL 12:56-58, November, 1976.

Hypokalemia and cardiac arrhythmia associated with prostaglandin-induced abortion, by R. L. Burt, et al. OBSTETRICS AND GYNECOLOGY 50(1 Suppl):45S-46S, July, 1977.

Identification by Q and G bands of chromosome anomalies in spontaneous abortion, by J. Boué, et al. ANNALES DE GENETIQUE 19(4):233-239, December, 1976.

The immunobiology of abortion [editorial] , by R. T. Smith. NEW ENGLAND JOURNAL OF MEDICINE (22):1249-1250, November 25, 1976.

Immunologic reactivity in infectious diseases following labor and abortion, by V. I. Kulakov, et al. AKUSHERSTVO I GINEKOLOGIIA (Moscow) (4):32-35, April, 1976.

Immunological characteristics of women with an interrupted pregnancy of unexplained etiology, by V. V. Kovalenko, et al. PEDIATRIIA AKUSHERSTVO I GINEKOLOGIIA (2):41-43, March-April, 1977.

Implications of fertility patterns in the Republic of Korea: a study by computer simulation, by C. J. Mode, et al. INTERNATIONAL JOURNAL OF BIO-MEDICAL COMPUTING 7(4):289-305, 1976. (Bio. Abstrs. February, 1977, 23761)

Improvement of the surgical technic in induced abortions using a supplementary instrument (special handgrip with revolving support for interruption cannulas), by W. Anton, et al. ZENTRALBLATT FUR GYNAEKOLOGIE 98(22):1401-1403, 1976.

In necessity and sorrow [book] . A review, by N. E. Zinberg. THE NEW YORK TIMES January 9, VII, p. 6, 1977.

In search of conscience on abortion. THE NEW YORK TIMES
June 22, 22:1, 1977.

Incidence of abortive ova in abortion material, by P. Emmrich,
et al. ZENTRALBLATT FUR GYNAEKOLOGIE 99(9):
541-546, 1977.

Incidence of post-abortion psychosis: a prospective study, by
C. Brewer. BRITISH MEDICAL JOURNAL 1:476-477,
February 19, 1977.

Incidence of repeated legal abortion [letter], by C. Brewer, et
al. BRITISH MEDICAL JOURNAL 2(6048):1382, Decem-
ber 4, 1976.

Inconsistencies in therapeutic abortion report [letter], by T. B.
MacLachian. CANADIAN MEDICAL ASSOCIATION JOUR-
NAL 117(3):220-222, August 6, 1977.

Increased reporting of menstrual symptoms among women who
used induced abortion, by L. H. Roht, et al. AMERICAN
JOURNAL OF OBSTETRICS AND GYNECOLOGY 127(4):
356-362, 1977.

Indication for pregnancy interruption in patients with heart
diseases, by Y. Hatano. FORTSCHRITTE DU MEDIZIN
95(11):685-689, March 17, 1977.

Indications for amniocentesis for prenatal fetal karyotype determination, by I. V. Lur'e. TSITOLOGIIA I GENETIKA
10(3):198-200, 1976. (Bio. Abstrs. January, 1977, 8195)

Induced abortion and brain damage, by A. Rett. WIENER
MEDIZINISCHE WOCHENSCHRIFT 126(49-50):700-702,
December 3, 1976.

Induced abortion and sterilization among women who became
mothers as adolescents, by J. F. Jekel, et al. AMERICAN
JOURNAL OF PUBLIC HEALTH 67:621-625, July, 1977.

Induced abortion in the 8-9th week of pregnancy with vaginally
administered 15-methyl PGF2 methyl ester, by A. Leader, et

al. PROSTAGLANDINS 12(4):631-637, 1976. (Bio. Abstrs. February, 1977, 22692)

Induced abortion with intramuscular administration of 15(S)-15methyl-prostaglandin F 2 alpha, by H. Halle, et al. ZENTRALBLATT FÜR GYNAEKOLOGIE 99(9):537-540, 1977.

Induction of abortion and labor by extraamniotic isotonic saline, with or without addition of oxytocin, in cases of missed abortion, missed labor and antepartum fetal death, by M. Blum, et al. INTERNATIONAL SURGERY 62(2):95-96, February, 1977.

Induction of abortion in the 2d and 3d trimester with prostaglandins, PGE2 and PGF2 alpha. Indications for differences between the effect of PGE2 and PGF2 alpha on the pregnant uterus, by M. Cornely. MEDIZINISCHE MONATSSCHRIFT 31(2):73-79, February, 1977.

Induction of first and second trimester abortion by the vaginal administration of 15-methyl-PGF2alpha methyl ester, by M. Bygdeman, et al. ADVANCES IN PROSTAGLANDIN AND THROMBOXANE RESEARCH 2:693-704, 1976.

Induction of labor in patients with missed abortion and fetal death in utero with prostaglandin E2 suppositories, by N. H. Lauersen, et al. AMERICAN JOURNAL OF OBSTETRICS AND GYNECOLOGY 127(6):609-611, 1977. (Bio. Abstrs. August, 1977, 16534)

Induction of midtrimester abortion by the combined method of continuous extravovular infusion of prostaglandin F2a and intracervical laminaria tents, by J. E. Hodgson, et al. FERTILITY AND STERILITY 27(12):1359-1365, 1976. (Bio. Abstrs. June, 1977, 70935)

Induction of mid-trimester abortion with intra-amniotic injection of prostaglandin F-2alpha, by A. J. Horowitz. MINNESOTA MEDICINE 60(7 Pt. 1):509-512, July, 1977.

Induction of midtrimester abortion with intra-amniotic urea

and intravenous oxytocin, by W. G. Smith, et al. AMERI-
CAN JOURNAL OF OBSTETRICS AND GYNECOLOGY
127(3):228-231, 1977. (Bio. Abstrs. May, 1977, 59034)

Inequities in abortion law found result of attitudes in people and
institutions, by J. S. Bennett. CANADIAN MEDICALE
ASSOCIATION JOURNAL 116(5):553-554, March 5, 1977.

Infant survival following uterine rupture and complete abruptio
placentae, by S. Semchyshyn, et al. OBSTETRICS AND
GYNECOLOGY 50(1 Suppl):74S-75S, July, 1977.

Infection in newborn siblings, by P. H. Azimi, et al. AMERICAN
JOURNAL OF DISEASES OF CHILDREN 131(4):398-399,
1977. (Bio. Abstrs. September, 1977, 27613)

Inflammation of the placenta in threatened abortion, by M. Iu.
Makkaveeva, et al. AKUSHERSTVO I GINEKOLOGIIA
(Moscow) (4):51-54, April, 1977.

Influence of enflurane on blood loss from the pregnant uterus,
by C. Van Damme, et al. ACTA ANAESTHESIOLOGICA
BELIGCA 27(Suppl):259-261, 1976.

Influence of the kind of anesthesia and length of hospitalization
on the frequency of early complications of abortion, by L.
Andolsek, et al. JUGOSLOVENSKA GINEKOLOGIJA I
OPSTETRICIJA 16(3):175-183, May-June, 1976.

Influence of personality attributes on abortion experiences, by
E. W. Freeman. AMERICAN JOURNAL OF ORTHOPSY-
CHIATRY 47:503-513, July, 1977.

The influence of physicians' attitudes on abortion performance,
patient management and professional fees, by C. A. Nathanson, et al. FAMILY PLANNING PERSPECTIVES 9(4):158-
163, July-August, 1977.

International trends. . .pregnancy and the unmarried girl, by H.
P. David. JOURNAL OF PSYCHIATRIC NURSING AND
MENTAL HEALTH SERVICES 15:40-42, February, 1977.

Interruption before and after March 9, 1972, by E. Heyer. ZENTRALBLATT FUR GYNAEKOLOGIE 98(20):1248-1251, 1976.

Interruption of early pregnancy by a new vacuum aspiration method, by S. Mihaly, et al. ORVOSI HETILAP 117(45): 2731-2734, November 7, 1976.

Interview follow-up of abortion applicant dropouts, by M. E. Swiger, et al. SOCIAL PSYCHIATRY 11(3):135-143, 1976. (Psycho. Abstrs. 1977, 3120)

Intra-amniotic administration of 15(S)-15-methyl-prostaglandin F2a for the induction of mid-trimester abortion, by J. R. Dingfelder, et al. AMERICAN JOURNAL OF OBSTETRICS AND GYNECOLOGY 125(6):821-826, 1976. (Bio. Abstrs. February, 1977, 17300)

Intra-amniotic prostaglandin F2a and urea for midtrimester abortion, by L. Wellman, et al. FERTILITY AND STERILITY 27(12):1374-1379, 1976. (Bio. Abstrs. June, 1977, 70933)

Intra-amniotic urea and prostaglandin F2a for midtrimester abortion: a modified regimen, by R. T. Burkman, et al. AMERICAN JOURNAL OF OBSTETRICS AND GYNECOLOGY 126(3):328-333, 1976. (Bio. Abstrs. February, 1977, 22702)

Intramuscular prostaglandin (15S)-15-methyl PGF2a (THAM) in midtrimester abortion, by E. S. Henriques, et al. PROSTAGLANDINS 13(1):183-191, 1977. (Bio. Abstrs. May, 1977, 59036)

Intrauterine adhesions secondary to elective abortion: hysteroscopic diagnosis and management, by C. M. March, et al. OBSTETRICS AND GYNECOLOGY 48(4):422-424, 1976. (Bio. Abstrs. February, 1977, 23565)

The intrauterine device and deaths from spontaneous abortion, by W. Cates, Jr., et al. NEW ENGLAND JOURNAL OF MEDICINE 294(21):1155-1159, 1976. (Bio. Abstrs. March, 1977, 35535)

Intrauterine device should be removed during pregnancy. LAKARTIDNINGEN 73(5):4541, December 15, 1976.

Intrauterine extra-amnial administration of prostaglandin F 2 alpha for the induction of abortion in primigravidae and problem cases, by G. Göretzlehner, et al. ZENTRALBLATT FUR GYNAEKOLOGIE 98(20):1252-1257, 1976.

Intrauterine extra-amniotic 15(S)-15-methyl prostaglandin F2a for induction of early midtrimester abortion, by A. G. Shapiro. FERTILITY AND STERILITY 27(9):1024-1028, 1976. (Bio. Abstrs. March, 1977, 28805)

Intrauterine prostaglandin E2 as an postconceptional abortifacient, by I. Z. Mackenzie, et al. ADVANCES IN PROSTAGLANDIN AND THROMBOXANE RESEARCH 2:687-691, 1976.

Introduction of second trimester abortions with 15-(S)-methyl prostaglandin F2alpha by intra-uterine and intramuscular routes, by V. Haingorani, et al. JOURNAL OF THE INDIAN MEDICAL ASSOCIATION 66(11):279-283, June 1, 1976.

The Irish emigrant and the abortion crisis. WORLD OF IRISH NURSING 4(10):1-2, October, 1975.

Is the concept of "habitual abortion" fiction? by W. Vlaanderen. NEDERLANDS TIJDSCHRIFT VOOR GENEESKUNDE 121(11):439-442, March 12, 1977.

Is there any evidence that the maternal HPL serum-concentration is of prognostic value in cases of threatened abortion? by P. Berle, et al. ZEITSCHRIFT FUR GEBURTSCHILFE UND PERINATOLOGIE 181(3):211-217, June, 1977.

The isolation of Actinobacillus equuli from equine abortion [letter], by R. F. Webb, et al. AUSTRALIAN VETERINARY JOURNAL 52(2):100-101, February, 1976.

The isolation of a leptospire from an aborted bovine fetus, by W. A. Ellis, et al. VETERINARY RECORD 99(23):458-

459, December 4, 1976.

Isolation of mycoplasmas from an aborted equine foetus [letter] , by A. R. Moorthy, et al. AUSTRALIAN VETERINARY JOURNAL 52(8):385, August, 1976.

Isolation of Spirillum/Vibrio-like organisms from bovine fetuses, by W. A. Ellis, et al. VETERINARY RECORD 100(21): 451-452, May 21, 1977.

The isolation of a strain of Leptospira serogroup icterohaemor-rhagiae from an aborted bovine foetus, by W. A. Ellis, et al. BRITISH VETERINARY JOURNAL 133(1):108-109, Jan-uary-February, 1977.

Israel selects middle-ground abortion law. THE NEW YORK TIMES (M) February 6, IV, 7:1, 1977.

The Israeli dilemma in the generation game, by E. Silver. GUAR-DIAN p. 11, February 1, 1977.

Isthmico-cervical insufficiency as a cause of habitual miscarriage, by A. P. Kiriushchenkov. FEL'DSKER I AKUSHERKA 41(8):25-28, August, 1976.

It will not go away. ECONOMIST 262:26, February 5, 1977.

Italy turns down an abortion bill. THE NEW YORK TIMES (S) June 12, IV, 4:2, 1977.

Italy's abortion bill. THE NEW YORK TIMES (S) January 23, IV, 2:2, 1977.

Jain and Judaeo-Christian respect for life, by J. A. Miles, Jr. AMERICAN ACADEMY OF RELIGION JOURNAL 44: 453-457, September, 1976.

Joseph Califano's "Alarming Words" [letter] , by S. Raphael. THE NEW YORK TIMES January 26, 22:6, 1977.

Just for the rich? ECONOMIST 263:44+, June 25, 1977.

Killing with kindness, by K. Marquart. CONCORDIA THEOLO-
GY QUARTERLY 41:44-49, January, 1977.

The kinetics of extraamniotically injected prostaglandins to in-
duce midtrimester abortion, by I. Z. MacKenzie, et al.
PROSTAGLANDINS 13(5):975-986, 1977. (Bio. Abstrs.
October, 1977, 40678)

Kitchen-table justice, by T. Wilker. THE NEW YORK TIMES
June 28, 31:5, 1977.

LCWR thinks no effective anti-abortion law possible, by J.
Kennedy. OUR SUNDAY VISITOR 66:2, August 21, 1977.

Laboratory studies in the diagnosis of early missed abortion, by
J. Krajewski, et al. WIADOMOSCI LEKARSKIE 29(23):
2111-2114, December 1, 1976.

Laparoscopic observation of the female pelvis following abortions by suction curettage, by P. K. Khan. INTERNATION-
AL SURGERY 62(2):77-78, February, 1977.

Late sequelae of interrupted pregnancy, by G. Venzmer.
KRANKENPFLEGE 30(10):290-291, October, 1976.

Law for the nurse supervisor. Action for wrongful life, by H.
Creighton. SUPERVISOR NURSE 8:12-15, April, 1977.

Law of abortion with special reference to Commonwealth Caribbean, by P. K. Menon. THE ANGLO-AMERICAN LAW
REVIEW 5:311-345, October-December, 1976.

Legal abortion, by H. P. Tarnesby. MINERVA GINECOLOGIA
28(5):458-473, May, 1976.

Legal abortion, by C. Tietze, et al. SCIENTIFIC AMERICAN
236:21-27, January, 1977.

Legal abortion among New York City residents: an analysis according to socioeconomic and demographic characteristics,
by M. J. Kramer. FAMILY PLANNING PERSPECTIVES
7(3):128-137, 1975. (Socio. Abstrs. 1977, 7717343)

Legal abortion: are American black women healthier because of it? [conference paper] by W. Cates, Jr. PHYLON 38:267-281, September, 1977.

Legal abortion during the first trimester of pregnancy at the University Hospital for Women in Novi Sad (1960-1975), by B. M. Beric, et al. ZENTRALBLATT FUR GYNAEKOLOGIE 99(6):371-376, 1977.

Legal abortion: a half-decade of experience, by J. Pakter, et al. FAMILY PLANNING PERSPECTIVES 7(6):248-257, 1975. (Socio. Abstrs. 1977, 7717028)

Legal abortion in Telemark, by P. Hoglend. TIDSSKRIFT FOR DEN NORSKE LAEGEFORENING 97(3):130-133, January 30, 1977.

Legal abortion in the United States, 1975-1976, by E. Sullivan, et al. FAMILY PLANNING PERSPECTIVES 9(3):116-129, May-June, 1977.

Legal abortion mortality in the United States: epidemiologic surveillance 1972-1974, by W. Cates, Jr., et al. JAMA; JOURNAL OF THE AMERICAN MEDICAL ASSOCIATION 237(5):452-455, 1977. (Bio. Abstrs. May, 1977, 59845)

Legal abortion: trends in various parts of the world, by C. Tietze, et al. SCIENTIFIC AMERICAN 236:21-27, January, 1977.

Legal abortions and trends in age-specific marriage rates, by K. E. Bauman, et al. AMERICAN JOURNAL OF PUBLIC HEALTH 67:52-53, January, 1977.

Legal abortions in the United States: rates and ratios by race and age, 1972-1974, by C. Tietze. FAMILY PLANNING PERSPECTIVES 9:12-15, January-February, 1977.

Legal aspects of menstrual regulation: some preliminary observations, by L. T. Lee, et al. JOURNAL OF FAMILY LAW 14(2):181-221, 1975. (Socio. Abstrs. 1977, 7714360)

Legal considerations and prenatal genetic diagnosis, by L. F. Hifman, 3d. CLINICAL OBSTETRICS AND GYNECOLOGY 19(4):965-972, December, 1976.

Legal enforcement, moral pluralism and abortion, by R. T. De George. PROCEEDINGS OF THE AMERICAN CATHOLIC PHILOSOPHICAL ASSOCIATION 49:171-180, 1975.

Legislators say abortion study invades privacy, by R. J. Meislin. THE NEW YORK TIMES (M) May 12, 1:4, 1977.

Lesson in judicial abdication: Roe v. Arizona Board of Regents [(Ariz) 549 P 2d 150] and the right of privacy. ARIZONA STATE LAW REVIEW 1976:499-524, 1976.

Let them eat cake, by G. J. Annas. HASTINGS CENTER REPORT 7(4):8-9, August, 1977.

Liberalized abortion bill in Italy passes in chamber, goes to senate, by A. Shuster. THE NEW YORK TIMES (M) January 22, 1:2, 1977.

A life threatening pregnancy, by E. Moult. MATERNAL-CHILD NURSING JOURNAL 4(3):207-211, Fall, 1975.

Lithopedion. An anatomo-clinical study apropos of 1 case, by B. Ait-Ouyahia, et al. JOURNAL OF GYNECOLOGIE, OBSTETRIQUE ET BIOLOGIE DE LA REPRODUCTION 6(2):233-238, March, 1977.

Lobbying on abortion issue intensifies as conferees remain deadlocked, by M. Tolchin. THE NEW YORK TIMES (M) September 15, II, 16:3, 1977.

Lobbyist on women's rights press congress for action. THE NEW YORK TIMES (M) August 13, 9:1, 1977.

The logic of abortion, by B. Williams. LISTENER 98:258-260, September 1, 1977.

The Lombardy Society of Obstetrics and Gynecology: oral ballot on the problem of abortion. ANNALI DI OSTETRICIA,

GINECOLOGIA, MEDICINA PERINATALE 97(3):133-136, May-June, 1976.

Love, sex, permissiveness and abortion: a test of alternative models, by A. M. Mirande, et al. ARCHIVES OF SEXUAL BEHAVIOR 5(6):553-566, 1976. (Bio. Abstrs. May, 1977, 53780 and Soc. Abstrs. 1977, 77I9674)

Malpractice decisions you should know about. Is a husband's consent necessary for abortion? MEDICAL TIMES 104(10): 160-162, October, 1976.

Management of the abortion problem in an English city, by J. B. Lawson. LANCET 2(7998):1288-1291, 1976. (Bio. Abstrs. May, 1977, 59877)

Management of the endotoxic shock in abortion, by G. Del Rio, et al. REVISTA CHILENA DE OBSTETRICIA Y GINE-COLOGIA 41(3):166-173, 1976.

The management of midtrimester abortion failures by vaginal evacuation, by R. T. Burkman, et al. OBSTETRICS AND GYNECOLOGY 49(2):233-236, February, 1977.

The management of septic abortion in an intensive care unit, by R. D. Cane, et al. EUROPEAN JOURNAL OF INTENSIVE CARE 2(3):135-138, November, 1976.

Marches call for abortion bar. THE NEW YORK TIMES (S) January 24, 29:3, 1977.

Markov chain model for events following induced abortion, by R. H. Shachtman, et al. OPERATIONS RESEARCH 24:916-932, September, 1976.

Massachusetts Supreme Judicial Court reverses conviction of Dr. Kenneth Edelin, by L. H. Glantz. MEDICO-LEGAL BULLE-TIN 5:3-4, Winter, 1977.

Maternal death and the I.U.D. [editorial]. LANCET 2(7997): 1234, December 4, 1976.

Maternal death and the I.U.D. [letter] , by R. A. Sparks, et al.
LANCET 1(8002):98, January 8, 1977.

Maternal-fetal relation. Absence of an immunologic blocking
factor from the serum of women with chronic abortions, by
R. E. Rocklin, et al. NEW ENGLAND JOURNAL OF MED-
ICINE 295(22):1209-1213, 1976. (Bio. Abstrs. April, 1977,
38754)

Maternal indications for abortion, by M. Mall-Haefeli. WIENER
MEDIZINISCHE WOCHENSCHRIFT 127(1):5-9, 1977.

Maternal primary hyperpara-thyroidism of pregnancy: successful
treatment by parathyroidectomy, by R. F. Gaeke, et al.
JAMA; JOURNAL OF THE AMERICAN MEDICAL ASSO-
CIATION 238(6):508-509, 1977. (Bio. Abstrs. December,
1977, 62119)

Maternal serum alpha-fetoprotein and spontaneous abortion, by
N. Wald, et al. BRITISH JOURNAL OF OBSTETRICS AND
GYNAECOLOGY 84(5):357-362, May, 1977.

Maternal serum alpha-fetoprotein in abnormal pregnancies and
during induced abortion, by D. M. Hay, et al. JOURNAL
OF REPRODUCTIVE MEDICINE 19(2):75-78, August,
1977.

Maternal serum alpha-feto-protein: its value in antenatal diagnosis of genetic disease and in obstetrical-gynaecological care,
by Z. A. Habib. ACTA OBSTETRICIA ET GYNECOLOGICA
SCANDINAVICA. SUPPLEMENT 8(16):1-90, 1976. (Bio.
Abstrs. October, 1977, 47804)

Maternal serum and amniotic fluid alpha-fetoprotein as a marker
of acute fetal distress in a midtrimester abortion model, by
R. R. Weiss, et al. OBSTETRICS AND GYNECOLOGY
48(6):718-722, December, 1976.

The mechanism of midtrimester abortion induced by intra-
amniotic instillation of hypertonic saline: a modification of
Gustavii's lysosomal hypothesis, by L. H. Honore. AMERI-
CAN JOURNAL OF OBSTETRICS AND GYNECOLOGY

126(8):1011-1015, 1976. (Bio. Abstrs. April, 1977, 47767)

Medicaid assistance for elective abortions: the statutory and constitutional issues. ST. JOHN'S LAW REVIEW 50:751-770, Summer, 1976.

Medicaid-funded abortions not mandated by federal law: U.S. Supreme Court. HOSPITALS 51:17-18, August 1, 1977.

Medicaid is banned in some abortions, by W. H. Waggoner. THE NEW YORK TIMES (S) June 28, 67:4, 1977.

Medical and social aspects of pregnancy among adolescents. Part II. Comparative study of abortions and deliveries, by E. Rautanen, et al. ANNALES CHIRURGIAE ET GYNAE-COLOGIAE FENNIAE 66(3):122-130, 1977.

Medical and surgical methods of early termination of pregnancy, by G. M. Filshie. PROCEEDINGS OF THE ROYAL SO-CIETY OF LONDON; B: BIOLOGICAL SCIENCES 195 (1118):115-127, December 10, 1976.

Medical ethics: fact or fantasy? by A. Doyle. AORN JOUR-NAL 23:827-831, April, 1976.

Medical genetic consultation in congenital developmental anomalies and aborted pregnancy, by V. A. Shileiko, et al. PEDIATRIIA AKUSHERSTVO I GINECOLOGIIA (2):45-46, March-April, 1977.

Medical opinion on abortion in Jamaica: a national Delphi survey of physician, nurses, and midwives, by K. A. Smith, et al. STUDIES IN FAMILY PLANNING 7(12):334-339, December, 1976.

Medical termination of midtrimester pregnancy in a community hospital, by P. E. Stroup. JOURNAL OF THE MEDICAL SOCIETY OF NEW JERSEY 74(9):747-752, September, 1977.

Medical termination of pregnancy—its status, achievements and lacunae, by S. Grewal. JOURNAL OF THE INDIAN MEDI-

CAL ASSOCIATION 66(11):269-275, June 1, 1976.

Medico-legal aspects of therapeutic abortion, by P. Zangani. MINERVA GINECOLOGIA 28(9):703-705, September, 1976.

Men's reactions to their partners' elective abortions, by A. A. Rothstein. AMERICAN JOURNAL OF OBSTETRICS AND GYNECOLOGY 128(8):831-837, August 15, 1977.

Menstrual regulation (M.R.) service (a preliminary report), by A. R. Khan, et al. BANGLADISH MEDICAL RESEARCH COUNCIL BULLETIN 1(2):90-96, October, 1975.

Method of payment—relation to abortion complications, by R. G. Smith, et al. HEALTH AND SOCIAL WORK 1(2):5-28, May, 1976.

Methodist women to meet only where E.R.A. wins. THE NEW YORK TIMES (S) April 27, 18:6, 1977.

Methods of artificial termination of pregnancy with special consideration of the use of prostaglandin, by R. Kepp. GEBURT-SHILFE UND FRAUENHEILKUNDE 36(9):700-705, September, 1976.

Mid-trimester abortion and its complications [editorial] . MEDICAL JOURNAL OF AUSTRALIA 1(4):82-83, January 22, 1977.

Mid-trimester abortion by dilatation and evacuation: a safe and practical alternative, by D. A. Grimes, et al. NEW ENGLAND JOURNAL OF MEDICINE 296(20):1141-1145, 1977. (Bio. Abstrs. September, 1977, 35546)

Midtrimester abortion by intraamniotic prostaglandin F2alpha. Safer than saline? by D. A. Grimes, et al. OBSTETRICS AND GYNECOLOGY 49(5):612-616, May, 1977.

Midtrimester abortion: a comparison of intraamniotic prostaglandin F2a and hypertonic saline, by M. I. Ragab, et al. INTERNATIONAL JOURNAL OF GYNAECOLOGY AND

OBSTETRICS 14(5):393-396, 1976. (Bio. Abstrs. October, 1977, 40668)

Mid-trimester abortions [letter]. NEW ENGLAND JOURNAL OF MEDICINE 297(9):511-512, September 1, 1977.

Midtrimester and missed abortion treated with intramuscular 15 (s)-15 methyl PGF2alpha, by A. P. Lange, et al. PROSTA-GLANDINS 14(2):389-395, August, 1977.

Minimizing the risk of amniocentesis for prenatal diagnosis, by A. I. Goldstein, et al. JAMA; JOURNAL OF THE AMERICAN MEDICAL ASSOCIATION 237(13):1336-1338, 1977. (Bio. Abstrs. July, 1977, 7600)

Mobilizing for abortion rights, by J. Benshoof. THE CIVIL LIBERTIES REVIEW 4:76-79, September-October, 1977.

Modification of the rate of complications in the inflammatory adnexa process and pregnancy interruption, by W. Franz, et al. ZENTRALBLATT FUR GYNAEKOLOGIE 99(2):113-116, 1977.

The monstrous regiments battle for and against abortion. ECON-OMIST 264:19-20, July 16, 1977.

Morbidity and mortality associated with legal abortion [letter], by M. Potts. MEDICAL JOURNAL OF AUSTRALIA 2(1): 30-31, July 3, 1976.

More abortion patients are young, unmarried, nonwhite; proce-dures performed earlier, and by suction; 1/5 repeats. FAMI-LY PLANNING PERSPECTIVES 9(3):130-131, May-June, 1977.

Morgentaler [Morgentaler v. Regina (1975) 43 D L R (3d) 161] case: criminal process and abortion law, by B. M. Dickens. OSGOODE HALL LAW JOURNAL 14:229-274, October, 1976.

Mormon turnout overwhelms women's conference in Utah, by J. M. Crewdson. THE NEW YORK TIMES (M) July 25,

26:4, 1977.

Mother with D/D translocation in genetic counseling, by J. Stepien, et al. GINEKOLOGIA POLASKA 48(3):285-288, March, 1977.

Motivation for induced abortion and post-interruption sequelae, by V. Bebjakova. CESKOSLOVENSKA GYNEKOLOGIE 41(9):692-693, November, 1976.

Motives, process and consequences of abortion among the population attending the Obstetrical Emergency Unit of the Maternal Health Service, by E. B. Farina. REVISTA DA ESCOLA DE ENFERMAGEN DA UNIVERSIDADE DE SAO PAULO 9(2):323-346, August, 1975.

Mr. Benyon's gift, by D. Gould. NEW STATESMAN 93:457, April 8, 1977.

Mr. Carter's cruel abortion plan. THE NEW YORK TIMES June 13, 28:1, 1977.

A mucosal disease virus as a cause of abortion hairy birth coat and unthriftiness in sheep. 1. Infiction of pregnant ewes and observations on aborted foetuses and lambs dying before one week of age, by J. W. Plant, et al. AUSTRALIAN VETERINARY JOURNAL 52(2):57-63, February, 1976.

Must we accept either the conservative or the liberal view on abortion?, by H. V. McLachlan. ANALYSIS 37:197-204, June, 1977.

National survey of doctors, nurses and social workers on liberalization of the Barbados abortion law, by M. D. Hoyos, et al. WEST INDIAN MEDICAL JOURNAL 26(4):2-11, March, 1977.

Never again! Never again? Can we lose our right to abortion? by R. B. Gratz. MS MAGAZINE 6:54-55, July, 1977.

The new abortion debate. COMMONWEAL 104:451-452, July 22, 1977.

A new ethical approach to abortion and its implications for the euthanasia dispute, by R. F. R. Gardner. JOURNAL OF MEDICAL ETHICS 1:127-131, September, 1975.

New findings on the physiology of reproduction in the dog and cat: consequences for the control of estrus, contraception abortion and therapy, by W. Jöchle. DEUTSCHE TIERAERZ-TLICHE WOCHENSCHRIFT 83(12):564-569, December 5, 1976.

A new immunochemical tube test for pregnancy using the latex-agglutination inhibition reaction. II. Clinical results, by H. Hepp, et al. DEUTSCHE MEDIZINSCHE WOCHENSCHRIFT 101(45):1639-1643, November 5, 1976.

New Jersey briefs: timing of abortion. THE NEW YORK TIMES (S) April 25, 67:1, 1977.

New Jersey court rules hospitals cannot prohibit abortions. HOSPITALS 51:20-21, January 1, 1977.

New regulations on legal abortion, by A. Hollmann. DEUTSCHE MEDIZINISCHE WOCHENSCHRIFT 102(7):252-254, February 18, 1977.

A new role for nurses. . .abortion counselling. . .Toronto General Hospital, by B. Easterbrook, et al. CANADIAN NURSE 73:28-30, January, 1977.

Newer fashions in illegitimacy, by R. H. Edmunds, et al. BRITISH MEDICAL JOURNAL 1(6062):701-703, March 12, 1977.

Nurses and abortion, by M. J. Tobin. THE NEW YORK TIMES January 30, XXI, 18:1, 1977.

Nurses and abortion: more viewpoints [letters]. THE NEW YORK TIMES March 13, XXI, 27:1, 1977.

Nursing decisions. Experiences in clinical problem solving. Series 2, Part 8: H. Joyce, an elective abortion patient, by R. De Tornyay, et al. RN; NATIONAL MAGAZINES FOR NURSES 40:55-61, June, 1977.

Obsessive-compulsive neurosis after viewing the fetus during therapeutic abortion, by S. Lipper, et al. AMERICAN JOURNAL OF PSYCHOTHERAPY 30(4):666-674, 1976. (Psycho. Abstrs. 1977, 8587)

Of abortion and the unfairness of life, by L. Morrow. TIME 110:49, August 1, 1977.

Of abortion, the law and Califano's views [letter], by K. P. Carroll. THE NEW YORK TIMES February 5, 18:6, 1977.

Of ballots and morality, by Msgr. F. B. Donnelly. THE NEW YORK TIMES March 21, 26:5, 1977.

OH research at Northwick Park, by M. Hamilton. OCCUPA-TIONAL HEALTH (London) 29:108-112, March, 1977.

On abortion, the houses still remain miles apart, by M. Tolchin. THE NEW YORK TIMES (M) November 27, IV, 4:3, 1977.

On ecumenical approach to abortion; statement by the Los Angeles Catholic-Jewish Respect Life Committee, by R. Casey. NATIONAL CATHOLIC REPORTER 14:2, November 11, 1977.

On funding abortions, by F. S. Jaffe. THE NEW YORK TIMES July 29, 20:4, 1977.

On seeking abortion counseling [letter], by W. Cates, Jr., et al. AMERICAN JOURNAL OF PUBLIC HEALTH 67(8):780-781, August, 1977.

One-third of Nassau pregnancies end in abortion, by R. R. Silver. THE NEW YORK TIMES (M) July 31, 21:1, 1977.

Operation of the abortion law [letter], by O. A. Schmidt. CANADIAN MEDICAL ASSOCIATION JOURNAL 117(3): 214, August 6, 1977.

Opinion to the vibrodilatation of the cervix in induced abor-tions—report of 2 years of experiences with the Soviet vibro-dilatator WG-I, by P. Landschek, et al. ZENTRALBLATT

FUR GYNAEKOLOGIE 98(17):1049-1053, 1976.

Opponents on abortion issue gear for a new battle, by M. Tolchin. THE NEW YORK TIMES (M) December 9, 16:1, 1977.

Order barring woman's abortion arrives too late to halt surgery. THE NEW YORK TIMES (M) April 23, 51:5, 1977.

Organization of specialized medical aid to women with habitual miscarriage in the Andizhan region, by N. T. Gudakova, et al. AKUSHERSTVO I GINEKOLOGIIA (Moscow) (5):54-55, May, 1977.

Organisms associated with abortion and reproductive problems in cattle, by I. H. Siddique, et al. MODERN VETERINARY PRACTICE 57(10):809-811, October, 1976.

Origin of the extra chromosome in trisomy 16, by J. G. Lauritsen, et al. CLINICAL GENETICS 10(3):156-160, 1976. (Bio. Abstrs. March, 1977, 32669)

Origin of triploidy and tetraploidy in man: 11 cases with chromosomes markers, by T. Kajii, et al. CYTOGENETICS AND CELL GENETICS 18(3):109-125, 1977.

Orthodoxy and attitudes of clergymen towards homosexuality and abortion, by T. C. Wagenaar, et al. REVIEW OF RELIGIOUS RESEARCH 18(2):114-125, 1977. (Socio. Abstrs. 1977, 77I8158)

Outcome of pregnancy among women in anaesthetic practice, by P. O. D. Pharoah, et al. LANCET 1(8001):34-36, 1977. (Bio. Abstrs. June, 1977, 72223)

Ovarian abscess associated with incomplete abortion and intrauterine contraceptive device, by A. Neri, et al. ISRAEL JOURNAL OF MEDICAL SCIENCES 13(3):305-308, 1977. (Bio. Abstrs. October, 1977, 41530)

Ovine enzootic abortion diagnosis [letter], by P. A. Bloxham, et al. VETERINARY RECORD 100(17):371-372, April 23, 1977.

Parent and child—right of unwed minor to obtain abortion without parental consent. JOURNAL OF FAMILY LAW 14: 637-643, 1975-1976.

The parliamentary scene, by T. Smith. JOURNAL OF MEDICAL ETHICS 3(2):100-101, June, 1977.

Party line, by A. Mah. NATIVE PEOPLE (10):7, February 18, 1977.

Pathogenesis of mycotic abortion in cows, by E. P. Kremlev. VETERINARIIA (7):71-74, July, 1977.

Patient's view of the role of the primary care physician in abortion, by R. H. Rosen. AMERICAN JOURNAL OF PUBLIC HEALTH 67:863-865, September, 1977.

Pattern of chorionic gonadotropins and placental lactogens during treatment of threatened and habitual abortion, by E. Samochowiec, et al. GINEKOLOGIA POLASKA 47(12): 1363-1370, December, 1976.

Pelvic abcess: a sequela of first trimester abortion, by C. B. Gassner, et al. OBSTETRICS AND GYNECOLOGY 48(6): 716-717, 1976. (Bio. Abstrs. April, 1977. 39387)

Performing abortions; excerpt from In necessity and sorrow: life and death in an abortion hospital, by M. Denes. COMMENTARY 62:4+, December, 1976; 63:18+, January; 22+ February, 1977.

Perinatal foal mortality. Causes of foal death in Switzerland, by J. Hösli. SCHWEIZER ARCHIV FUR TIERHEILKUNDE 119(3):103-110, March, 1977.

Personal defeat, private hell [editorial]. THE NEW YORK TIMES January 31, 20:1, 1977.

Personality characteristics associated with contraceptive behavior in women seeking abortion under liberalized California law, by L. D. Noble. DISSERTATION ABSTRACTS INTERNATIONAL 35(7-B):3589-3590, 1975. (Psycho. Abstrs. 1977, 3141)

Pharmacokinetic studies on 15-methyl-PGF2alpha and its methyl ester after administration to the human via various routes for induction of abortion, by K. Gréen, et al. ADVANCES IN PROSTAGLANDIN AND THROMBOXANE RESEARCH 2:719-725, 1976.

Physician acquitted of abortion conviction: Boston. HOSPITALS 51:20+, February 1, 1977.

Physicians of Quebec: majority of favor of abortion, by C. Lalonde. CANADIAN MEDICAL ASSOCIATION JOURNAL 115(11):1134-1143, December 4, 1976.

Pituitary response to luteinizing hormone-releasing hormone after induced abortion in the first and second trimesters, by M. E. Domenzain, et al. FERTILITY AND SETERILITY 28(5):531-534, 1977. (Bio. Abstrs. October, 1977, 37959)

Placental insufficiency; a Scylla and Charybdis situation, by P. J. Boerrigter, et al. NEDERLANDS TIJDSCHRIFT VOOR GENEESKUNDE 121(6):210-215, February 5, 1977.

Placental morphology in spontaneous human abortuses with normal and abnormal karyotypes, by L. H. Honoré, et al. TERATOLOGY 14(2):151-166, October, 1976.

Planned parenthood begins abortion aid drive, by J. Cummings. THE NEW YORK TIMES (M) July 10, 23:3, 1977.

Planned Parenthood v. Danforth (96 Sup. Ct. 2831): resolving the antinomy. OHIO NORTHERN UNIVERSITY LAW REVIEW 4:425-440, 1977.

Plasma progesterone in women with a history of recurrent early abortions, by S. K. Yip, et al. FERTILITY AND STERILITY 28(2):151-155, 1977. (Bio. Abstrs. June, 1977, 62721)

The politics of abortion, by J. Armstrong. CHRISTIAN CENTURY p. 215, March 10, 1976.

The politics of abortion; from the Supreme Court, Congress, and the Department of Health, Education and Welfare, by

P. Steinfels. COMMONWEAL 104:456, July 22, 1977.

The politics of pregnancy, by L. Edmunds. DAILY TELE-
GRAPH p. 15, February 23, 1977.

Policlinical abortions using the Karman-catheter without anesthesia of cervix dilatation. LAKARTIDNINGEN 74(23):2281-
2283, June 8, 1977.

Poll at synod finds liberal views on sex, by G. Dugan. THE NEW
YORK TIMES (M) July 3, 32:1, 1977.

Pope equates abortion with "murder" of young. THE NEW
YORK TIMES (S) January 2, 5:1, 1977.

Population growth and abortion legislation, by K. Sundström-
Feigenberg. LAKARTIDNINGEN 73(44):3747-3752,
October 27, 1976.

A possible association of long Y chromosomes and fetal loss, by
S. R. Patil, et al. HUMAN GENETICS 35(2):233-235, 1977.
(Bio. Abstrs. July, 1977, 2275)

Possible correlation between the blood groups of the ABO system and Rh(D) factors and abortion, by M. Furfaro, et al.
MINERVA GINECOLOGIA 29(4):309-310, April, 1977.

Possible immunologic factors in natural selection of the sexes, by
B. Seguy. JOURNAL DE GYNECOLOGIE, OBSTETRIQUE
ET BIOLOGIE DE LA REPRODUCTION 5(5):617-620,
July-August, 1976.

Possible role of feline T-strain mycoplasmas in cat abortion, by
R. J. Tan, et al. AUSTRALIAN VETERINARY JOURNAL
50(4):142-145, April, 1974.

Possibilities and limits of tocolytic treatment, by R. Brütigam,
et al. WIENER MEDIZINISCHE WOCHENSCHRIFT 127
(10):320-326, May 30, 1977.

Postabortal amenorrhea due to cervical stenosis, by E. Hakim-
Elahi. OBSTETRICS AND GYNECOLOGY 48(6):723-724,

1976. (Bio. Abstrs. March, 1977, 35625)

Postabortal laparoscopic tubal sterilization. Results in comparison to interval procedures, by I. M. Hernandez, et al. OBSTETRICS AND GYNECOLOGY 50(3):356-358, September, 1977.

Postcoital contraception [letter], by H. C. McLaren. BRITISH MEDICAL JOURNAL 1(6057):377, February 5, 1977.

Postimplantation pregnancy disruption in Microtus ochrogaster, M. pennsulvanicus and Peromyscus maniculatus, by A. M. Kenney, et al. JOURNAL OF REPRODUCTION AND FERTILITY 49(2):365-367, March, 1977.

Post-irradiation abortion: a slaughter of innocents? by G. V. Dalrymple, et al. JOURNAL OF THE ARKANSAS MEDICAL SOCIETY 73(11):474-476, April, 1977.

Postpartum and postabortion sterilization, by B. N. Purandare. INTERNATIONAL JOURNAL OF GYNAECOLOGY AND OBSTETRICS 14(1):65-70, 1976. (Bio. Abstrs. February, 1977, 23556)

Preceding pregnancy loss as an index of risk of stillbirth or neonatal death in the present pregnancy, by J. Fedrick, et al. BIOLOGY OF THE NEONATE 31(1-2):84-93, 1977.

Predictive factors in emotional response to abortion: King's termination study, by E. M. Belsey, et al. SOCIAL SCIENCE AND MEDICINE 11:71-82, January, 1977.

Pregnancies of Irish residents terminated in England and Wales in 1974, by D. Walsh. IRISH MEDICAL JOURNAL 70(3): 64, March 19, 1977.

Pregnancy and hyperthyroidism, by N. H. Kyung. KOREAN CENTRAL JOURNAL OF MEDICINE 29(6):633-636, 1975. (Bio. Abstrs. July, 1977, 8200)

Pregnancy during the hysterogram cycle, by R. L. Goldenberg, et al. FERTILITY AND STERILITY 27(11):1274-1276,

1976. (Bio. Abstrs. March, 1977, 35650)

Pregnancy in patients with heart diseases. Indications for interruption, control of pregnancy and condition of labor in the German Federal Republic, by P. Stoll. FORTSCHRITTE DU MEDIZIN 95(11):690, March 17, 1977.

Premature detachment of a normally situated placenta, by A. S. Egorov, et al. PEDIATRIIA AKUSHERSTVO I GINEKOLOGIIA (4):43-45, July-August, 1976.

Prenatal diagnosis and selective abortion, by T. Jenkins, et al. SOUTH AFRICAN MEDICAL JOURNAL 50(53):2091-2095, December 11, 1976.

Prenatal diagnosis: distributive justice and the quality of life, by K. Lebacqz. HARVARD THEOLOGICAL REVIEW 68:392-393, July-October, 1975.

Prenatal diagnosis of genetic disorders, by M. F. Niermeijer, et al. JOURNAL OF MEDICAL GENETICS 13(3):182-194, 1976. (Bio. Abstrs. October, 1977, 37423)

Preoperative cervical dilatation by oral PGE2, by A. S. Van Den Bergh. CONTRACEPTION 14(6):631-638, 1976. (Bio. Abstrs. April, 1977, 41035)

President defends court's action curbing federal aid for abortion, by L. Foreman. THE NEW YORK TIMES (M) July 13, 1:4, 1977.

Preventing pregnancy after mismating in dogs. MODERN VETERINARY PRACTICE 47(12):1041-1042, December, 1976.

Prevention and treatment of habitual abortion, by S. Hong. KOREAN CENTURY JOURNAL OF MEDICINE 29(6): 546-548, 1976. (Bio. Abstrs. April, 1977, 43615)

Prevention of abortion and premature labor in cattle and horses, by M. Vandeplassche, et al. DEUTSCHE TIEROERZLICHE WOCHENSCHRIFT 83(12):554-556, December 5, 1976.

Prevention of the abortifacient action of antiprogesterone serum by progesterone, by A. I. Csapo, et al. AMERICAN JOURNAL OF OBSTETRICS AND GYNECOLOGY 128(2):212-214, May 15, 1977.

Prevention of the pathology of fertility in cows, by E. P. Kremlev, et al. VETERINARIIA (9):60-62, 1976.

Prevention of spontaneous abortion by cervical suture of the malformed uterus, by M. Blum. INTERNATIONAL SURGERY 62(4):213-215, April, 1977.

Preventive long term hospitalization in habitual abortion, by H. Ruwisch. MEDIZINISCHE WELT 28(6):282-286, February 11, 1977.

The price of advice, by D. Mundy. NURSING TIMES 73(35): 1344-1345, September 1, 1977.

Principles of the current legal regulations on pregnancy interruption. Results of the decision of the Federal constitutional court of 25 February, 1975, by G. Brenner. DEUTSCHE KRANKENPFLEGE-ZEITSCHRIFT 29(12):671-676, December, 1976.

Principles of medical genetic consultation in spontaneous abortions in women, by V. P. Kulazhenko, et al. AKUSHERSTVO I GINEKOLOGIIA (Moscow) (12):36-40, December, 1976.

A private practice management of mid-trimester abortion, by J. W. Tidwell, 2nd, et al. NORTH CAROLINA MEDICAL JOURNAL 38(3):148-150, March, 1977.

A probabilistic justification for abortion, by J. R. Greenwell. PHILOSOPHY RESEARCH ARCHIVES 2:1136, 1976.

Problem of family planning in women in the textile industry. An analysis of social indications for pregnancy interruption, by A. Zdziennicki. POLSKI TYGODNIK LEKARSKI 31(46): 1993-1994, November 15, 1976.

Problems and risks of the legalization of abortion, by A. Andriani. MINERVA GINECOLOGIA 28(9):736-737, September, 1976.

Problems of abortion in Britain: Aberdeen, a case study, by B. Thompson. POPULATION STUDIES 31(1):143-154, 1977. (Bio. Abstrs. October, 1977, 47974)

Pro-"choice" groups lobby against abortion fund ban; language of senate amendment called crucial [concerning use of medicaid funds to pay for abortions for poor women], by B. M. Hager. CONGRESSIONAL QUARTERLY WEEKLY REPORT 35:1286-1287, June 25, 1977.

The profilactic and therapeutic attitude in abortion, by C. Tatic, et al. VIATA MEDICALA; REVISTA DE INFORMORE PROFESIONALA SI STUNTIFICA A CODRELAR MEDII SANITARE 23(9):57-60, September, 1975.

Progesterone levels in amniotic fluid and maternal plasma in prostaglandin F2a-induced midtrimester abortion, by Z. Koren, et al. OBSTETRICS AND GYNECOLOGY 48(4):473-474, 1976. (Bio. Abstrs. February, 1977, 22682)

The prognostic value of human placental lactogen levels in threatened abortion in general practice, by D. W. Gau, et al. JOURNAL OF THE ROYAL COLLEGE OF GENERAL PRACTITIONERS 27(175):91-92, February, 1977.

Prolactin and human placental lactogen changes in maternal serum and amniotic fluid in midtrimester induced abortions, by R. R. Weiss, et al. AMERICAN JOURNAL OF OBSTETRICS AND GYNECOLOGY 129(1):9-13, September 1, 1977.

Pro-life target: women's year meetings; Minnesota conference disrupted, by M. Papa. NATIONAL CATHOLIC REPORTER 13:20, June 17, 1977.

Prophecy and politics: abortion in the election of 1976, by J. Hitchcock. WORLDVIEW 20:25-26+, March, 1977.

Proposed laws on abortion for the consideration of Parliament, by V. S. Pesce. MINERVA GINECOLOGIA 28(9):732-736, Setpember, 1976.

Prostaglandin E2 in a diaphragm. A further note, by H. Schulman, et al. PROSTAGLANDINS 13(4):751-753, April, 1977.

Prostaglandin E2 induction of labor for fetal demise, by D. R. Kent, et al. OBSTETRICS AND GYNECOLOGY 48(4): 475-478, 1976. (Bio. Abstrs. February, 1977, 22681)

Prostaglandin F2alpha, hypertonic saline, and oxytocin in midtrimester abortion, by A. Adachi, et al. NEW YORK STATE JOURNAL OF MEDICINE 77(1):46-49, January, 1977.

Prostaglandin F2alpha induced luteolysis, hypothermia, and abortions in beagle bitches, by P. W. Concannon, et al. PROSTAGLANDINS 13(3):533-542, March, 1977.

Prostaglandin impact, by A. I. Csapo. ADVANCES IN PROSTAGLANDIN AND THROMBOXANE RESEARCH 2:705-718, 1976.

The prostaglandins, by J. M. Beazley. NURSING TIMES 72: 1800-1803, November 18, 1976.

Prostaglandins and post abortion luteolysis in early pregnancy, by A. Leader, et al. PROSTAGLANDINS 10(5):889-897, 1976. (Bio. Abstrs. January, 1977, 4174)

Proteinuria and the renal lesion in preeclampsia and abruptio placentae, by J. S. Robson. PERSPECTIVES IN NEPHROLOGY AND HYPERTENSION 5:61-73, 1976.

Psychologic impact on nursing students of participation in abortion, by A. Hurwitz, et al. NURSING RESEARCH 26:112-120, March-April, 1977.

Psychological aspects in medical termination of pregnancy, by J. Joseph. CHRISTIAN NURSE pp. 20-22, June, 1976.

Psychological effects of abortion (a study of 1739 cases), by

W. F. Tsoi, et al. SINGAPORE MEDICAL JOURNAL 17(2):68-73, June, 1976.

Psychological sequelae of abortion, by A. V. Gordon. NEW ZEALAND PSYCHOLOGIST 5(1):37-47, 1976. (Psycho. Abstrs. 1977, 6201)

Psychoprophylaxis in midtrimester abortions, by C. Anderson, et al. JOGN; JOURNAL OF OBSTETRIC, GYNECOLOGIE AND NEONATAL NURSING 5:29-33, November-December, 1976.

Psychosocial characteristics of 13,365 women studied with regard to abortion, by A. G. de Wit Greene, et al. NEUROOGIA, NEUROCIRU, PSIQUIATRIA 16(2):109-136, 1975. (Psycho. Abstrs. 1977, 3090)

Psychosocial correlates of delayed decisions to abort, by M. B. Bracken, et al. HEALTH EDUCATION MONOGRAPHS 4(1):6-44, Spring, 1976.

The psychosocial factors of the abortion experience: a critical review. PSYCHOLOGY OF WOMEN QUARTERLY 1(1): 79-103, February, 1976. (Soc. Abstrs. 1977, 77I5928)

Publicity and the public health: the elimination of IUD-related abortion deaths, by W. Cates, Jr., et al. FAMILY PLANNING PERSPECTIVES 9(3):138-140, May-June, 1977.

Q and G banding techniques in the identification of chromosome anomalies in spontaneous abortions, by J. Bove, et al. ANNALES DE GENETIQUE 19(4):233-239, 1976. (Bio. Abstrs. July, 1977, 2248)

Quantitative interference with the right to life: abortion and Irish law, by M. Mathews. CATHOLIC LAWYER 22:344-358, Autumn, 1976.

A question of conscience [letter]. BRITISH MEDICAL JOURNAL 2(6029):234-235, July 24, 1976.

Radiation-induced teratogen effects and therapeutic abortion, by

F. E. Stieve. ROENTGENBLAETTER 29(10):465-482, October, 1976.

Real dialogue in Los Angeles; Los Angeles Roman Catholic-Jewish Repsect Life Committee. AMERICA 137:324, November 12, 1977.

Reasons for the artificial interruption of pregnancy, by I. Dimitrov. AKUSHERSTVO I GINEKOLOGIIA (Sofia) 16(3): 177-179, 1977.

Reasons for criminal abortion and complications of patients at Ramathibodi Hospital, 1975, by U. Kabusa. THAI JOURNAL OF NURSING 25(2):153-155, April, 1976.

Recent changes in the emotional reactions of therapeutic abortion applicants, by S. Meikle, et al. CANADIAN PSYCHIATRIC ASSOCIATION JOURNAL 22(2):67-70, March, 1977.

Recovery of uterine embryos in Rhesus monkeys, by P. R. Hurst, et al. BIOLOGY OF REPRODUCTION 15(4):429-434, November, 1976.

Recurrent abortion associated with a balanced 22;22 translocation, or isochromosome 22q in a monozygous twin, by B. V. Lewis, et al. HUMAN GENETICS 37(1):81-85, June 10, 1977.

Redefining the issues in fetal experimentation; reprint from The Journal of the American Medical Association, July 19, 1976, by E. Diamond. LINACRE 44:148-154, May, 1977.

Reimbursement for abortions. FEDERAL REGISTER 42: 40486, August 10, 1977.

The relationship of immediate post-abortal intrauterine device insertion to subsequent endometritis. A case-control study, by R. T. Burkman, et al. CONTRACEPTION 15(4):435-444, 1977. (Bio. Abstrs. August, 1977, 23522)

Relative safety of midtrimester abortion methods. MEDICAL LETTER ON DRUGS AND THERAPEUTICS 19(6):25-26,

March 25, 1977.

Religious tension in Saint Cloud; refusal of United Way funds to agencies making abortion referrals, by J. M. Wall. CHRISTIAN CENTURY 94:1019-1020, November 9, 1977.

Repeat abortion in Denmark: an analysis based on national record linkage, by R. L. Somers. STUDIES IN FAMILY PLANNING 8(6):142-147, June, 1977.

The repeat abortion patient, by J. Leach. FAMILY PLANNING PERSPECTIVES 9:37-39, January-February, 1977.

Repeated extra-amniotic administration of prostaglandin F2a for midtrimester abortion, by M. Ragab, et al. INTERNATIONAL JOURNAL OF GYNAECOLOGY AND OBSTETRICS 14(4):337-340, 1976. (Bio. Abstrs. September, 1977, 34567)

Report of the committee on the operation of the abortion law, by V. Hunter. QUILL AND QUIRE 43(5):44, 1977.

The report of the royal commission on contraception, sterilisation and abortion: a comparison with health professional policies, by D. Wills. NURSING FORUM (Auckland) 5:4-6, April-May, 1977.

Reported live births following induced abortion: two and one-half years' experience in upstate New York, by G. Stroh, et al. AMERICAN JOURNAL OF OBSTETRICS AND GYNECOLOGY 126(1):83-90, 1976. (Bio. Abstrs. March, 1977, 31315)

Reprise. THE NEW YORK TIMES July 14, 38:1, 1977.

Reproductive counseling in patients who have had a spontaneous abortion, by B. J. Poland, et al. AMERICAN JOURNAL OF OBSTETRICS AND GYNECOLOGY 127(7):685-691, 1977. (Bio. Abstrs. August, 1977, 17466)

Request for abortion during the 2d pregnancy trimester, by P. E. Treffers, et al. NEDERLANDS TIJDSCHRIFT VOOR

GENEESKUNDE 120(5):2255-2262, December 18, 1976.

Requests for abortion: a psychiatrist's view, by R. Mester. ISRAEL ANNALS OF PSYCHIATRY AND RELATED DISCIPLINES 14(3):294-299, 1976. (Psycho. Abstrs. 1977, 13126)

Research of antibodies against toxoplasma gondii in subjects with repeated abortions, perinatal mortality and malformed newborns, by A. S. Castro, et al. ANNALI SCLAVO 18(1):75-81, 1976. (Bio. Abstrs. March, 1977, 29539)

Respect life, by K. Keron. SAIRAANHOITAJA (23-24):10-11, December 7, 1976.

Restricting medicaid funds for abortions: projections of excess mortality for women for childbearing age, by D. B. Petitti, et al. AMERICAN JOURNAL OF PUBLIC HEALTH 67(9): 860-862, September, 1977.

Results of five-year survey on causes of bovine abortions, by K. Wohlgemuth, et al. PROCEEDINGS—ANNUAL MEETING OF THE UNITED STATES ANIMAL HEALTH ASSOCIA-TION (77):509-514, 1974.

Results of the overall treatment of patients suffering from miscarriages, by E. L. Maizel', et al. VOPROSY OKHRANY MATERINSTVA I DETSTVA 21(11):59-62, November, 1976.

Resumption of menstruation and fertility after cesarean section, by D. Dang. ANNALES DE BIOLOGIE ANIMALE BIO-CHIMIE BIOPHYSIQUE 17(3A):325-329, 1977. (Bio. Abstrs. November, 1977, 59934)

Review of induced-abortion technics in Czechoslovakia, by F. Havranek. CESKOSLOVENSKA GYNEKOLOGIE 41(8): 616-620, October, 1976.

A review of the progress of psychiatric opinion regarding emotional complications of therapeutic abortion, by G. W. Hubbard. SOUTHERN MEDICAL JOURNAL 70(5):558-560,

May, 1977.

Rh immunoglobulin utilization after spontaneous and induced abortion, by D. A. Grimes, et al. OBSTETRICS AND GYNE-COLOGY 50(3):261-263, September, 1977.

Rheography and rheometry of the internal genital organs in early normal pregnancy and in threatened abortion, by F. A. Syrovatko, et al. VOPROSY OKHRANY MATERINSTVA I DETSTVA 21(4):74-75, April, 1976.

Right to abortion: the end of parental and spousal consent requirements. ARKANSAS LAW REVIEW 31:122-126, Spring, 1977.

Right to an abortion—problems with parental and spousal consent. NEW YORK LAW SCHOOL LAW REVIEW 22:65-86, 1976.

Right to life committee challenges health department: Rhode Island, by W. A. Regan. HOSPITAL PROGRESS 58:30+, February, 1977.

Right to life of potential persons, by E.-H. W. Kluge. DALHOU-SIE LAW JOURNAL 3:837-848, January, 1977.

The right to life; two messages of the Italian Episcopal Conference. THE POPE SPEAKS 22:260-263, November 3, 1977.

Right to medicaid payment for abortion, by P. A. Butler. HAST-INGS LAW JOURNAL 29:931-977, March, 1977.

Risks and sequelae of induced abortion, by G. Giocoli-Nacci. MINERVA GINECOLOGIA 28(9):721-725, September, 1976.

Risks of miscarriage after amniocentesis, by C. O. Carter. JOUR-NAL OF MEDICAL GENETICS 13(5):351, October, 1976.

Roe vs. Ward: the rhetoric of fetal life. CENTRAL STATES SPEECH JOURNAL 27(3):192-199, February, 1976.

Role and responsibility of the obstetrician in performing an abortion, by A. Coletta. MINERVA GINECOLOGIA 28(9):706-712, September, 1976.

Role and cerclage in the prevention of abortion and premature labor, by J. Kubinyi, et al. ZENTRALBLATT FUR GYNAE-KOLOGIE 98(17):1043-1048, 1976.

The role of chromosome abnomalities in failures in reproduction, by A. Bove. JOURNAL DE GYNECOLOGIE, OBSTE-TRIQUE ET BIOLOGIE DE LA REPRODUCTION 6(1): 5-21, 1977. (Bio. Abstrs. September, 1977, 26662)

Role of mycoplasma infections in repeat abortions [letter], by C. Alexandre, et al. NOUVELLE PRESSE MEDICALE 5(39): 2631, November, 1976.

Role of the obstetrician in performing an abortion. Objections of conscience, by N. Damiani. MINERVA GINECOLOGIA 28(9):728-732, September, 1976.

Role of psychotherapy in complex treatment of spontaneous abortions, by A. Z. Khasin, et al. AKUSHERSTVO I GINE-KOLOGIIA (Moscow) (10):35-39, October, 1976.

Role of small doses of estrogens and progesterone in prevention of early abortions, by V. I. Bodiazhina, et al. AKUSHER-STVO I GINAKOLOGIIA (Moscow) (10):31-35, October, 1976.

Rural women resist old oppression, by S. Hassan. GUARDIAN p. 15, March 28,1 977.

The sacred rights of life, by J. Basile. C.I.C.I.A.M.S. NOU-VELLES (3):25-37, 1976.

Safety of abortion [letter], by W. V. Dolan. JAMA; JOURNAL OF THE AMERICAN MEDICAL ASSOCIATION 237(24): 2601-2602, June 13, 1977.

The safety of local anesthesia and outpatient treatment: a controlled study of induced abortion by vacuum aspiration, by

L. Andolsek, et al. STUDIES IN FAMILY PLANNING 8(5):118-124, May, 1977.

Saline abortion: a retrospective study, by R. A. Kronstadt. JOURNAL OF THE AMERICAN OSTEOPATHIC ASSOCIATION 76(4):276-281, December, 1976.

Saline induction of labor: a review with a report of a maternal death, by F. W. Tysoe. TRANSACTIONS OF THE PACIFIC COAST OBSTETRICAL AND GYNECOLOGICAL SOCIETY 43:31-36, 1976.

Scholars call pro-abortion statement irresponsible; a call to concern, constitutes a cause for concern, according to an interfaith grouping. OUR SUNDAY VISITOR 66:2, November 13, 1977.

Scope of the indications for abortion, by E. Martella. MINERVA GINECOLOGIA 28(9):694-697, September, 1976.

Second trimester abortion: single dose intraamniotic injection of prostaglandin F2a with intravenous oxytocin augmentation, by G. Perry, et al. PROSTAGLANDINS 13(5):987-994, 1977. (Bio. Abstrs. October, 1977, 40677)

Second trimester abortion with intramuscular injections of 15-methyl prostaglandin F2a, by C. A. Ballard, et al. CONTRACEPTION 14(5):541-550, 1976. (Bio. Abstrs. March, 28800)

Semantics, future generations, and the abortion problem: comments on a fallacious case against the morality of abortion, by J. Narveson. SOCIAL THEORY AND PRACTICE 3(4): 461-485, 1975. (Socio. Abstrs. 1977, 7718254)

Senate, in payroll plight, continues abortion curb, by M. Tolchin. THE NEW YORK TIMES (M) November 5, 9:2, 1977.

Senate panel softens abortion provision: publicly funded abortions not required, high court says [the supreme court, June 20, ruled that states and cities did not have to spend public funds for abortions of an elective or nontherapeutic nature, by M. E. Eccles. CONGRESSIONAL QUARTERLY WEEKLY

REPORT 35:1284-1285+, June 25, 1977.

Senate vote forbids using federal funds for most abortions, by A. Clymer. THE NEW YORK TIMES (M) June 30, 1:1, 1977.

Senate votes pregnancy benefits in disability plan for workers. THE NEW YORK TIMES (M) September 17, 8:1, 1977.

Senators elucidate shift on abortions, by M. Tolchin. THE NEW YORK TIMES (M) July 1, 24:1, 1977.

Septic abortion due to invasive salmonella agona, by A. P. Ball, et al. POSTGRADUATE MEDICAL JOURNAL 53(617): 155-156, March, 1977.

Septic shock in obstetric-gynecologic practice, by I. T. Riabtseva, et al. AKUSHERSTVO I GINEKOLOGIIA (Moscow) (4): 40-43, April, 1976.

Septicemia and abortion with the CU-7, by M. B. Viechnicki. AMERICAN JOURNAL OF OBSTETRICS AND GYNE-COLOGY 127(2):203, January 15, 1977.

Several years of diagnostic studies on the EHV 1 abortion in thoroughbred studs following the introduction of vaccination, by C. von Benten, et al. BERLINER UND MUNC-HENER TIERARZTLICHE WOCHENSCHRIFT 90(9):176-180, May 1, 1977.

Sex guilt and contraceptive use in abortion patients, by C. O. Gerrard. DISSERTATION ABSTRACTS INTERNATION-AL 35(8-B):4143, 1975. (Psycho. Abstrs. 1977, 8142)

Sex guilt in abortion patients, by M. Gerrard. JOURNAL OF CONSULTING AND CLINICAL PSYCHOLOGY 45(4): 708, August, 1977.

Sexology and abortion with respect to their psychological and socioeconomic repercussions, by A. De Leonardis. MINER-VA GINECOLOGIA 28(9):737-379, September, 1976.

Sexual experimentation and pregnancy in young black adoles-

cents, by M. Gispert, et al. AMERICAN JOURNAL OF OB-
STETRICS AND GYNECOLOGY 126(4):459-466, 1976.
(Bio. Abstrs. February, 1977, 23255)

Showdown seems near, by J. M. Naughton. THE NEW YORK
TIMES (M) June 26, IV, 1:4, 1977.

Silence is broken, by L. Clements. RISK 13(1):1-63, 1977.

Smallpox vaccination and pregnancy [letter], by M. Luisi.
AMERICAN JOURNAL OF OBSTETRICS AND GYNE-
COLOGY 128(6):700, July 15, 1977.

Smoking: a risk factor for spontaneous abortion, by J. Kline,
et al. NEW ENGLAND JOURNAL OF MEDICINE 297(15):
793-796, October 13, 1977.

Social and demographic determinants of abortion in Poland, by
D. P. Mazur. POPULATION STUDIES 29(1):21-35, 1975.
(Socio. Abstrs. 1977, 7717345)

Social factors in the choice of contraceptive method: a comparison of first clinic attenders accepting oral contraceptives with
those accepting intrauterine devices, by S. U. Kingsley, et al.
JOURNAL OF BIOSOCIAL SCIENCE 9(2):153-162, 1977.
(Bio. Abstrs. September, 1977, 29735)

Social hygiene aspects of criminal abortions among women of the
city of Kalinin, by V. L. Krasnenkov. ZDRAVOOKHRAN-
ENIE ROSSIISKOI FEDERATSII (5):19-22, 1977.

Social-hygienic characteristics of abortions in Lenningrad, by I.
V. Poliakov, et al. SOVETSKAE ZDRAVOOKHRANENIE
(12):43-46, 1976.

Social policy and social psychology. "Social welfare interaction"
analyzed from three theoritical perspectives, by A. Sellerberg. ACTA SOCIOLOGICA 19(3):263-272, 1976. (Socio.
Abstrs. 1977, 7716255)

Sociologic, ethical and psychological aspects of abortion, by R.
De Vicienti. MINERVA GINECOLOGIA 28(9):739-741,

September, 1976.

Somatic complications after induced abortion in hospitals in Telemark county, by P. Hoglend, et al. TIDSSKRIFT FOR DEN NORSKE LAEGEFORENING 97(3):134-136, January 30, 1977.

Sombrevin anesthesia in short-duration gynecological operations, by A. R. Volchenkova, et al. AKUSHERSTVO I GINE-KOLOGIIA (Moscow) (2):56-57, 1977.

Some comments on the demographic and social influence of the 1967 Abortion Act, by R. Leete. JOURNAL OF BIO-SOCIAL SCIENCE 8(3):229-251, 1976. (Socio. Abstrs. 1977, 77I4000)

Some comments to the interruption statute novelized in 1973, by J. Presl. CESKOSLOVENSKA GYNEKOLOGIA 42(5): 338-341, June, 1977.

Some laws relating to population growth: laws directly affecting fertility, by K. K. S. Wee. THE NURSING JOURNAL OF SINGAPORE 17:20-24, May, 1977.

Special aspects of blood circulation in the organs of the pelvis minor in threatening uterine abortion and disturbed tubal pregnancy, by V. M. Zdanovskii, et al. VOPROSY OKHRA-NY MATERINSTVA I DETSTVA 22(5):59-62, May, 1977.

Spina bifida and anencephaly: are miscarriages a possible cause? by K. M. Laurence, et al. BRITISH MEDICAL JOURNAL 2(6083):361-362, August 6, 1977.

Spring clip sterilization: one-year follow-up of 1079 cases, by J. F. Hulka, et al. AMERICAN JOURNAL OF OBSTE-TRICS AND GYNECOLOGY 125(8):1039-1043, 1976. (Bio. Abstrs. January 1977, 5275)

State insists that bar on medicaid for abortion conforms to U.S. law, by W. H. Waggoner. THE NEW YORK TIMES (M) July 19, 75:1, 1977.

State limitations upon the availability and accessibility of abortions after Wade and Bolton. KANSAS LAW REVIEW 25:87-107, Fall, 1976.

State panel votes to restrict the use of medicaid funds for abortions, by A. Clymer. THE NEW YORK TIMES (M) June 22, 17:3, 1977.

State protection of the viable unborn child after Roe v. Wade: how litte, how late? LOUISIANA LAW REVIEW 37:270-282, Fall, 1976.

State senate passes bill allowing municipal courts to define obsenity and asks U.S. abortion action, by A. A. Narvaez. THE NEW YORK TIMES (M) January 25, 75:1, 1977.

Statistical analysis of first-trimester pregnancy terminations in an ambulatory surgical center, by N. Bozorgi. AMERICAN JOURNAL OF OBSTETRICS AND GYNECOLOGY 127 (7):763-768, April 1, 1977.

Statistics on maternal and child health: induced abortion, by T. Nakahara. JAPANESE JOURNAL FOR MIDWIVES 30(11): 691, November, 1976.

Stillbirth and abortion in hamsters by experimental infection with Japanese encephalitis virus. I. Occurrence of stillbirth and abortion, by K. Takehara, et al. VIRUS 25(4):253-260, 1975.

Studies on the gonadotropin response after administration of LH/FSH-releasing hormone (LRH) during pregnancy and after therapeutic abortion in the second trimester, by S. Jeppsson, et al. AMERICAN JOURNAL OF OBSTETRICS AND GYNECOLOGY 125(4):484-490, June 15, 1976.

Studies on hereditary spherocytosis in Iceland, by O. Jensson, et al. ACTA MEDICA SCANDINAVICA 201(3):187-195, 1977. (Bio. Abstrs. September, 1977, 26642)

Studies on the mechanisms of abortion induction by Trichosanthin. SCIENTIA SINICA 19(6):811-830, November-December, 1976.

Studies on prostaglandin-induced abortion in guinea pigs, by W. Elger, et al. ADVANCES IN PROSTAGLANDIN AND THROMBOXANE RESEARCH 2:673-677, 1976.

A study of abortion and problems in decision-making, by M. Cotronco, et al. JOURNAL OF MARRIAGE AND FAMILY COUNSELING 3(1):69-76, 1977. (Socio. Abstrs. 1977, 7718557)

A study of abortion in countries where abortions are legally restricted, by I. C. Chi, et al. JOURNAL OF REPRODUCTIVE MEDICINE 18(1):15-26, January, 1977.

A study of the pathogenesis of experimental salmonella dublin abortion in cattle, by G. A. Hall, et al. JOURNAL OF COMPARATIVE PATHOLOGY 87(1):53-65, January, 1977.

A study on status of maternal and child health in urban and rural areas, by K. Cho. KOREAN CENTRAL JOURNAL OF MEDICINE 31(6):641-647, 1976. (Bio. Abstrs. November, 1977, 59835)

A study of the status of maternal health in Kwang-Ju area, by S. Park. KOREAN CENTRAL JOURNAL OF MEDICINE 31(3):297-302, 1976. (Bio. Abstrs. November, 1977, 52819)

Study of therapeutic abortion committees in British Columbia, by W. J. Harris, et al. UNIVERSITY OF BRITISH COLUMBIA LAW REVIEW 11:81-118, 1977.

Subclinical spontaneous abortion, by G. D. Braunstein, et al. OBSTETRICS AND GYNECOLOGY 50(1 Suppl):41S-44S, July, 1977.

Submission to the Royal Commission on contraception, sterilization and abortion, by New Zealand Psychological Society. NEW ZEALAND PSYCHOLOGIST 5(1):48-56, 1976. (Psycho. Abstrs. 1977, 6215)

Suboptimal pregnancy outsome among women with prior abortions and premature births, by S. J. Funderburk, et al. AMERICAN JOURNAL OF OBSTETRICS AND GYNE-COLOGY 126(1):55-60, 1976. (Bio. Abstrs. January, 1977, 11577)

Subsequent fertility in heifers aborted using prostaglandins at 45-60 days of pregnancy [letter] , by R. I. Thain. AUSTRA-LIAN VETERINARY JOURNAL 53(4):198, April, 1977.

Substantive due process revisited: reflections on (and beyond) recent cases, by M. J. Perry. NORTHWESTERN UNIVER-SITY LAW REVIEW 71:417-469, September-October, 1976.

Successful pregnancy in acute monocytic leukaemia, by R. Gokal, et al. BRITISH JOURNAL OF CANCER 34(3):299-302, 1976. (Bio. Abstrs. November, 1977, 51360)

Summarizing data on bovine abortions with the aid of a computer, by W. T. Hubbert, et al. PROCEEDINGS—ANNUAL MEETING OF THE UNITED STATES ANIMAL HEALTH ASSOCIATION (77):500-508, 1974.

A summary of some of the pathogenetic mechanisms involved in bovine abortion, by R. B. Miller. CANADIAN VETERIN-ARY JOURNAL 18(4):87-95, April, 1977.

Summary of supreme court actions: abortions. THE NEW YORK TIMES (S) May 24, 22:5, 1977.

Supreme court abortion decisions—a challenge to use political process, by E. J. Schulte. HOSPITAL PROGRESS 58:22-23, August, 1977.

Supreme court activities—abortion. THE NEW YORK TIMES (S) June 28, 15:1, 1977.

Supreme court ignites a fiery abortion debate. TIME 110:6-8, July 4, 1977.

Supreme court June 20, 1977 abortion decisions, by M. Fisk. TRIAL 13:14-16+, August, 1977.

Supreme court on medicare and abortion; medicaid-funding of nontherapeutic abortions. ORIGINS 7:86-90, June 30, 1977.

Supreme court retreats from activist, public policy abortion stance, by E. J. Schulte. HOSPITAL PROGRESS 58:19, July, 1977.

Supreme court ruling sparks moves to halt medicaid abortions, by G. Dullea. THE NEW YORK TIMES June 27, 32:1, 1977.

Supreme court: states need not pay for "nonthereapeutic" abortions via medicaid; public hospitals can deny service. FAMILY PLANNING PERSPECTIVES 9:177-179+, July-August, 1977.

The supreme court's abortion decisions and public opinion in the United States, by J. Blake. POPULATION AND DEVELOP-MENT REVIEW 3:45-62, March-June, 1977.

Supreme court's abortion rulings and social change, by D. W. Brady, et al. SOCIAL SCIENCE QUARTERLY 57:535-546, December, 1976.

Surgical treatment of habitual abortion, by V. Krstajic, et al. SRPSKI ARHIV ZA CELOKUPNO LEKARSTVO 104(7-8):527-529, July-August, 1976.

A survey in a local urban area of induced abortion performed in women and their marital status, by Y. J. Kim. KOREAN NURSE 15(4):70-80, August 25, 1976.

Surviving trophoblastic giant cells and ovarian function after prostaglandin-induced abortion in the golden hamster, by R. Pijnenborg. JOURNAL OF ENDOCRINOLOGY 71(2): 271-272, November, 1976.

Suspected sarcocystis infections of the bovine placenta and foetus, by B. L. Munday, et al. ZEITSCHRIFT FUR PARA-SITENKUNDE 51(1):129-132, December 30, 1976.

The susceptibility of the postpartum and postabortal cervix and uterine cavity to infection with attenuated rubella virus, by R. J. Bolognese, et al. AMERICAN JOURNAL OF OBSTETRICS AND GYNECOLOGY 125(4):525-527, June 15, 1976.

The Swedish children born to women denied abortion study: a radical criticism, by P. Cameron, et al. PSYCHOLOGICAL REPORTS 39(2):391-394, 1976. (Psycho. Abstrs. 1977, 8095)

Swiss voters asked to resolve abortion dispute, by V. Lusinchi. THE NEW YORK TIMES (M) May 6, 27:1, 1977.

Swiss voters to decide on allowing abortions. THE NEW YORK TIMES (S) June 28, 34:2, 1977.

Swiss voters uphold abortion ban. THE NEW YORK TIMES (M) September 26, 4:3, 1977.

Switzerland voting on abortion reform. THE NEW YORK TIMES (M) September 24, 45:1, 1977.

The synergistic effect of calcium and prostaglandin F2a in second trimester abortion: a pilot study, by L. Weinstein, et al. OBSTETRICS AND GYNECOLOGY 48(4):469-471, 1976. (Bio. Abstrs. February, 1977, 22683)

Tactics in the management of patients with septic abortion, by S. A. Omarov, et al. AKUSHERSTVO I GINEKOLOGIIA (Moscow) (4):46-48, April, 1976.

Talks aborted. ECONOMIST 264:48, September 3, 1977.

Ten-minute abortions, by W. O. Goldthorp. BRITISH MEDICAL JOURNAL 2:562-564, August 27, 1977.

Termination of abnormal intrauterine pregnancies with intramuscular administration of dihomo 15 methyl prostaglandin F 2alpha, by S. M. Karim, et al. BRITISH JOURNAL OF OBSTETRICS AND GYNAECOLOGY 83(11):885-889, November, 1976.

Termination of pregnancy in the midtrimester using a new technic. Preliminary report, by S. T. DeLee. INTERNATIONAL SURGERY 61(20):545-546, October, 1976.

Termination of pregnancy with prostaglandin analogues, by S. M. Karim, et al. ADVANCES IN PROSTAGLANDIN AND THROMBOXANE RESEARCH 2:727-736, 1976.

Termination of pregnancy with vaginal administration of 16, 16 dimethyl prostaglandin E2 p-benzaldehyde semicarbazone ester, by S. M. Karim, et al. BRITISH JOURNAL OF OBSTETRICS AND GYNAECOLOGY 84(2):135-137, February, 1977.

That controversial anti-abortion ad—Grey nuns were behind it, by J. Dunlop. MARKETING 82:2, January 10, 1977.

Theologian: we can't outlaw abortion, by M. Winiarski. NATIONAL CATHOLIC REPORTER 14:1-2, October 28, 1977.

Therapeutic abortion and its aftermath, by M. Stone. MIDWIFE, HEALTH VISITOR AND COMMUNITY NURSE 11(10):335-338, October, 1975.

Therapeutic abortion and psychiatric disturbance in Canadian women, by E. R. Greenglass. CANADIAN PSYCHIATRIC ASSOCIATION JOURNAL 21(7):453-460, November, 1976.

Therapeutic abortion: extensions and restrictions of current indications, by T. Wierdis. MINERVA GINECOLOGIA 28(9): 716-719, September, 1976.

Therapeutic abortion, fertility plans, and psychological sequelae, by E. R. Greenglass. AMERICAN JOURNAL OF ORTHOPSYCHIATRY 47:119-126, January, 1977.

Therapeutic intra-amniotic, transabdominal induction of abortion in the 2nd trimenon using prostaglandin F 2alpha, by E. Sacha, et al. GYNAEKOLOGISCHE RUNDSCHAW 16(4):261-263, 1976.

There are some in media and congress who see abortion as money-saver for public, by J. Castelli. OUR SUNDAY VISITOR 66: 3, July 24, 1977.

Third party consent to abortions before and after Danforth (Planned Parenthood of Cent. Mo. v. Danforth, 96 Sup. Ct. 2831): a theoretical analysis. JOURNAL OF FAMILY LAW 15:508-536, 1976-1977.

Third time unlucky: a study of women who have three or more legal abortions, by C. Brewer. JOURNAL OF BIOSOCIAL SCIENCE 9(1):99-195, 1977. (Bio. Abstrs. December, 1977, 65346)

Though legal, abortions are not always available, by T. Schultz. THE NEW YORK TIMES (M) January 2, IV, 8:3, 1977.

Three levels of discussion about abortion, by J. Carlson. CATHO-LIC MIND p. 22, November, 1976.

Three states are likely to continue abortion funding for medicaid patient. MODERN HEALTHCARE, SHORT-TERM CARE EDITION 7(8):26, August, 1977.

Thymus-dependent lymphocyte activity during the normal course of pregnancy an in spontaneous premature interruption of pregnancy, by S. D. Bulienko, et al. AKUSHER-STVO I GINEKOLOGIIA (Moscow) 5:50-53, May, 1976.

A tissue-selective prostaglandin E2 analog with potent anti-fertility effects, by H. J. Hess, et al. EXPERIENTIA 33(8): 1076-1077, August 15, 1977.

To have or to have not—promotion and prevention of childbirth in gynaecological work, by S. Macintyre. SOCIOLOGICAL REVIEW: MONOGRAPHS (22):176-193, March, 1976.

Tocolysis in obstetrics, by W. Grabensberger. OSTERREICHI-SCHE KRANKENPFLEGE-ZEITSCHRIFT 26(11):358-364, 1976.

Tocolysis in prevention of spontaneous abortion, by V. Sulovic,

et al. JUGOSLOVENSKA GINEKOLOGIJA I OPSTETRI-
CIJA 16(5-6):411-419, 1976.

Top women aides tell president why they appose him on abortion, by B. Gamarekian. THE NEW YORK TIMES (M)
August 27, 22:1, 1977.

Toward a context for the ethics of abortion, by W. O. Cross.
ANGLICAN THEOLOGICAL REVIEW 59:212-220, April,
1977.

Towards a practical implementation of the abortion decision:
the interests of the physician, the woman and the fetus.
DE PAUL LAW REVIEW 25:676-706, Spring, 1976.

Toxoplasmosic endometritis, by A. Viglione, et al. MINERVA
GINECOLOGIA 29(4):253-260, April, 1977.

Toxoplasmosis in sheep. The relative importance of the infection
as a cause of reproductive loss in sheep in Norway, by H.
Waldeland. ACTA VETERINARIA SCANDINAVICA
17(4):412-425, 1976.

Toxoplasmosis: its role in abortion, by C. R. Mahajan, et al.
INDIAN JOURNAL OF MEDICAL RESEARCH 64(6):797-
800, 1976. (Bio. Abstrs. February, 1977, 22293)

Treatment of cervix incompetence in pregnant women by means
of Mayer's pessary. Discussion contribution on the paper of
K. Jiratek, et al. "Directed therapy of threatened premature
abortion—comparison of treatment results using cerclage and
pessary", by E. Bechinie. CESKOSLOVENSHA GYNE-
KOLOGIE 42(3):205-206, April, 1977.

Treatment of endometritis after artificial abortion, by A. A.
Vorontsov, et al. PEDIATRIIA AKUSHERSTVO I GINE-
KOLOGIIA (1):53-56, January-February, 1977.

Treatment of habitual abortion with caprovestrol, by L. G.
Kovtumova, et al. VOPROSY OKHRANY MATERINSTVA
I DETSTVA 21(5):72-75, May, 1976.

Treatment of preclinical forms of threatened abortion in women with genital infantilism, by N. K. Moskvitina. AKUSHER-STVO I GINEKOLOGIIA (Moscow) 5:53-56, May, 1976.

The treatment of threatened abortion, by P. Berle, et al. GE-BURTSHILFE UND FRAUENHEILKUNDE 37(2):139-142, February, 1977.

Treatment of threatened abortion with Gravibinan, by Z. Sterna-del, et al. GINEKOLOGIA POLASKA 48(5):509-512, May, 1977.

Treatment of threatened and habitual abortion with human chorionic gonadotrophin. The role of serum human placental lactogen determination, by C. Z. Vorster, et al. SOUTH AFRICAN MEDICAL JOURNAL 51(6):165-166, February 5, 1977.

Treatment of threatening abortion with Diaphylline, by G. Illei, et al. ORVOSI HETILAP 118(21):1239-1240, May 22, 1977.

Trisomy 5 in two abortuses, by K. Ohama, et al. JAPANESE JOURNAL OF HUMAN GENETICS 21(1):1-4, June, 1976.

Trisomy 17 in two abortuses, by K. Ohama, et al. JAPANESE JOURNAL OF HUMAN GENETICS 21(4):257-260, March, 1977.

Two measures of nurses' attitudes toward abortion as modified by experience, by D. V. Allen, et al. MEDICAL CARE 15:849-857, October, 1977.

Tying abortion to the death penalty; study by Paul Cameron, by J. Horn. PSYCHOLOGY TODAY 11:43+, November, 1977.

Ultrasonic diagnosis of abortion of torpid evolution, by R. Comino, et al. ACTA OBSTETRICA Y GINECOLOGICA HISPANA-LUSITANA 24(1):5-15, January, 1976.

Unbiased consideration of applicants to medical schools, by R. S.

Schweiker. HOSPITAL PROGRESS 58(5):8, May, 1977.

Unborn child in Canadian law, by K. M. Weiler, et al. OSGOODE HALL LAW JOURNAL 14:643-659, December, 1976.

Unsuccessful termination of pregnancy in an unrecognized case of uterus bicornis/unicollis, by P. E. Andersen, Jr. UGESKRIFT FOR LAEGER 139(12):713-714, March 21, 1977.

Untreated endocervical gonorrhea and endometritis following elective abortion, by R. T. Burkman, et al. AMERICAN JOURNAL OF OBSTETRICS AND GYNECOLOGY 126 (6):648-651, 1976. (Bio. Abstrs. April, 1977, 41724)

Urinary excretion of chorionic gonadotropin, estrogens and pregnanediol in threatened abortion, by O. N. Savchenko, et al. AKUSHERSTVO I GINEKOLOGIIA (Moscow) (8):52-56, August, 1976.

U.S. abortion panel disbanded by chief. THE NEW YORK TIMES (M) November 27, 1:1, 1977.

The use of cloprostenol for the termination of pregnancy and the expulsion of mummified fetus in cattle, by P. S. Jackson, et al. VETERINARY RECORD 100(17):361-363, April 23, 1977.

Use of combination prostaglandin F2a and hypertonic saline for midtrimester abortion, by M. Borten. PROSTAGLANDINS 12(4):625-630, 1976. (Bio. Abstrs. February, 1977, 22694)

Use of prostaglandins in obstetrics, by W. Wells, et al. REVISTA CHILENA DE OBSTETRICIA Y GINECOLOGIA 40(6): 343-359, 1975.

Uterine perforation in connection with vacuum aspiration for legal abortion, by P. J. Moberg. INTERNATIONAL JOURNAL OF GYNAECOLOGY AND OBSTETRICS 14(1):77-80, 1976. (Bio. Abstrs. February, 1977, 53573)

Uterine rupture following midtrimester abortion by laminaria, prostaglandin F2alpha, and oxytocin: report of two cases,

by D. Propping, et al. AMERICAN JOURNAL OF OBSTE-
TRICS AND GYNECOLOGY 128(6):689-690, July 15,
1977.

Uterine toxoplasma infections and repeated abortions, by B.
Stray-Pedersen, et al. AMERICAN JOURNAL OF OBSTE-
TRICS AND GYNECOLOGY 128(7):716-721, August 1,
1977.

Uterine trauma associated with midtrimester abortion induced by
intra-amniotic prostaglandin F2a with and without concomitant use of oxytocin, by G. Perry, et al. PROSTAGLANDINS
13(6):1147-1160, 1977. (Bio. Abstrs. December, 1977,
72336)

Vacuum extraction in interruption of pregnancy using a jagged
cannula, by N. Gudac. JUGOSLOVENSKA GINEKOLOGI-
JA I OPSTETRICIJA 16(5-6):407-410, 1976.

Vaginal administration of a single dose of 16, 16 dimethyl
prostaglandin E2 p-benzaldehyde semicarbazone ester for
pre-operative cervical dilatation in first trimester nulliparae,
by S. M. Karim, et al. BRITISH JOURNAL OF OBSTE-
TRICS AND GYNAECOLOGY 84(4):269-271, April, 1977.

Vaginal cytology after intra-amniotic injection of hypertonic
urea for interruption of pregnancy during the second trimester, by B. Bercovici, et al. ARCHIVES D'ANATOMIE ET
DE CYTOLOGIE PATHOLOGIQUE 25(2):81-85, 1977.

Vaginal hysterectomy for therapeutic abortion and simultaneous
sterilization, by K. A. Walz, et al. GEBURTSHILFE UND
FRAUENHEILKUNDE 36(10):868-871, October, 1976.

Vaginal prostaglandin E2 for missed abortion and intrauterine
fetal death, by A. Rutland, et al. AMERICAN JOURNAL
OBSTETRICS AND GYNECOLOGY 128(5):503-506, 1977.
(Bio. Abstrs. December, 1977, 64654)

The vaginal transverse low segment hysterotomy for second
trimester therapeutic abortion, by G. Schariot, et al. GE-
BURTSHILFE UND FRAUENHEILKUNDE 36(8):687-690,

August, 1976.

Validity of parental consent statutes after planned parenthood (Planned Parenthood of Cent. Mo. v. Danforth, 96 Sup. Ct. 2831). UNIVERSITY OF DETROIT JOURNAL OF URBAN LAW 54:127-164, Fall, 1976.

Value sheets for health education, by P. C. Dunn. HEALTH EDUCATION 8(3):42-43, May-June, 1977.

Vatican bids Italy's senate amend abortion bill. THE NEW YORK TIMES (S) January 23, 7:1, 1977.

Very young adolescent women in Georgia: has abortion or contraception lowered their fertility? by J. D. Shelton. AMERICAN JOURNAL OF PUBLIC HEALTH 67:616-620, July, 1977.

Vexing abortion issue, by L. Fellows. THE NEW YORK TIMES (M) July 3, XXIII, 10:1, 1977.

Viability, values, and the vast cosmos, by D. J. Horan. CATHOLIC LAWYER 22:1-37, Winter, 1976.

Vitamins C and E in spontaneous abortion, by J. S. Vobecky, et al. INTERNATIONAL JOURNAL FOR VITAMIN AND NUTRITION RESEARCH 46(3):291-296, 1976. (Bio. Abstrs. June, 1977, 61970)

Voluntary interruption of pregnancy, by A. Harlay. L'INFIRMIERE FRANCAIS (181):11, January, 1977.

WHO: excessive dilation may affect later pregnancy. FAMILY PLANNING PERSPECTIVES 9:134-135, May-June, 1977.

The wages of sin? ECONOMIST 265:36, December 10, 1977.

We did it for the women. TIME 109:32, January 31, 1977.

Welcome prepared, by E. Schaeffer. CHRISTIANITY TODAY 21:28-29, April 1, 1977.

What price abortion now! by S. Carlton. OBSERVER p. 22, August 14, 1977.

When does life begin? by S. Chandrasekhar. POPULATION REVIEW 15(1-2):50-59, 1971. (Socio. Abstrs. 1977, 7715952)

White house backs subsidy for adopting unwanted children, by D. E. Rosenbaum. THE NEW YORK TIMES (M) July 9, 1:4, 1977.

Whose interests? by J. Turner. NURSING TIMES 71(45):1763, November 6, 1975.

Why a constitutional convention is needed; human life amendment, by E. J. McMahon. AMERICA 137:12-14, July 2, 1977.

Why is abortion wrong, by J. Donceel. AMERICAN p. 65, August 16, 1975.

Woman's meeting Friday in Albany will have a national focus, by N. Robertson. THE NEW YORK TIMES (M) July 5, 34:1, 1977.

Women at Albany meeting vote to support abortion, by J. Dunning. THE NEW YORK TIMES (M) July 11, 31:2, 1977.

Women end parley with plan for rights, by A. Quindlen. THE NEW YORK TIMES (M) November 22, 1:1, 1977.

Women hail attack on government over abortion, by R. Lindsey. THE NEW YORK TIMES (M) September 11, 27:1, 1977.

Women in administration protest Carter opposition to abortion aid. THE NEW YORK TIMES (M) July 16, 7:3, 1977.

Work in progress. Menstrual induction with vaginal infusion of the PGF2 alpha analogue ICI 81008, by P. Mocsary. PROSTAGLANDINS 13(4):807-808, April, 1977.

Working together for Christ: facing the antilife challenge, by W. F. Sullivan. HOSPITAL PROGRESS 58(5):82-84+, May, 1977.

Wrongful birth in the abortion context—critique of existing case law and proposal for future actions. DENVER LAW JOURNAL 53:501-520, 1976.

The young must learn actions have results [letter], by G. M. Middlemiss. THE NEW YORK TIMES January 30, XXI, 19:5, 1977.

PERIODICAL LITERATURE

SUBJECT INDEX

ABNORMALITIES
see: Complications

ABORTION (GENERAL)
Abortion alert, by G. Steinem. MS MAGAZINE 6:118, November, 1977.

Abortion: the risk, by C. Brewer. NEW SOCIETY p. 281, February 10, 1977.

Countdown to an abortion, by T. Ashford. AMERICA 136:128-130, February 12, 1977.

Party line, by A. Mah. NATIVE PEOPLE [10]:7, February 18, 1977.

Silence is broken, by L. Clements. RISK 13(1):1-63, 1977.

ABORTION ACT
see: Laws and Legislation

ABORTION: AUSTRIA

ABORTION: BARBADOS
National survey of doctors, nurses and social workers on liberalization of the Barbados abortion law, by M. D. Hoyos, et al. WEST INDIAN MEDICAL JOURNAL 26(4):2-11, March, 1977.

ABORTION: BELGIUM

ABORTION: BRAZIL
Conspiracy of silence facilitates abortion in Brazil, by M. Galanternick. THE NEW YORK TIMES (M) May 28, 46:1, 1977.

ABORTION: CANADA
Abortion law: a study of R. v. Morgentaler [(1975) 53 D L R (3d) 161]. SASKATCHEWAN LAW REVIEW 39:259-284, 1974-1975.

The Canadian abortion law [letter]. CANADIAN MEDICAL ASSOCIATION JOURNAL 116(3):238+, February 5, 1977.

How many trials will Morgentaler face? by E. Farkas. LAST POST 5:13-14, December, 1976.

Morgentaler [Morgentaler v. Regina (1975) 53 D L R (3d) 161] case: criminal process and abortion law, by B. M. Dickens. OSGOODE HALL LAW JOURNAL 14:229-274, October, 1976.

A new role for nurses. . .abortion counselling. . .Toronto General Hospital, by B. Easterbrook, et al. CANADIAN NURSE 73:28-30, January, 1977.

Physicians of Quebec: majority in favor of abortion, by C. Lalonde. CANADIAN MEDICAL ASSOCIATION JOURNAL 115(11):1134-1143, December 4, 1976.

Study of therapeutic abortion committees in British Columbia, by W. J. Harris, et al. UNIVERSITY OF BRITISH COLUMBIA LAW REVIEW 11:81-118, 1977.

Therapeutic abortion and psychiatric disturbance in Canadian women, by E. R. Greenglass. CANADIAN PSYCHIATRIC ASSOCIATION JOURNAL 21(7):453-460, November, 1976.

Unborn child in Canadian law, by K. M. Weiler, et al. OS-
GOODE HALL LAW JOURNAL 14:643-659, December,
1976.

ABORTION: CAROLINE ISLANDS

ABORTION: CHILE

ABORTION: CHINA
Abortion in Chinese law, by B. H-k Luk. AMERICAN JOUR-
NAL OF COMPARATIVE LAW 25:372-392, Spring,
1977.

ABORTION: CUBA

ABORTION: CZECHOSLOVAKIA
Children born to women denied abortion, by Z. Dytrych, et
al. FAMILY PLANNING PERSPECTIVES 7(4):165-
171, 1975. (Socio. Abstrs. 1977, 7717333)

Review of induced-abortion technics in Czechoslovakia, by
F. Havranek. CESKOSLOVENSKA GYNEKOLOGIE
41(8):616-620, October, 1976.

ABORTION: DENMARK
Abortion views and practices among Danish family physi-
cians, by M. Gammeltoft, et al. JOURNAL OF BIO-
SOCIAL SCIENCE 8(3):287-292, July, 2976. (Socio.
Abstrs. 1977, 7713508)

Repeat abortion in Denmark: an analysis based on national
record linkage, by R. L. Somers. STUDIES IN FAMILY
PLANNING 8:142-147, June, 1977.

ABORTION: EUROPE

ABORTION: FINLAND

ABORTION: FRANCE
Abortion. Report of a commission of the Paris Academy of

Medicine, by M. R. Merger. GYNAEKOLOGISCHE
RUNDSCHAU 16(3):185-191, 1976.

ABORTION: GERMANY
Abortion, abstract norms, and social control: the decision of
the West Germans federal constitutional court, by H.
Gerstein, et al. EMORY LAW JOURNAL 25:849-878,
Fall, 1976.

Abortion and constitution: United States and West Germany,
by D. P. Kommers. AMERICAN JOURNAL OF COM-
PARATIVE LAW 25:255-285, Spring, 1977.

Abortion statistics for the Federal Republic of Germany—
notification requirements for the physician performing
the abortion, by W. Christian. OEFFENTLICHE GE-
SUNDHEITSWESEN 38(11):676-680, November, 1976.

Pregnancy in patients with heart diseases. Indications for
interruption, control of pregnancy and condition of labor
in the German Federal Republic, by P. Stoll, FORT-
SCHRITTE DU MEDIZIN 95(11):690, March 17, 1977.

ABORTION: GHANA

ABORTION: HUNGARY
Abortion and family-building models: fertility limitation in
Hungary, by K. Ford. DEMOGRAPHY 13:495-505,
November, 1976.

ABORTION: INDIA
Psychological aspects in medical termination of pregnancy,
by J. Joseph. CHRISTIAN NURSE pp. 20-22, June,
1976.

Toxoplasmois—its role in abortion, by R. C. Mahajan, et al.
INDIAN JOURNAL OF MEDICAL RESEARCH 64(6):
797-800, June, 1976. (Bio. Abstrs. February, 1977,
22293)

ABORTION: IRAN
The effect of industrialization on spontaneous abortion in
Iran, by N. Kavoussi. JOURNAL OF OCCUPATIONAL
MEDICINE 19(6):419-423, June, 1977. (Bio. Abstrs.
November, 1977, 59812)

ABORTION: ITALY
Almost legal. ECONOMIST 262:42+, January 29, 1977.

Epidemiology of rubella during 1971-1975. Comparison
with abortus cases and malformed newborn in Lombardia (Italy), by V. Carreri, et al. ANNALI SCLAVO
18(5):714-719, September-October, 1976.

Italy turns down an abortion bill. THE NEW YORK TIMES
(S) June 12, IV, 4:2, 1977.

Italy's abortion bill. THE NEW YORK TIMES (S) January
23, IV, 2:2, 1977.

Liberalized abortion bill in Italy passes in chamber, goes to
senate, by A. Shuster. THE NEW YORK TIMES (M)
January 22, 1:2, 1977.

The right to life; two messages of the Italian Episcopal Conference. THE POPE SPEAKS 22:260-263, November 3,
1977.

Vatican bids Italy's senate amend abortion bill. THE NEW
YORK TIMES (S) January 23, 7:1, 1977.

We did it for the women. TIME 109:32, January 31, 1977.

What price abortion now! by S. Carlton. OBSERVER p. 22,
August 14, 1977.

ABORTION: JAMAICA
Medical opinion on abortion in Jamaica: a national Delphi
survey of physician, nurses, and midwives, by K. A.
Smith, et al. STUDIES IN FAMILY PLANNING 7(12):

334-339, December, 1976.

ABORTION: JAPAN

ABORTION: KOREA
Abdominal pain in early pregnancy and its treatment by C.
Yi. KOREAN CENTRAL JOURNAL OF MEDICINE
29(6):543-545, 1976. (Bio. Abstrs. April, 1977, 47773)

Causes of abortions, by S. Chang. KOREAN CENTRAL
JOURNAL OF MEDICINE 29(2):123-124, 1975. (Bio.
Abstrs. April, 1977, 43617)

Diagnosis and treatment of abortions, by Y. Chang. KOREAN
CENTRAL JOURNAL OF MEDICINE 29(2):125-127,
1976. (Bio. Abstrs. April, 1977, 43616)

Early pregnancy hemorrhages and their management, by M.
Shin. KOREAN CENTRAL JOURNAL OF MEDICINE
29(1):5-8, 1975. (Bio. Abstrs. April, 1977, 41853)

Family planning. KOREAN CENTRAL JOURNAL OF
MEDICINE 31(6):649-650, 1976. (Bio. Abstrs. December, 1977, 66070)

Implications of fertility patterns in the Republic of Korea: a
study by computer simulation, by C. J. Mode, et al.
INTERNATIONAL JOURNAL OF BIO-MEDICAL COMPUTING 7(4):289-305, 1976. (Bio. Abstrs. February,
1977, 23761)

Pregnancy and hyperthyroidism, by N. H. Kyung. KOREAN
CENTRAL JOURNAL OF MEDICINE 29(6):633-636,
1975. (Bio. Abstrs. July, 1977, 8200)

Prevention and treatment of habitual abortion, by S. Hong.
KOREAN CENTRAL JOURNAL OF MEDICINE 29(6):
546-548, 1976. (Bio. Abstrs. April, 1977, 43615)

A study of the status of maternal health in Kwang-Ju area, by

S. Park. KOREAN CENTRAL JOURNAL OF MEDI-
CINE 31(3):297-302, 1976. (Bio. Abstrs. November,
1977, 52819)

A study on status of maternal and child health in urban and
rural areas, by K. Cho. KOREAN CENTRAL JOURNAL
OF MEDICINE 31(6):641-647, 1976. (Bio. Abstrs.
November, 1977, 59835)

ABORTION: MALAYSIA

ABORTION: MEXICO
Births aborted among the users of the voluntary family
planning program of the Instituto Mexicano del Seguro
Social, by J. E. Garcia de Alba, et al. GINECOLOGIA
Y OBSTETRICIA DE MEXICO 41(245):235-242, March,
1977.

ABORTION: NETHERLANDS
Clinic and client: an investigation into the experiences of
Dutch women in outpatient abortion clinics, by A.
Schroeder. STIMEZO-RESEARCH 1:85, 1975. (Psycho.
Abstrs. 1977, 8832)

The Dutch on abortion: opinions on terminating life in the
case of abortion, euthanasia, acts of war and punishment,
by R. Veenhoven, et al. STIMEZO-RESEARCH 3:70,
1975. (Psycho. Abstrs, 1977, 10068)

Talks aborted. ECONOMIST 264:48, September 3, 1977.

ABORTION: NEW ZEALAND
Abortion practice in NZ public hospitals. NURSING FORUM
(Auckland) 3(4):5-7, November-December, 1975.

The report of the royal commission on contraception,
sterilisation and abortion: a comparison with health
professional policies, by D. Wills. NURSING FORUM
(Auckland) 5:4-6, April-May, 1977.

ABORTION: NIGERIA

ABORTION: NORWAY
Legal abortion in Telemark, by P. Hoglend. TIDSSKRIFT
FOR DEN NORSKE LAEGEFORENING 97(3):130-
133, January 30, 1977.

Somatic complications after induced abortion in hospitals in
Telemark county, by P. Hoglend, et al. TIDSSKRIFT
FOR DEN NORSKE LAEGEFORENING 97(3):134-
136, January 30, 1977.

ABORTION: PAKISTAN

ABORTION: PALESTINE
Abortion law is approved in Israel, by W. Farrell. THE NEW
YORK TIMES (M) February 1, 11:1, 1977.

Israel selects middle-ground abortion law. THE NEW YORK
TIMES (M) February 6, IV, 7:1, 1977.

The Israeli dilemma in the generation game, by E. Silver.
GUARDIAN p. 11, February 1, 1977.

Requests for abortion: a psychiatrist's view, by R. Mester.
ISRAEL ANNALS OF PSYCHIATRY AND RELATED
DISCIPLINES 14(3):294-299, 1976. (Psycho. Abstrs.
1977, 13126)

ABORTION: POLAND
Social and demographic determinants of abortion in Poland,
by D. P. Mazur. POPULATION STUDIES 29(1):21-35,
1975. (Socio. Abstrs. 1977, 7717345)

ABORTION: PORTUGAL

ABORTION: PUERTO RICO

ABORTION: RHODESIA

ABORTION: ROMANIA

ABORTION: SCANDINAVIA

ABORTION: SINGAPORE
Abortions in Singapore, by S. C. Chew. THE NURSING
JOURNAL OF SINGAPORE 17:18-19, May, 1977.

Psychological effects of abortion (a study of 1739 cases), by
W. F. Tsoi, et al. SINGAPORE MEDICAL JOURNAL
17(2):68-73, June, 1976.

Some laws relating to population growth: laws directly affecting fertility, by K. K. S. Wee. THE NURSING JOUR-
NAL OF SINGAPORE 17:20-24, May, 1977.

ABORTION: SWEDEN
Dutch tolerance of illegal abortions draws clients from all
over Europe. THE NEW YORK TIMES (M) June 18,
48:4, 1977.

Social policy and social psychology: social welfare interaction analysed from three theoretical perspectives, by A.
M. Sellerberg. ACTA SOCIOLOGICA 19(3):263-272,
1976. (Socio. Abstrs. 1977, 7716255)

Swedish children born to women denied abortion study: a
radical criticism, by P. Cameron, et al. PSYCHOLOGI-
CAL REPORTS 39:391-394+, October, 1976.

Swiss voters asked to resolve abortion dispute, by V. Lusinchi.
THE NEW YORK TIMES (M) May 6, 27:1, 1977.

Swiss voters to decide on allowing abortions. THE NEW
YORK TIMES (S) June 28, 34:2, 1977.

Swiss voters uphold abortion ban. THE NEW YORK TIMES
(M) September 26, 4:3, 1977.

Switzerland voting on abortion reform. THE NEW YORK

TIMES (M) September 24, 45:1, 1977.

ABORTION: TAIWAN
Don't know: item ambiguity or respondent uncertainty? by C. H. Coombs, et al. PUBLIC OPINION QUARTERLY 40:497-514, Winter, 1976-1977.

ABORTION: THAILAND
Abortion in Bangkok, by S. Kaedsawang. THAI JOURNAL OF NURSING 25(3):209-217, July, 1976.

Attitudes of rural Thai women towards induced abortion, by R. G. Burnight, et al. JOURNAL OF BIOSOCIAL SCIENCE 9(1):61-72, January, 1977.

ABORTION: UGANDA
Abortion in Mulago Hospital, Kampala, by C. Lwanga. EAST AFRICAN MEDICAL JOURNAL 54(3):142-148, March, 1977.

ABORTION: UNITED KINGDOM
Abortion and democratic politics, by M. Simms. NEW HUMANIST 93:15-17, May-August, 1977.

Abortion: the fall, by C. Francome. NEW SOCIETY pp. 234-235, February 3, 1977.

Abortion in England, 1890-1914, by A. McLaren. VICTORIAN STUDIES 20:379-400, Summer, 1977.

Abortion: an issue that won't go away, by P. Ferris. OBSERVER p. 13, January 30, 1977.

Abortion: it will not go away [Britain]. ECONOMIST 262: 26, February 5, 1977.

Abortion trail, by J. Turner. NEW SOCIETY p. 123, October 20, 1977.

Abortion: why the doctors are closing ranks against new

curbs, by P. Healy. TIMES p. 14, July 8, 1977.

Abortions: public and private facilities [Great Britain].
LABOUR RESEARCH (London) 66:106-107, May,
1977.

Are there too many advantages already for the wealthy
woman? by G. Hill. TIMES p. 16, February 25, 1977.

The birth of a bill restricting a women's rights, by J. Turner.
GUARDIAN p. 11, February 17, 1977.

The clinic over the sea, by A. McHardy. GUARDIAN p. 9,
October 31, 1977.

Dilemmas and pressures. On patients and nurses—abortion
legislation. Part 2, by E. Donachie. WORLD OF IRISH
NURSING 6:1+, June, 1977.

How many illegal abortions? by C. Francome. THE BRITISH
JOURNAL OF CRIMINOLOGY 16(4):389-392, 1976.
(Socio. Abstrs. 1977, 7718243)

The Irish emigrant and the abortion crisis. WORLD OF
IRISH NURSING 4(10):1-2, October, 1975.

It will not go away. ECONOMIST 262:26, February 5,
1977.

Management of the abortion problem in an English city, by
J. B. Lawson. LANCET 2(7998):1288-1291, 1976.
(Bio. Abstrs. May, 1977, 59877)

Monstrous regiments battle for and against abortion. ECON-
OMIST 264:19-20, July 16, 1977.

Mr. Benyon's gift, by D. Gould. NEW STATESMAN 93:457,
April 8, 1977.

The politics of pregnancy, by L. Edmunds. DAILY TELE-

GRAPH p. 15, February 23, 1977.

Pregnancies of Irish residents terminated in England and Wales in 1974, by D. Walsh. IRISH MEDICAL JOURNAL 70(3):64, March 19, 1977.

Problems of abortion in Britain: Aberdeen, a case study, by B. Thompson. POPULATION STUDIES 31(1):143-154, 1977. (Bio. Abstrs. October, 1977, 47974)

Quantitative interference with the right to life: abortion and Irish law, by M. Mathews. CATHOLIC LAWYER 22: 344-358, Fall, 1976.

ABORTION: UNITED STATES
ARIZONA
Abortion—action by nineteen year-old unmarried female against the Arizona board of regents to determine the the constitutionality of a state statute prohibiting nontherapeutic abortions at the university hospital. JOURNAL OF FAMILY LAW 15:113-118, 1976-1977.

ARKANSAS

CALIFORNIA
Contraceptive risk taking and abortion: results and implications of a San Francisco bay area study, by K. Luker. STUDIES IN FAMILY PLANNING 8:190-196, August, 1977.

On ecumenical approach to abortion: statement by the Los Angeles Catholic-Jewish Respect Life Committee, by R. Casey. NATIONAL CATHOLIC REPORTER 14:2, November 11, 1977.

Personality characteristics associated with contraceptive behavior in women seeking abortion under liberalized California law, by L. D. Noble. DISSERTATION ABSTRACTS INTERNATIONAL 35(7-B):3589-3590,

CALIFORNIA
1975. (Psycho. Abstrs. 1977, 3141)

Real dialogue in Los Angeles; Los Angeles Roman Catholic-Jewish Respect Life Committee. AMERICA 137: 324, November 12, 1977.

CHICAGO

CINCINNATI

COLORADO

CONNECTICUT
Edelin decision revisited: a survey of the reactions of Connecticut's OB/GYNs, by G. Affleck, et al. CONNECTICUT MEDICINE 41:637-640, October, 1977.

FLORIDA

GEORGIA

HAWAII

ILLINOIS

INDIANA

IOWA

LOUISIANA

MARYLAND

MASSACHUSETTS
After Edelin: little guidance, by J. A. Robertson. HASTINGS CENTER REPORT 7(3):15-17+, June, 1977.

Edelin case rekindles right-to-life hopes, by R. Adam. FAITH FOR THE FAMILY p. 9, November-Decem-

MASSACHUSETTS
    ber, 1975.

    Massachusetts Supreme Judicial Court reverses conviction
        of Dr. Kenneth Edelin, by L. H. Glantz. MEDICO-
        LEGAL BULLETIN 5:3-4, Winter, 1977.

    Physician acquitted of abortion conviction: Boston.
        HOSPITALS 51:20+, February 1, 1977.

MICHIGAN

MINNESOTA
    Pro-life target: women's year meetings; Minnesota con-
        ference disrupted, by M. Papa. NATIONAL CATHO-
        LIC REPORTER 13:20, June 17, 1977.

MISSISSIPPI

MISSOURI
    Abortion—possible alternatives to unconstitutional spou-
        sal and parental consent provisions of Missouri's
        abortion law. MISSOURI LAW REVIEW 42:291-
        297, Spring, 1977.

MONTANA

NEBRASKA

NEW HAMPSHIRE

NEW JERSEY
    Abortion foes urged to join new causes. THE NEW YORK
        TIMES (M) March 28, 63:4, 1977.

    Antiabortion bill stirs new debate, by M. Waldron. THE
        NEW YORK TIMES (M) February 27, XI, 1:1, 1977.

    New Jersey briefs: timing of abortion. THE NEW YORK
        TIMES (S) April 25, 67:1, 1977.

NEW JERSEY
New Jersey court rules hospitals cannot prohibit abortions. HOSPITALS 51:20-21, January 1, 1977.

NEW YORK
Abortion-fund fight expected in Albany, by R. J. Meislin. THE NEW YORK TIMES (M) December 9, 16:4, 1977.

Albany bars a halt in abortions study, by R. J. Meislin. THE NEW YORK TIMES (S) May 24, 39:6, 1977.

Albany senate passes court bill but its enactment is still distant: anti-abortion amendment, by R. J. Meislin. THE NEW YORK TIMES (S) May 25, II, 2:2, 1977.

Contraceptive practice in the context of a non-restrictive abortion law: age-specific pregnancy rates in New York City, 1971-1973, by C. Tietze. FAMILY PLANNING PERSPECTIVES 7(5):192-202, 1975. (Socio. Abstrs. 1977, 7717046)

The effect of legalization of abortion on population growth and public health, by C. Tietze. FAMILY PLANNING PERSPECTIVES 7(3):123-127, 1975. (Socio. Abstrs. 1977, 7717047)

Legal abortion among New York City residents: an analysis according to socioeconomic and demographic characteristics, by M. J. Kramer. FAMILY PLANNING PERSPECTIVES 7(3):128-137, 1975. (Socio. Abstrs. 1977, 7717343)

One-third of Nassau pregnancies end in abortion, by R. R. Silver. THE NEW YORK TIMES (M) July 31, 21:1, 1977.

Reported live births following induced abortion: two and one-half years' experience in upstate New York, by G. Stroh, et al. AMERICAN JOURNAL OF OBSTE-

NEW YORK
     TRICS AND GYNECOLOGY 126(1):83-90, 1976.
     (Bio. Abstrs. March, 1977, 31315)

NORTH CAROLINA

OKLAHOMA

OREGON

PENNSYLVANIA
     Abortion—Pennsylvania Medicaid regulations and proce-
     dures denying non-therapeutic abortions to indigent
     women held inconsistent with title XIX of the social
     security act. JOURNAL OF FAMILY LAW 15:587-
     592, 1976-1977.

RHODE ISLAND
     Anti-abortion petition. THE NEW YORK TIMES (S)
     April 21, 18:6, 1977.

     Right to life committee challenges health department:
     Rhode Island, by W. A. Regan. HOSPITAL PRO-
     GRESS 58:30+, February, 1977.

SOUTH CAROLINA
     Abortion in South Carolina, by D. N. Bishop, et al.
     JOURNAL OF THE SOUTH CAROLINA MEDICAL
     ASSOCIATION 72(12):455-459, December, 1976.

SOUTH DAKOTA

TENNESSEE
     Abortion in Tennessee—1975, by A. R. Hinman. JOUR-
     NAL OF THE TENNESSEE MEDICAL ASSOCIA-
     TION 70(3):163-167, March, 1977.

TEXAS

UTAH
Mormon turnout overwhelms women's conference in
Utah, by J. M. Crewdson. THE NEW YORK TIMES
(M) July 25, 26:4, 1977.

VERMONT

WISCONSIN

ABORTION: USSR
Opinion to the vibrodilatation of the cervix in induced abortions—report of 2 years of experiences with the Soviet
vibrodilatator WG-I, by P. Landschek, et al. ZENTRAL-
BLATT FUR GYNAEKOLOGIE 98(17):1049-1053,
1976.

Social hygiene aspects of criminal abortions among women
of the city of Kalinin, by V. L. Krasnenkov. ZDRA-
VOOKHRANENIE ROSSIISKOI FEDERATSII (5):19-
22, 1977.

Social-hygienic characteristics of abortions in Leningrad, by
I. V. Poliakov, et al. SOVETSKAE ZDRAVOOKHRA-
NENIE (12):43-46, 1976.

ABORTION: YUGOSLAVIA
A comparison of flexible and nonflexible plastic cannulae
for performing first trimester abortion, by L. Andolsek,
et al. INTERNATIONAL JOURNAL OF GYNAECOLO-
GY AND OBSTETRICS 14(3):199-204, 1976.

ADOPTION
see: Family Planning

ALDOMET
Fetal outcome in trial of antihypertensive treatment in pregnancy, by C. W. G. Redman, et al. LANCET 2(7989):
753-756, 1976. (Bio. Abstrs. February, 1977, 13896)

ALUPENT

AMERICAN COLLEGE OF OBSTETRICIANS AND GYNE-
COLOGISTS

AMERICAN HOSPITAL ASSOCIATION

AMERICAN PUBLIC HEALTH ASSOCIATION

AMIKACIN
Amikacin for treatment of septic abortions: summary, by J.
Bravo-Scandoval, et al. JOURNAL OF INFECTIOUS
DISEASES 134(Suppl):S380, November, 1976.

Efficacy of amikacin in septic abortion: serum and urine
antibiotic concentrations, by J. Bravo-Sandoval, et al.
JOURNAL OF INTERNATIONAL MEDICAL RE-
SEARCH 4(4):223-227, 1976.

AMOGLANDIN

AMOXICILLIN

ANESTHESIA
see also: Induced Abortion
Therapeutic Abortion

Anesthesia for elective termination of pregnancy [letter], by
J. P. Annis. JAMA; JOURNAL OF THE AMERICAN
MEDICAL ASSOCIATION 236(23):2942-2943, Decem-
ber 27, 1976.

Anaesthetics as an occupational hazard [editorial]. MEDI-
CAL JOURNAL OF AUSTRALIA 1(13):427-428,
March 26, 1977.

Case of convulsions with late onset after ketalar anesthesia,
by A. Dimitrov, et al. AKUSHERSTVO I GINEKOLO-
GIIA (Sofia) 15(3):229-230, 1976.

Choice of analgesia or anesthesia for pain relief in suction curettage, by J. A. Rock, et al. OBSTETRICS AND GYNECOLOGY 49(6):721-723, June, 1977.

Comparative evaluation of different methods of general anesthesia during surgical termination of early pregnancy, by V. A. Glotova. VOPROSY AKHRANY MATERIN-STVA I DETSTVA 21(4):81-84, April, 1976.

Sombrevin anesthesia in short-duration gynecological operations, by A. R. Volchenkova, et al. AKUSHERSTVO I GINEKOLOGIIA (Moscow) (2):56-57, 1977.

ANTIBODIES
The association of maternal lymphocytotoxic antibodies with obstetric complications, by R. E. Harris, et al. OBSTETRICS AND GYNECOLOGY 48(3):302-304, 1976. (Bio. Abstrs. February, 1977, 20979)

Research of antibodies against toxoplasma gondii in subjects with repeated abortion, perinatal mortality and malformed newborns, by A. S. Castro, et al. ANNALI SCLAVO 18(1):75-81, 1976. (Bio. Abstrs. March, 1977, 29539)

ARACHIDONIC ACID

ARTIFICIAL ABORTION
see: Induced Abortion

ASPIRIN

BEHAVIOR
see: Sociology and Behavior

BIBLIOGRAPHY

BIRTH CONTROL
see also: Family Planning

Birth control: contraception, abortion, sterilization, by

Ferraris. MINERVA GINECOLOGIA 29(4):249-252, April, 1977.

To have or to have not—promotion and prevention of child-birth in gynaecological work, by S. Macintyre. SO-CIALOGICAL REVIEW: MONOGRAPHS (22):176-193, March, 1976.

BLOOD

Comparison of vaginal cytology with plasma progesterone levels in early human pregnancy, by I. Khanna, et al. INDIAN JOURNAL OF MEDICAL RESEARCH 64(9): 1267-1271, September, 1976. (Bio. Abstrs. May, 1977, 50500)

Evaluation of hypercoagulability in septic abortion, by H. Graeff. HAEMOSTASIS 5(5):284-294, 1976. (Bio. Abstrs. June, 1977, 63772)

Functional state of the blood coagulation and anticoagulation systems in women in missed abortion or labor, by M. M. Kligerman, et al. PEDIATRIIA AKUSHERSTVO I GINEKOLOGIIA (4):37-39, July-August, 1976.

Maternal serum alpha-fetoprotein and spontaneous abortion, by N. Wald, et al. BRITISH JOURNAL OF OBSTE-TRICS AND GYNAECOLOGY 84(5):357-362, May, 1977.

Plasma progesterone in women with a history of recurrent early abortions, by S. K. Yip, et al. FERTILITY AND STERILITY 28(2):151-155, February, 1977. (Bio. Abstrs. June, 1977, 62721)

Possible correlation between the blood groups of the ABO system and Rh(D) factors and abortion, by M. Furfaro, et al. MINERVA GINECOLOGIA 29(4):309-310, April, 1977.

Vitamins C and E in spontaneous abortion, by J. S. Vobecky,

et al. INTERNATIONAL JOURNAL FOR VITAMIN
AND NUTRITION RESEARCH 46(3):291-296, 1976.
(Bio. Abstrs. June, 1977, 61970)

CAMPAIGN ISSUES
see: Politics

CANDIDIASIS
see: Complications

CAPROVESTROL
Treatment of habitual abortion with caprovestrol, by L. G.
Kovtumova, et al. VOPROSY OKHRANY MATERIN-
STVA I DETSTVA 21(5):72-75, May, 1976.

CARDIOVASCULAR SYSTEM
see: Complications

CEPHALOTHIN

CERVICAL INCOMPETENCE AND INSUFFICIENCY
Cervical pregnancy: report of three cases and a review of the
literature, by H. Khosravi, et al. INTERNATIONAL
JOURNAL OF GYNAECOLOGY AND OBSTETRICS
14(3):237-240, 1976. (Bio. Abstrs. June, 1977, 71947)

Isthmico-cervical insufficiency as a cause of habitual miscarriage, by A. P. Kiriushchenkov. FEL'DSKER I AKU-
SHERKA 41(8):25-28, August, 1976.

Treatment of cervix incompetence in pregnant women by
means of Mayer's pessary. Discussion contribution on
the paper of K. Jiratek, et al. "Directed therapy of
threatened premature abortion—comparison of treatment
results using cerclage and pessary," by E. Bechinie.
CESKOSLOVENSKA GYNEKOLOGIE 42(3):205-206,
April, 1977.

CHLORMADINONE

CLINICAL ASPECTS
Clinic and client: an investigation into the experiences of
Dutch women in outpatient abortion clinics, by A.
Schroeder. STIMEZO-RESEARCH 1:85, 1975. (Psycho.
Abstrs. 1977, 8832)

Clinical and pathomorphological study on placentae during
abortions in the second trimester, by A. Sed'ova, et al.
CESKOSLOVENSKA GYNEKOLOGIE 41(8):569-571,
October, 1976.

Clinical and x-ray studies on the relationship between interruption of pregnancy and premature labor, by R. Voigt,
et al. ZENTRALBLATT FUR GYNAEKOLOGIE
98(25):1589-1593, 1976.

Clinical aspects of premature detachment of normally functioning placentas, by Z. N. Zaidieva. AKUSHERSTVO I
GINEKOLOGIIA (Moscow) (1):56-59, 1977.

Clinical comparison of abortifacient activity of vaginally
administered prostaglandin E2 in two dosage forms, by
T. J. Roseman, et al. AMERICAN JOURNAL OF OB-
STETRICS AND GYNECOLOGY 129(2):225-227,
September 15, 1977.

A clinical comparison of prostaglandin F2alpha and intra-
amniotic saline for induction of midtrimester abortion,
by G. S. Berger, et al. ANNALES CHIRURGIAE ET
GYNAECOLOGIAE FENNIAE 66(1):55-58, 1977.

Clinical details, cytogenic studies, and cellular physiology of
a 69, XXX fetus, with comments on the biological effect
of triploidy in man, by C. M. Gosden, et al. JOURNAL
OF MEDICAL GENETICS 13(5):371-380, October,
1976.

Clinical experiences with the gestagen Turinal in treating
threatened and habitual abortions, by A. Pociatek, et al.
BRATISLAUSKE LEKARSKE LISTY 67(1):87-91,

January, 1977.

Clinical experiences with prostaglandin E2 and F2 alpha in the termination of pregnancy and labor induction in intrauterine fetal death, by J. Kunz, et al. SCHWEIZERISCHE MEDIZINISCHE WOCHENSCHRIFT 107(22):757-763, June 4, 1977.

Clinical problems of ovulation defects, by A. Grant. INTERNATIONAL JOURNAL OF GYNECOLOGY AND OBSTETRICS 14(2):123-128, 1976. (Bio. Abstrs. April, 1977, 44075)

Clinical results of two-time abortion technics with special regard to ascending genital infections, by H. Kreibich, et al. ZENTRALBLATT FUR GYNAEKOLOGIE 99(12):755-762, 1977.

Contraceptive practice by women presenting to a free-standing abortion clinic, by S. Treloar, et al. MEDICAL JOURNAL OF AUSTRALIA 1(15):527-532, April 9, 1977.

Elective abortion: complications seen in a free-standing clinic, by G. J. L. Wulf, Jr., et al. OBSTETRICS AND GYNECOLOGY 49(3):351-357, 1977. (Bio. Abstrs. July, 1977, 5457)

Evolution of a women's clinic: an alternate system of medical care, by M. J. Gray, et al. AMERICAN JOURNAL OF OBSTETRICS AND GYNECOLOGY 126(7):760-768, December 1, 1976.

Infection in newborn siblings, by P. H. Azimi, et al. AMERICAN JOURNAL OF DISEASES OF CHILDREN 131(4): 398-399, 1977. (Bio. Abstrs. September, 1977, 27613)

Lithopedion. An anatomo-clinical study apropos of 1 case, by B. Ait-Ouyahia, et al. JOURNAL DE GYNECOLOGIE, OBSTETRIQUE ET BIOLOGIE DE LA REPRODUCTION 6(2):233-238, March, 1977.

Nursing decisions. Experience in clinical problem solving. Series 2, Part 8: H. Joyce, an elective abortion patient, by R. De Tornyay, et al. RN; NATIONAL MAGAZINES FOR NURSES 40:55-61, June, 1977.

CLOMIPHENE

COLLEGE WOMEN
see: Youth

COMPLICATIONS
see also: Hemorrhage

Abdominal pain in early pregnancy and its treatment, by C. Yi. KOREAN CENTRAL JOURNAL OF MEDICINE 29(6):543-545, 1976. (Bio. Abstrs. April, 1977, 47773)

Abdominal wall endometriosis following hypertonic saline abortion, by B. T. Ferrari, et al. JAMA; JOURNAL OF THE AMERICAN MEDICAL ASSOCIATION 238(1): 56-57, July 4, 1977.

Abortion and maternal deaths [letter], by I. Chalmers. BRITISH MEDICAL JOURNAL 2(6037):698, September 18, 1976.

An abortion stick in the duodenum and gallbladder, by G. M. Gandhi, et al. INTERNATIONAL SURGERY 61(11-12): 594-595, November-December, 1976.

Abortions at Nacka Hospital, 1975—somatic complications and preventive technics, by K. Sigurdsson. LAKAR-TIDNINGEN 74(5):318-321, February, 1977.

Abruptio placentae and perinatal death: a prospective study, by R. L. Naeye, et al. AMERICAN JOURNAL OF OB-STETRICS AND GYNECOLOGY 128(7):740-746, August 1, 1977.

Acute renal failure of obstetric origin, by K. S. Chugh, et al.

OBSTETRICS AND GYNECOLOGY 48(6):642-646, December, 1976.

The association of maternal lymphocytotoxic antibodies with obstetric complications, by R. E. Harris, et al. OBSTETRICS AND GYNECOLOGY 48(3):302-304, 1976. (Bio. Abstrs. February, 1977, 20979)

The association of multiple induced abortions with subsequent prematurity and spontaneous abortion, by L. H. Roht, et al. ACTA OBSTETRICA ET GYNAECOLOGICA JAPONIA 23(2):140-145, April, 1976.

Avulsion of the ureter from both ends as a complication of interrutpion of pregnancy with vacuum aspirator, by C. Dimopoulos, et al. JOURNAL OF UROLOGY 118(1 Pt 1):108, July, 1977.

Cervical pregnancy: report of three cases and a review of the literature, by H. Khosravi, et al. INTERNATIONAL JOURNAL OF GYNAECOLOGY AND OBSTETRICS 14(3):237-240, 1976. (Bio. Abstrs. June, 1977, 71947)

Changes in congenital oral cleft incidence in relation to induced abortions, by A. P. Polednak, et al. AMERICAN JOURNAL OF OBSTETRICS AND GYNECOLOGY 126(6):734-735, November 15, 1976.

Clinical and x-ray studies on the relationship between interruption of pregnancy and premature labor, by R. Voigt, et al. ZENTRALBLATT FUR GYNAEKOLOGIE 98(25):1589-1593, 1976.

Clinical aspects of premature detachment of normally functioning placentas, by Z. N. Zaidieva. AKUSHERSTVO I GINEKOLOGIIA (Moscow) (1):56-59, 1977.

Coagulopathy with midtrimester induced abortion: association with hyperosmolar urea administration, by R. T. Burkman, et al. AMERICAN JOURNAL OF OBSTE-

TRICS AND GYNECOLOGY 127(5):533-536, March 1, 1977. (Bio. Abstrs. August, 1977, 23526)

Complications following induced abortion by vacuum aspiration: patient characteristics and procedures, by M. Cheng, et al. STUDIES IN FAMILY PLANNING 8(5):125-129, May, 1977.

Complications in induced abortions, by H. Kirchhoff. WIENER MEDIZINISCHE WOCHENSCHRIFT 126(49-50):696-699, December 3, 1976.

The course of pregnancy and outcome of labor in women with chronic pyelonephritis, by L. S. Koval' chuk. AKUSHERSTVO I GINEKOLOGIIA (Moscow) (10):47-50, October, 1976.

Death after legal abortion by catheter placement, by D. A. Grimes, et al. AMERICAN JOURNAL OF OBSTETRICS AND GYNECOLOGY 129(1):107-108, September 1, 1977.

The development of coagulopathy in missed abortion, by H. Heyes, et al. GEBURTSHILFE UND FRAUENHEIL-KUNDE 37(7):595-599, July, 1977.

Developmental anomalies of the umbilical vessels (arteria umbilicalis singularis) and spontaneous abortion, by E. Horak, et al. ORVOSI HETILAP 118(29):1721-1726, July 17, 1977.

A developmental approach to post-abortion depression, by F. M. Burkle, Jr. PRACTITIONER 218(1304):217-225, February, 1977.

Ectopic pregnancies and the use of intrauterine device and low dose progestogen contraception, by P. Rantakyla, et al. ACTA OBSTETRICIA ET GYNECOLOGICA SCANDINAVICA 56(1):61-62, 1977. (Bio. Abstrs. July, 1977, 5564)

Effect of interruption on the prognosis of children from the following pregnancy, by J. Ringel, et al. CESKOSLO-VENSKA PEDIATRIE 31(8):442-445, August, 1976.

Elective abortion. Complications seen in a free-standing clinic, by G. J. Wulff, Jr., et al. OBSTETRICS AND GYNECOLOGY 49(3):351-357, March, 1977. (Bio. Abstrs. July, 1977, 5457)

Endotoxic shock in obstetrics, by R. Valle, et al. REVISTA CHILENA DE OBSTETRICIA Y GINECOLOGIA 41(3): 158-165, 1976.

Factors minimising mortality and morbidity from infection after intra-amniotic saline infusion for medical termination of pregnancy, by R. N. Ghosh, et al. JOURNAL OF THE INDIAN MEDICAL ASSOCIATION 66(11):283-285, June 1, 1976.

Fever in a 22 years old woman. PRAXIS 65(38):1155-1156, September 21, 1976.

The frequency of uterine contractions in abruptio placentae, by H. J. Odendaal. SOUTH AFRICAN MEDICAL JOURNAL 50(54):2129-2131, December 18, 1976.

Glutamate dehydrogenase isoenzymes of the placenta and fetal membranes in normal pregnancy and pregnancy complicated by sex gland hypofunction, by T. N. Pogo-relova, et al. AKUSHERSTVO I GINEKOLOGIIA (Moscow) 5:64-66, May, 1976.

Hip prosthesis and post-abortion streptococcal infection in lupus, by P. Godeau, et al. SEMAINE DES HOPITAUX DE PARIS 53(10):633-635, March 9, 1977.

Hypokalemia and cardiac arrhythmia associated with prosta-glandin-induced abortion, by R. L. Burt, et al. OBSTE-TRICS AND GYNECOLOGY 50(1 Suppl):45S-46S, July, 1977.

Incidence of post-abortion psychosis: a prospective study, by C. Brewer. BRITISH MEDICAL JOURNAL 1:476-477, February 19, 1977.

Indication for pregnancy interruption in patients with heart diseases, by Y. Hatano. FORTSCHRITTE DU MEDIZIN 95(11):685-689, March 17, 1977.

Induced abortion and brain damage, by A. Rett. WIENER MEDIZINISCHE WOCHENSCHRIFT 126(49-50):700-702, December 3, 1976.

Infant survival following uterine rupture and complete abruptio placentae, by S. Semchyshyn, et al. OBSTE-TRICS AND GYNECOLOGY 50(1 Suppl):74S-75S, July, 1977.

Influence of the kind of anesthesia and length of hospitali-zation on the frequency of early complications of abor-tion, by L. Andolsek, et al. JUGOSLOVENSKA GINE-KOLOGIIA I OPSTETRICIJA 16(3):175-183, May-June, 1976.

Intrauterine device should be removed during pregnancy. LAKARTIDNINGEN 73(51):4541, December 15, 1976.

Late sequelae of interrupted pregnancy, by G. Venzmer. KRANKENPFLEGE 30(10):290-291, October, 1976.

Maternal primary hyperpara-thyroidism of pregnancy: suc-cessful treatment by parathyroidectomy, by R. F. Gaeke, et al. JAMA; JOURNAL OF THE AMERICAN MEDI-CAL ASSOCIATION 238(6):508-509, 1977. (Bio. Abstrs. December, 1977, 62119)

Medical genetic consultation in congenital developmental anomalies and aborted pregnancy, by V. A. Shileiko, et al. PEDIATRIIA AKUSHERSTVO I GINECOLOGIIA (2):45-46, March-April, 1977.

Method of payment—relation to abortion complications, by
R. G. Smith, et al. HEALTH AND SOCIAL WORK
1(2):5-28, May, 1976.

Mid-trimester abortion and its complications [editorial].
MEDICAL JOURNAL OF AUSTRALIA 1(4):82-83,
January 22, 1977.

Modification of the rate of complications in the inflam-
matory adnexa process and pregnancy interruption, by
W. Franz, et al. ZENTRALBLATT FUR GYNAEKOLO-
GIE 99(2):113-116, 1977.

Morbidity and mortality associated with legal abortion [let-
ter], by M. Potts. MEDICAL JOURNAL OF AUSTRALIA
2(1):30-31, July 3, 1976.

Motivation for induced abortion and post-interruption sequelae, by V. Bebjakova. CESKOSLOVENSKA GYNE-
KOLOGIE 41(9):692-693, November, 1976.

Ovarian abscess associated with incomplete abortion and
intrauterine contraceptive device, by A. Neri, et al.
ISRAEL JOURNAL OF MEDICAL SCIENCES 13(3):
305-308, 1977. (Bio. Abstrs. October, 1977, 41530)

Pelvic abscess. A sequela of first trimester abortion, by C.
B. Glassner, et al. OBSTETRICS AND GYNECOLOGY
48(6):716-717, December, 1976. (Bio. Abstrs. April,
1977, 39387)

Postabortal amenorrhea due to cervical stenosis, by E. Hakim-
Elahi. OBSTETRICS AND GYNECOLOGY 48(6):
723-724, 1976. (Bio. Abstrs. March, 1977, 35625)

Postimplantation pregnancy disruption in Microtus ochrogaster, M. pennsulvanicus and Peromyscus maniculatus,
by A. M. Kenney, et al. JOURNAL OF REPRODUC-
TION AND FERTILITY 49(2):365-367, March, 1977.

Preceding pregnancy loss as an index of risk of stillbirth or neonatal death in the present pregnancy, by J. Fedrick, et al. BIOLOGY OF THE NEONATE 31(1-2):84-93, 1977.

Pregnancy during the hysterogram cycle, by R. L. Goldenberg, et al. FERTILITY AND STERILITY 27(11):1274-1276, 1976. (Bio. Abstrs. March, 1977, 35650)

Premature detachment of a normally situated placenta, by A. S. Egorov, et al. PEDIATRIIA AKUSHERSTVO I GINEKOLOGIIA (4):43-45, July-August, 1976.

Proteinuria and the renal lesion in preeclampsia and abruptio placentae, by J. S. Robson. PERSPECTIVES IN NEPHROLOGY AND HYPERTENSION 5:61-73, 1976.

Reasons for criminal abortion and complications of patients at Ramathibodi Hospital, 1975, by U. Kabusa. THAI JOURNAL OF NURSING 25(2):153-155, April, 1976.

Resumption of menstruation and fertility after cesarean section, by D. Dang. ANNALES DE BIOLOGIE ANIMALE BIOCHIMIE BIOPHYSIQUE 17(3A):325-329, 1977. (Bio. Abstrs. November, 1977, 59934)

Safety of abortion [letter], by W. V. Dolan. JAMA; JOURNAL OF THE AMERICAN MEDICAL ASSOCIATION 237(24):2601-2602, June 13, 1977.

Septic shock in obstetric-gynecologic practice, by I. T. Riabtseva, et al. AKUSHERSTVO I GINEKOLOGIIA (Moscow) (4):40-43, April, 1976.

Smallpox vaccination and pregnancy [letter], by M. Luisi. AMERICAN JOURNAL OF OBSTETRICS AND GYNECOLOGY 128(6):700, July 15, 1977.

Somatic complications after induced abortion in hospitals in Telemark county, by P. Hoglend, et al. TIDSSKRIFT

FOR DEN NORSKE LAEGEFORENING 97(3):134-
136, January 30, 1977.

Spina bifida and anencephaly: are miscarriages a possible
cause? by K. M. Laurence, et al. BRITISH MEDICAL
JOURNAL 2(6083):361-362, August 6, 1977.

Successful pregnancy in acute monocytic leukaemia, by R.
Gokal, et al. BRITISH JOURNAL OF CANCER 34(3):
299-302, 1976. (Bio. Abstrs. November, 1977, 51360)

The susceptibility of the postpartum and postabortal cervix
and uterine cavity to infection with attenuated rubella
virus, by R. J. Bolognese, et al. AMERICAN JOURNAL
OF OBSTETRICS AND GYNECOLOGY 125(4):525-
527, June 15, 1976.

Treatment of endometritis after artificial abortion, by A. A.
Vorontsov, et al. PEDIATRIIA AKUSHERSTVO I
GINEKOLOGIIA (1):53-56, January-February, 1977.

Treatment of preclinical forms of threatened abortion in
women with genital infantilism, by N. K. Moskvitina.
AKUSHERSTVO I GINEKOLOGIIA (Moscow) 5:53-
56, May, 1976.

Untreated endocervical gonorrhea and endometritis following elective abortion, by R. T. Burkman, et al. AMERI-
CAN JOURNAL OF OBSTETRICS AND GYNECOLO-
GY 126(6):648-651, 1976. (Bio. Abstrs. April, 1977,
41724)

Uterine perforation in connection with vacuum aspiration
for legal abortion, by P. J. Moberg. INTERNATIONAL
JOURNAL OF GYNAECOLOGY AND OBSTETRICS
14(1):77-80, 1976. (Bio. Abstrs. February, 1977,
53573)

WHO: excessive dilation may affect later pregnancy. FAMILY
PLANNING PERSPECTIVES 9:134-135, May-June, 1977.

CONTRACEPTION
Abortion or contraception? by C. Giannice. MINERVA GINECOLOGIA 28(7-8):671-675, July-August, 1976.

Birth control: contraception, abortion, sterilization, by Ferraris. MINERVA GINECOLOGIA 29(4):249-252, April, 1977.

Contraceptive use and subsequent fertility, by G. R. Huggins. FERTILITY AND STERILITY 28(6):603-612, 1977. (Bio. Abstrs. December, 1977, 71780)

Ectopic pregnancies and the use of intrauterine device and low dose progestogen contraception, by P. Rantakyla, et al. ACTA OBSTETRICIA ET GYNECOLOGICA SCANDINAVICA 56(1):61-62, 1977. (Bio. Abstrs. July, 1977, 5564)

Fetal loss, twinning and birth weight after oral-contraceptive use, by K. J. Rothman. NEW ENGLAND JOURNAL OF MEDICINE 297(9):468-471, September 1, 1977.

Personality characteristics associated with contraceptive behavior in women seeking abortion under liberalized California law, by L. D. Noble. DISSERTATION ABSTRACTS INTERNATIONAL 35(7-B):3589-3590, 1975. (Psycho. Abstrs. 1977, 3141)

Prostaglandin E2 in a diaphragm. A further note, by H. Schulman, et al. PROSTAGLANDINS 13(4):751-753, April, 1977.

The report of the royal commission on contraception, sterilisation and abortion: a comparison with health professional policies, by D. Wills. NURSING FORUM (Auckland) 5:4-6, April-May, 1977.

Sex guilt and contraceptive use in abortion patients, by C. O. Gerrard. DISSERTATION ABSTRACTS INTERNATIONAL 35(8-B):4143, 1975. (Psycho. Abstrs. 1977,

8142)

Social factors in the choice of contraceptive method: a comparison of first clinic attenders accepting oral contraceptives with those accepting intrauterine devices, by S. U. Kingsley, et al. JOURNAL OF BIOSOCIAL SCIENCE 9(2):153-162, 1977. (Bio. Abstrs. September, 1977, 29735)

Submission to the Royal Commission on contraception, sterlization and abortion, by New Zealand Psychological Society. NEW ZEALAND PSYCHOLOGIST 5(1):48-56, 1976. (Psycho. Abstrs. 1977, 6215)

CRIMINAL ABORTION
see: Laws and Legislation

DEMOGRAPHY
see also: Population

Abortion at the Felix Bulnes Hospital. Sociodemographic and medical data, by R. Viada, et al. REVISTA CHILENA DE OBSTETRICIA Y GINECOLOGIA 40(5): 235-241, 1975.

An attempt to evaluate the risk of death in utero, by C. Huraux-Rendu, et al. JOURNAL DE GYNECOLOGIE, OBSTETRIQUE ET BIOLOGIE DE REPRODUCTION 5(5):675-680, 1976. (Bio. Abstrs. April, 1977, 37255)

Legal abortion among New York City residents: an analysis according to socioeconomic and demographic characteristics, by M. J. Kramer. FAMILY PLANNING PERSPECTIVES 7(3):128-137, 1975. (Socio. Abstrs. 1977, 7717343)

The psychosocial factors of the abortion experience: a critical review. PSYCHOLOGY OF WOMEN QUARTERLY 1(1):79-103, February, 1976. (Soc. Abstrs. 1977, 7715928)

Social and demographic determinants of abortion in Poland, by D. P. Mazur. POPULATION STUDIES 29(1):21-35, 1975. (Socio. Abstrs. 1977, 7717345)

Some comments on the demographic and social influence of the 1967 Abortion Act, by R. Leete. JOURNAL OF BIO-SOCIAL SCIENCE 8(3):229-251, 1976. (Socio. Abstrs. 1977, 7714000)

DIAGNOSIS

Clinical aspects of premature detachment of normally functioning placentas, by Z. N. Zaidieva. AKUSHERSTVO I GINEKOLOGIIA (Moscow) (1):56-59, 1977.

Clinical problems of ovulation defects, by A. Grant. INTERNATIONAL JOURNAL OF GYNECOLOGY AND OBSTETRICS 14(2):123-128, 1976. (Bio. Abstrs. April, 1977, 44075)

Diagnosis and treatment of abortions, by Y. Chang. KOREAN CENTRAL JOURNAL OF MEDICINE 29(2):125-127, 1976. (Bio. Abstrs. April, 1977, 43616)

The diagnosis and treatment of threatened miscarriage, by B. Faris. AUSTRALASIAN NURSES JOURNAL 4(4): 7, October, 1975.

Diagnostic and prognostic importance of the chorionic gonadotropin test in threatened abortions, by D. I. Dimitrov. AKUSHERSTVO I GINEKOLOGIIA (Sofia) 16(3):220-221, 1977.

Eisenmenger's syndrome in pregnancy: does heparin prophylaxis improve the maternal mortality rate? by J. A. Pitts, et al. AMERICAN HEART JOURNAL 93(3):321-326, 1977. (Bio. Abstrs. November, 1977, 58782)

Failure to diagnose pregnancy as cause of late abortion [letter], by C. Brewer. LANCET 1(8001):46, January 1, 1977.

The fate of pregnancy after a cuneiform ovarian resection performed in cases of Stein-Leventhal syndrome clinically diagnosed, by F. Divila, et al. CESKOSLOVENSKA GYNEKOLOGIE 41(9):669-671, November, 1976.

Genetic counselling and prenatal diagnosis for chromosome anomalies. Use of study of spontaneous abortions, by J. Boué, et al. INTERNATIONAL JOURNAL OF GYNAECOLOGY AND OBSTETRICS 14(4):290-295, 1976. (Bio. Abstrs. September, 1977, 32528)

Glycosaminoglycans in the amniotic fluid in normal pregnancy and in cases of clinical signs of threatened fetus, by A. Bromboszcz, et al. GINEKOLOGIA POLASKA 47(11):1261-1267, November, 1976.

How to stimulate the placental function, by A. Fanard, et al. REPRODUCCION 3(1-2):15-25, January-June, 1976.

Intrauterine adhesions secondary to elective abortion: hysteroscopic diagnosis and management, by C. M. March, et al. OBSTETRICS AND GYNECOLOGY 48(4):422-424, 2976. (Bio. Abstrs. February, 1977, 23565)

Is there any evidence that the maternal HPL serum-concentration is of prognostic value in cases of threatened abortion? by P. Berle, et al. ZEITSCHRIFT FUR GEBURTSCHILFE UND PERINATOLOGIE 181(3):211-217, June, 1977.

Laboratory studies in the diagnosis of early missed abortion, by J. Krajewski, et al. WIADOMOSCI LEKARSKIE 29(23):2111-2113, December 1, 1976.

Maternal serum alpha-feto-protein: its value in antenatal diagnosis of genetic disaease and in obstetrical-gynaecological care, by Z. A. Habib. ACTA OBSTETRICIA ET GYNECOLOGICA SCANDINAVIA. SUPPLEMENT

8(16):1-90, 1976. (Bio. Abstrs. October, 1977, 47804)

Minimizing the risk of amniocentesis for prenatal diagnosis, by A. I. Goldstein, et al. JAMA; JOURNAL OF THE AMERICAN MEDICAL ASSOCIATION 237(13):1336-1338, 1977. (Bio. Abstrs. July, 1977, 7600)

A new immunochemical tube test for pregnancy using the latex-agglutination inhibition reaction. II. Clinical results, by H. Hepp, et al. DEUTSCHE MEDIZINSCHE WOCHENSCHRIFT 101(45):1639-1643, November 5, 1976.

Prenatal diagnosis and selective abortion, by T. Jenkins, et al. SOUTH AFRICAN MEDICAL JOURNAL 50(53): 2091-2095, December 11, 1976.

Prenatal diagnosis: distributive justice and the quality of life, by K. Lebacqz. HARVARD THEOLOGICAL REVIEW 68:392-393, July-October, 1975.

Prenatal diagnosis of genetic disorders, by M. F. Niermeijer, et al. JOURNAL OF MEDICAL GENETICS 13(3):182-194, 1976. (Bio. Abstrs. October, 1977, 37423)

The prognostic value of human placental lactogen levels in threatened abortion in general practice, by D. W. Gau, et al. JOURNAL OF THE ROYAL COLLEGE OF GENERAL PRACTITIONERS 27(175):91-92, February, 1977.

Subclinical spontaneous abortion, by G. D. Braunstein, et al. OBSTETRICS AND GYNECOLOGY 50(1 Suppl):41S-44S, July, 1977.

Ultrasonic diagnosis of abortion of torpid evolution, by R. Comino, et al. ACTA OBSTETRICA Y GINECOLOGICA HISPANA-LUSITANA 24(1):5-15, January, 1976.

DIAPHYLINE
Treatment of threatening abortion with diaphylline, by G.
Illei, et al. ORVOSI HETILAP 118(21):1239-1240,
May 22, 1977.

DIAZEPAM

DIETHYLSTILBESTROL

DINOPROST THOMETHAMINE

DIXYRAZINE
The antiemetic effect of dixyrazine in postoperative patients:
a double-blind study, by I. Kivalo, et al. ANNALES
CHIRURGIAE ET GYNAECOLOGIAE FENNIAE 65(4):
295-299, 1976. (Bio. Abstrs. May, 1977, 53319)

DOXICILLIN

DRUG THERAPY
see: Induced Abortion
Surgical Treatment and Management
Techniques of Abortion
Under Specific Drugs

E-AMINOCAPROIC ACID

EDUCATION
Bioethics and health education: some issues of the biological
revolution, by G. B. Fulton. JOURNAL OF SCHOOL
HEALTH 47:205-211, April, 1977.

Contraception, abortion and veneral disease: teenagers knowl-
edge and the effect of education, by P. A. Reichelt, et al.
FAMILY PLANNING PERSPECTIVE 7(2):83-88, 1975.
(Socio. Abstrs. 1977, 7717089)

Health education activities in the prevention of abortion, by
E. V. Smoliakova. FEL'DSKER I AKUSHERKA 42(1):
35-38, January, 1977.

Value sheets for health education by P. C. Dunn. HEALTH EDUCATION 8(3):42-43, May-June, 1977.

ENDOTOXIN

ESTRADIOL

ETHYL ALCOHOL

ETIDOCAINE

EUTHANASIA
Abortion and euthanasia: recent developments of the law, by D. J. Horan. FORUM 12:960-979, Summer, 1977.

A new ethical approach to abortion and its implications for the euthanasia dispute, by R. F. R. Gardner. JOURNAL OF MEDICAL ETHICS 1:127-131, September, 1975.

FAMILY PLANNING
see also: Sociology and Behavior

Abortion statutes after Danforth (Planned Parenthood of Cent. Mo. v. Danforth, 96 Sup Ct 2831): an examination. JOURNAL OF FAMILY LAW 15:537-567, 1976-1977.

Births aborted among the users of the voluntary family planning program of the Instituto Mexicano del Seguro Social, by J. E. Garcia de Alba, et al. GINECOLOGIA Y OBSTETRICIA DE MEXICO 41(245):235-242, March, 1977.

Comparative study of the causes of induced abortion and the knowledge of family planning, by M. D. Ramos Netto. REVISTA ENFERMAGEM EM NOVAS DIMENSOES 1(4):172, September-October, 1975.

Family planning. KOREAN CENTRAL JOURNAL OF MEDICINE 31(6):649-650, 2976. (Bio. Abstrs. December, 1977, 66070)

Family planning measures—their merits and demerits, by D. Roy. JOURNAL OF THE INDIAN MEDICAL ASSO-CIATION 66(11):265-268, June 1, 1976.

Problem of family planning in women in the textile industry. An analysis of social indications for pregnancy interruption, by A. Zdziennicki. POLSKI TYGODNIK LEKAR-SKI 31(46):1993-1994, November 15, 1976.

FAUSTAN

FEES AND PUBLIC ASSISTANCE
  see also: Laws and Legislation
              Sociology and Behavior

Abortion: who pays? by S. Fraker, et al. NEWSWEEK 90: 12-13, July 4, 1977.

FERTILITY
  see: Sterility

FETUS
  Abortion, fetal research, and the law, by J. M. Humber. SOCIAL THEORY AND PRACTICE 4:127-147, Spring, 1977.

  Case study: the unwanted child: caring for a fetus born alive after an abortion, by Bok, et al. HASTINGS CENTER REPORT 6:10-15, October, 1976.

  Redefining the issues in fetal experimentations; reprint from The Journal of the American Medical Association, July 19, 1976, by E. Diamond. LINACRE 44:148-154, May, 1977.

FLAVOXATE

FLUMETHASONE

GENETICS
Aetiology of spontaneous abortion: a cytogenetic and epidemiological study of 288 abortuses and their parents, by J. G. Lauritsen. ACTA OBSTETRICIA ET GYNECOLOGICA SCANDINAVICA. SUPPLEMENT 52:1-29, 1976. (Bio. Abstrs. March, 1977, 26401)

Balanced translocation t (3; 21) (q 11; q 21) as a cause of habitual abortions, by N. I. Smirnova, et al. TSITOLOGIIA I GENETIKA 11(1):74-76, January-February, 1977.

Chromosomal anomalies in early spontaneous abortion. (Their consequences on early embryogenesis and in vitro growth of embryonic cells), by J. G. Boué, et al. CURRENT TOPICS IN PATHOLOGY 62:193-208, 1976.

Chromosome anomalies and miscarriage, by Iu. I. Novikov, et al. AKUSHERSTVO I GINEKOLOGIIA (Moscow) (12):32-35, December, 1976.

Cytogenetic findings in fifty-five couples with recurrent fetal wastage, by J. R. Byrd, et al. FERTILITY AND STERILITY 28(3):246-250, March, 1977.

Cytogenetic studies in families with habitual abortions, by G. Bulkova, et al. AKUSHERSTVO I GINEKOLOGIIA (Sofia) 15(4):265-268, 1976.

Cytogenetic studies in spontaneous abortions, by S. Gilgenkrantz, et al. BULLETIN DE L'ASSOCIATION DES ANATOMISTES 60(169):357-365, 1976. (Bio. Abstrs. September, 1977, 26622)

Cytogenetic studies in sterility and miscarriage, by V. I. Kucharenko, et al. AKUSHERSTVO I GINEKOLOGIIA (Moscow) (5):1-4, May, 1977.

Cytogenetics of habitual abortion and other reproductive wastage, by M. A. Stenchever, et al. AMERICAN JOUR-

NAL OF OBSTETRICS AND GYNECOLOGY 127(2):
143-150, January 15, 1977.

Determination of prenatal sex ratio in man, by M. Yamamoto,
et al. HUMAN GENETICS 36(3):265-269, 1977. (Bio.
Abstrs. October, 1977, 38521)

Ethical considerations of prenatal genetic diagnosis, by J. F.
Tormey. CLINICAL OBSTETRICS AND GYNECOLOGY
19(4):957-963, December, 1976.

Eugenic indications in the current status of abortion, by G.
Giocoli. MINERVA GINECOLOGIA 28(9):700-703,
September, 1976.

Eugenic indications; problems provoked by present-day
genetics, by G. Mollica. MINERVA GINECOLOGIA
28(9):714-716, September, 1976.

Fertility in women with gonadal dysgenesis, by F. I. Reyes,
et al. AMERICAN JOURNAL OF OBSTETRICS AND
GYNECOLOGY 126(6):668-670, 1976. (Bio. Abstrs.
March, 1977, 32715)

A further chromosome analysis in induced abortions, by M.
Yamamoto, et al. HUMAN GENETICS 34(1):69-71,
1976. (Bio. Abstrs. March, 1977, 32690)

Fusion of homologous chromosomes (15q15q) as cause of
recurrent abortion [letter], by M. Bartsch-Sandhoff.
LANCET 1(8010):551, March 5, 1977.

Genetic counselling and prenatal diagnosis for chromosome
anomalies: use of study of spontaneous abortions, by J.
Boue, et al. INTERNATIONAL JOURNAL OF GYNAE-
COLOGY AND OBSTETRICS 14(4):290-295, 1976.
(Bio. Abstrs. September, 1977, 32528)

Genetically determined pathology of fertility in population
of couples with spontaneous (habitual) abortions, by

V. P. Kulazhenko, et al. GENETIKA 13(1):138-145, 1977. (Bio. Abstrs. October, 1977, 44940)

Identification by Q and G bands of chromosome anomalies in spontaneous abortion, by J. Boué, et al. ANNALES DE GENETIQUE 19(4):233-239, December, 1976.

Indications for amniocentesis for prenatal fetal karyotype determination, by I. V. Lur'e. TSITOLOGIIA I GENE-TIKA 10(3):198-200, 1976. (Bio. Abstrs. January, 1977, 8195)

Legal considerations and prenatal genetic diagnosis, by L. F. Hifman, 3d. CLINICAL OBSTETRICS AND GYNE-COLOGY 19(4):965-972, December, 1976.

Maternal serum alpha-feto-protein: its value in antenatal diagnosis of genetic disease and in obstetrical-gynaeco-logical care, by Z. A. Habib. ACTA OBSTETRICIA ET GYNECOLOGICA SCANDINAVICA. SUPPLEMENT 8(16):1-90, 1976. (Bio. Abstrs. October, 1977, 47804)

Medical genetic consultation in congenital developmental anomalies and aborted pregnancy, by V. A. Shileiko, et al. PEDIATRIIA AKUSHERSTVO I GINECOLOGIIA (2):45-46, March-April, 1977.

Mother with D/D translocation in genetic counseling, by J. Stepien, et al. GINEKOLOGIA POLASKA 48(3):285-288, March, 1977.

Origin of the extra chromosome in trisomy 16, by J. G. Lauritsen, et al. CLINICAL GENETICS 10(3):156-160, 1976. (Bio. Abstrs. March, 1977, 32669)

Origin of triploidy and tetraploidy in man: 11 cases with chromosomes markers, by T. Kajii, et al. CYTOGEN-ETICS AND CELL GENETICS 18(3):109-125, 1977.

A possible association of long Y chromosomes and fetal loss, by S. R. Patil, et al. HUMAN GENETICS 35(2):233-235, 1977. (Bio. Abstrs. July, 1977, 2275)

Prenatal diagnosis of genetic disorders, by M. F. Niermeijer, et al. JOURNAL OF MEDICAL GENETICS 13(3):182-194, 1976. (Bio. Abstrs. October, 1977, 37423)

Prevention and treatment of habitual abortion, by S. Hong. KOREAN CENTRAL JOURNAL OF MEDICINE 29(6): 546-548, 1976. (Bio. Abstrs. April, 1977, 43615)

Principles of medical genetic consultation in spontaneous abortions in women, by V. P. Kulazhenko, et al. AKU-SHERSTVO I GINEKOLOGIIA (Moscow) (12):36-40, December, 1976.

Q and G banding techniques in the identification of chromosome anomalies in spontaneous abortions, by J. Bove, et al. ANNALES DE GENETIQUE 19(4):233-239, 1976. (Bio. Abstrs. July, 1977, 2248)

Recurrent abortion associated with a balanced 22;22 translocation, or isochromosome 22q in a monozygous twin, by B. V. Lewis, et al. HUMAN GENETICS 37(1):81-85, June 10, 1977.

Role of chromosome abnormalities in reproduction failures, by A. Boué, et al. JOURNAL DE GYNECOLOGIE, OBSTETRIQUE ET BIOLOGIE DE LA REPRODUCTION 6(1):5-21, January, 1977.

Studies on hereditary spherocytosis in Iceland, by O. Jensson, et al. ACTA MEDICA SCANDINAVICA 201(3): 187-195, 1977. (Bio. Abstrs. September, 1977, 26642)

Trisomy 5 in two abortuses, by K. Ohama, et al. JAPANESE JOURNAL OF HUMAN GENETICS 21(1):1-4, June, 1976.

Trisomy 17 in two abortuses, by K. Ohama, et al. JAPANESE

JOURNAL OF HUMAN GENETICS 21(4):257-260, March, 1977.

GENTAMICIN GARAMYCIN

GESTANON

GONORRHEA
see: Complications

GRAVIBINAN
Treatment of threatened abortion with Gravibinan, by Z. Sternadel, et al. GINEKOLOGIA POLASKA 48(5):509-512, May, 1977.

GYNECOLOGY
Clinical application of prostaglandins in obstetrics and gynecology, by F. J. Brunnberg. ACTA BIOLOGICA ET MEDICA GERMANICA 35(8-9):1243-1247, 1976.

Ethical problems in obstetrics and gynaecology, by J. Bonnar. WORLD OF IRISH NURSING 6(4):1, April, 1977.

The Lombardy Society of Obstetrics and Gynecology: oral ballot on the problem of abortion. ANNALI DI OBSTETRICIA, GINECOLOGIA, MEDICINA PERINATALE 97(3):133-136, May-June, 1976.

GYNESTHESIN

HABITUAL ABORTION
Balanced translocation t (3; 21) (q 11; q 21) as a cause of habitual abortions, by N. I. Smirnova, et al. TSITOLOGIIA I GENETIKA 11(1):74-76, January-February, 1977.

Clinical experiences with the gestagen. Turinal in treating threatened and habitual abortions, by A. Pociatek, et al. BRATISLAUSKE LEKARSKE LISTY 67(1):87-91, January, 1977.

Clinical problems of ovulation defects, by A. Grant. INTER-NATIONAL JOURNAL OF GYNECOLOGY AND OB-STETRICS 14(2):123-128, 1976. (Bio. Abstrs. April, 1977, 44075)

Common HLA antigens in couples with repeated abortions, by L. Komlos, et al. CLINICAL IMMUNOLOGY AND IMMUNOPATHOLOGY 7(3):330-335, May, 1977.

Correlation of sex hormone levels with target tissue reaction in deficiency of the lutein phase of the menstrual cycle, by O. N. Savchenko, et al. VOPROSKY OKHRANY MATERINSTVA I DETSTVA 21(10):68-72, October, 1976.

Cytogenetic findings in fifty-five couples with recurrent fetal wastage, by J. R. Byrd, et al. FERTILITY AND STE-RILITY 28(3):246-250, March, 1977.

Cytogenetic studies in families with habitual abortions, by G. Bulkova, et al. AKUSHERSTVO I GINEKOLOGIIA (Sofia) 15(4):265-268, 1976.

Cytogenetics of habitual abortion and other reproductive wastage, by M. A. Stenchever, et al. AMERICAN JOUR-NAL OF OBSTETRICS AND GYNECOLOGY 127(2): 143-150, January 15, 1977.

Developmental anomalies of the umbilical vessels (arteria umbilicalis singularis) and spontaneous abortion, by E. Horak, et al. ORVOSI HETILAP 118(29):1721-1726, July 17, 1977.

Direct evidence of luteal insufficiency in women with habitual abortion, by J. L. Horta, et al. OBSTETRICS AND GYNECOLOGY 49(6):705-708, June, 1977.

The fate of pregnancy after a cuneiform ovarian resection performed in cases of Stein-Leventhal syndrome clinically diagnosed, by F. Divila, et al. CESKOSLOVENSKA

GYNEKOLOGIE 41(9):669-671, November, 1976.

Glutamate dehydrogenase isoenzymes of the placenta and
fetal membranes in normal pregnancy and pregnancy
complicated by sex gland hypofunction, by T. N. Pogo-
relova, et al. AKUSHERSTVO I GINEKOLOGIIA (Moscow) 564-66, May, 1976.

Gravibinon "Schering" in the treatment of habitual abortion
and prevention of abortion in uterus hypoplasticus, by I.
Shurkalev, et al. AKUSHERSTVO I GINEKOLOGIIA
(Sofia) 15(4):255-259, 1976.

An habitual aborter's self-concept during the course of a
successful pregnancy, by Y. M. Chao. MATERNAL-
CHILD NURSING JOURNAL 6:165-175, Fall, 1977.

How to stimulate the placental function, by A. Fanard, et
al. REPRODUCTION 3(1-2):15-25, January-June,
1976.

The immunobiology of abortion [editorial], by R. T. Smith.
NEW ENGLAND JOURNAL OF MEDICINE (22):1249-
1250, November 25, 1976.

Incidence of repeated legal abortion [letter], by C. Brewer,
et al. BRITISH MEDICAL JOURNAL 2(6048):1382,
December 4, 1976.

Is the concept of "habitual abortion" fiction? by W. Vlaanderen. NEDERLANDS TIJDSCHRIFT VOOR GENEE-
SKUNDE 121(11):439-442, March 12, 1977.

Isthmico-cervical insufficiency as a cause of habitual miscarriage, by A. P. Kirlushchenkov. FEL'DSKER I AKU-
SHERKA 41(8):25-28, August, 1976.

Maternal-fetal relation. Absence of an immunologic blocking
factor from the serum of women with chronic abortions,
by R. E. Rocklin, et al. NEW ENGLAND JOURNAL

OF MEDICINE 295(22):1209-1213, November 25, 1976. (Bio. Abstrs. April, 1977, 38754)

Mother with D/D translocation in genetic counseling, by J. Stepien, et al. GINEKOLOGIA POLASKA 48(3):285-288, March, 1977.

Organization of specialized medical aid to women with habitual miscarriage in the Andizhan region, by N. T. Gudakova, et al. AKUSHERSTVO I GINEKOLOGIIA (Moscow) (5):54-55, May, 1977.

Pattern of chorionic gonadotropins and placental lactogens during treatment of threatened and habitual abortion, by E. Samochowiec, et al. GINEKOLOGIA POLASKA 47(12):1363-1370, December, 1976.

Plasma progesterone in women with a history of recurrent early abortions, by S. K. Yip, et al. FERTILITY AND STERILITY 28(2):151-155, February, 1977. (Bio. Abstrs. June, 1977, 62721)

Prevention and treatment of habitual abortion, by S. Hong. KOREAN CENTRAL JOURNAL OF MEDICINE 29(6): 546-548, 1976. (Bio. Abstrs. April, 1977, 43615)

Preventive long term hospitalization in habitual abortion, by H. Ruwisch. MEDIZINISCHE WELT 28(6):282-286, February 11, 1977.

Recurrent abortion associated with a balanced 22;22 translocation, or isochromosome 22q in a monozygous twin, by B. V. Lewis, et al. HUMAN GENETICS 37(1):81-85, June 10, 1977.

The repeat abortion patient, by J. Leach. FAMILY PLANNING PERSPECTIVES 9:37-39, January-February, 1977.

Role of mycoplasma infections in repeat abortions [letter],

by C. Alexandre, et al. NOUVELLE PRESSE MEDI-
CALE 5(39):2631, November, 1976.

Surgical treatment of habitual abortion, by V. Krstajic, et
al. SRPSKI ARHIV ZA CELOKUPNO LEKARSTVO
104(7-8):527-529, July-August, 1976.

Treatment of habitual abortion with caprovestrol, by L. G.
Kovtumova, et al. VOPROSY OKHRANY MATERIN-
STVA I DETSTVA 21(5):72-75, May, 1976.

Treatment of threatened and habitual abortion with human
chorionic gonadotrophin. The role of serum human
placental lactogen determination, by C. Z. Vorster, et al.
SOUTH AFRICAN MEDICAL JOURNAL 51(6):165-
166, February 5, 1977.

Uterine toxoplasma infections and repeated abortions, by B.
Stray-Pedersen, et al. AMERICAN JOURNAL OF OB-
STETRICS AND GYNECOLOGY 128(7):716-721,
August 1, 1977.

HALOTHANE

HEMORRHAGE
see also: Complications

Early pregnancy hemorrhages and their management, by M.
Shin. KOREAN CENTRAL JOURNAL OF MEDICINE
29(1):5-8, 1975. (Bio. Abstrs. April, 1977, 41853)

HEPARIN
Eisenmenger's syndrome in pregnancy: does heparin prophylaxis improve the maternal mortality rate? by J. A. Pitts,
et al. AMERICAN HEART JOURNAL 93(3):321-326,
1977. (Bio. Abstrs. November, 1977, 58782)

HEXENAL

HISTORY
Abortion: a philosophical and historical analysis, by J. R. Connery. HOSPITAL PROGRESS 58(4):49-50, April, 1977.

HORMONES
Correlation of sex hormone levels with target tissue reaction in deficiency of the lutein phase of the menstrual cycle, by O. N. Savchenko, et al. VOPROSKY OKHRANY MATERINSTVA I DETSTVA 21(10):68-72, October, 1976.

Effect of 15(s)15-methyl-PGF2alpha-methyl ester vaginal suppositories on circulating hormone levels in early pregnancy, by C. P. Puri, et al. PROSTAGLANDINS 13(2): 363-373, February, 1977.

Hormone changes in relation to the time of fetal death after prostaglandin-induced abortion, by I. S. Fraser, et al. PROSTAGLANDINS 13(6):1161-1167, June, 1977. (Bio. Abstrs. November, 1977, 58981)

Hormone therapy in threatened abortion and premature labor, by G. Kikawa. JAPANESE JOURNAL FOR MIDWIVES 30(12):750-752, December, 1976.

Pituitary response to luteinizing hormone-releasing hormone after induced abortion in the first and second trimesters, by M. E. Domenzain, et al. FERTILITY AND STERILITY 28(5):531-534, 1977. (Bio. Abstrs. October, 1977, 37959)

Studies on the gonadotropin response after administration of LH/FSH-releasing hormone (LRH) during pregnancy and after therapeutic abortion in the second trimester, by S. Jeppsson, et al. AMERICAN JOURNAL OF OBSTETRICS AND GYNECOLOGY 125(4):484-490, June 15, 1976.

HOSPITALS
Abortion and the law: the impact on hospital policy of the
Roe and Doe decisions, by K. A. Kemp, et al. JOURNAL
OF HEALTH POLITICS, POLICY AND LAW 1:319-
337, Fall, 1976.

Abortion clinic damaged by fire. THE NEW YORK TIMES
(S) February 25, D, 14:3, 1977.

Abortion practice in NZ public hospitals. NURSING FORUM
(Auckland) 3(4):5-7, November-December, 1975.

Courts rule on constitutionality of hospital bans on elective
abortions. HOSPITAL LAW 10:3-4, January, 1977.

Performing abortions; excerpt from In necessity and sorrow:
life and death in an abortion hospital, by M. Denes. COM-
MENTARY 62:4+, December, 1976; 63:18+, January;
22+ February, 1977.

IMMUNITY
The association of maternal lymphocytotoxic antibodies
with obstetric complications, by R. E. Harris, et al.
OBSTETRICS AND GYNECOLOGY 48(3):302-304,
1976. (Bio. Abstrs. February, 1977, 20979)

Cellular and humoral immune aspects in mixed wife-husband
leukocyte cultures in spontaneous abortions, by I. Halbrecht, et al. ACTA EUROPAEA FERTILITATIS
7(3):249-255, September, 1976.

Common HLA antigens in couples with repeated abortions,
by L. Komlos, et al. CLINICAL IMMUNOLOGY AND
IMMUNOPATHOLOGY 7(3):330-335, May, 1977.

The immunobiology of abortion [editorial], by R. T. Smith.
NEW ENGLAND JOURNAL OF MEDICINE (22):1249-
1250, November 25, 1976.

Immunologic reactivity in infectious diseases following labor

and abortion, by V. I. Kulakov, et al. AKUSHERSTVO
I GINEKOLOGIIA (Moscow) (4):32-35, April, 1976.

Immunological characteristics of women with an interrupted
pregnancy of unexplained etiology, by V. V. Kovalenko,
et al. PEDIATRIIA AKUSHERSTVO I GINEKOLOGIIA
(2):41-43, March-April, 1977.

Maternal-fetal relation. Absence of an immunologic blocking factor from the serum of women with chronic abortions, by R. E. Rocklin, et al. NEW ENGLAND JOUR-
NAL OF MEDICINE 295(22):1209-1213, 1976. (Bio.
Abstrs. April, 1977, 38754)

Possible immunologic factors in natural selection of the
sexes, by B. Seguy. JOURNAL DE GYNECOLOGIE,
OBSTETRIQUE ET BIOLOGIE DE LA REPRODUC-
TION 5(5):617-620, July-August, 1976.

Rh immunoglobulin utlization after spontaneous and induced
abortion, by D. A. Grimes, et al. OBSTETRICS AND
GYNECOLOGY 50(3):261-263, September, 1977.

Thymus-dependent lymphocyte activity during the normal
course of pregnancy an in spontaneous premature interruption of pregnancy, by S. D. Bulienko, et al. AKU-
SHERSTVO I GINEKOLOGIIA (Moscow) 5:50-53,
May, 1976.

INDOMETHACIN

INDUCED ABORTION
see also: Techniques of Abortion

Abdominal wall endometriosis following hypertonic saline
abortion, by B. T. Ferrari, et al. JAMA; JOURNAL OF
THE AMERICAN MEDICAL ASSOCIATION 238(1):
56-57, July 4, 1977.

The abortifacient and oxytocic effects of an intravaginal

silicone rubber device containing a 0.5% concentration of 15(S)-15-methyl-prostaglandin F2alpha methyl ester, by N. H. Lauersen, et al. AMERICAN JOURNAL OF OBSTETRICS AND GYNECOLOGY 127(7):784-787, April 1, 1977.

The abortifacient effectiveness and plasma prostaglandin concentrations with 15(S)-15-methyl prostaglandin F2alpha methyl ester-containing vaginal silastic devices, by N. H. Lauersen, et al. FERTILITY AND STERILITY 27(12):1366-1373, December, 1976.

Abortion and family-binding models: fertility limitation in Hungary, by K. Ford. DEMOGRAPHY 13(4):495-505, November, 1976.

Abortion and maternal deaths [letter]. BRITISH MEDICAL JOURNAL 2(6029):232, July 24, 1976.

—, by A. Cartwright. BRITISH MEDICAL JOURNAL 2(6039):813, October 2, 1976.

Abortion and the Supreme Court: some are more equal than others, by M. C. Segers. HASTINGS CENTER REPORT 7(4):5-6, August, 1977.

Abortion applicants: characteristics distinguishing dropouts remaining pregnant and those having abortion, by M. E. Swigar, et al. AMERICAN JOURNAL OF PUBLIC HEALTH 67(2):142-146, February, 1977.

Abortion as a public health argument, by G. Ciasca. MINERVA GINECOLOGIA 28(9):719-721, September, 1976.

Abortion as a reality, by H. Schmidt-Matthiesen. THERA-PEUTISCHE UMSCHAW 33(4):289-293, April, 1976.

Abortion at the Felix Bulnes Hospital. Sociodemographic and medical data, by R. Viada, et al. REVISTA CHILENA

DE OBSTETRICIA Y GINECOLOGIA 40(5):235-241, 1975.

Abortion deaths associated with the use of prostaglandin F2a, by W. Cates, Jr., et al. AMERICAN JOURNAL OF OBSTETRICS AND GYNECOLOGY 127(3):219-222, 1977. (Bio. Abstrs. June, 1977, 65533)

Abortion in the moral reflections of the Catholic physician, by N. Miccolis. MINERVA GINECOLOGIA 28(9):742-746, September, 1976.

Abortion in Mulago Hospital, Kampala, by C. Lwanga. EAST AFRICAN MEDICAL JOURNAL 54(3):142-148, March 1977.

Abortion induced through massage, by F. Havranek. CESKO-SLOVENSKA GYNEKOLOGIE 42(7):532, August, 1977.

Abortion. Report of a commission of the Paris Academy of Medicine, by M. R. Merger. GYNAEKOLOGISCHE RUNDSCHAU 16(3):185-191, 1976.

Abortion statistics for the Federal Republic of Germany— notification requirements for the physician performing the abortion, by W. Christian. OEFFENTLICHE GE-SUNDHEITSWESEN 38(11):676-680, November, 1976.

An abortion stick in the duodenum and gallbladder, by G. M. Gandhi, et al. INTERNATIONAL SURGERY 61(11-12): 594-595, November-December, 1976.

Abortions at Nacka Hospital, 1975—somatic complications and preventive technics, by K. Sigurdsson. LAKAR-TIDNINGEN 74(5):318-321, February, 1977.

Abortions in Singapore, by C. S. Chai. THE NURSING JOURNAL OF SINGAPORE 17(1):18-19, May, 1977.

Abortions in Tennessee—1975, by A. R. Hinman. JOURNAL OF THE TENNESSEE MEDICAL ASSOCIATION 70(3): 163-167, March, 1977.

Absence of chronoperiodic response following intra-amniotic instillation of hypertonic saline, by D. A. Edelman, et al. AMERICAN JOURNAL OF OBSTETRICS AND GYNE- COLOGY 127(4):446-447, February 15, 1977.

Acute renal failure of obstetric origin, by K. S. Chugh, et al. OBSTETRICS AND GYNECOLOGY 48(6):642-646, December, 1976.

Amniotic fluid adenosine 3' 5'—monophosphate in prosta- glandin-induced midtrimester abortions, by P. R. Weiss, et al. OBSTETRICS AND GYNECOLOGY 49(2):223- 226, February, 1977. (Bio. Abstrs. July, 1977, 4344)

Amniotic fluid removal prior to saline abortion, by A. C. Mehta, et al. ANNALES CHIRURGIAE ET GYNAE- COLOGIAE FENNIAE 65(1):68-71, 1976. (Bio. Abstrs. February, 1977, 23550)

Analysis of statistical data concerning artificial abortions in a number of foreign countries, by I. P. Katkova. SOVET- SKAE ZDRAVOOKHRANENIE (7):30-34, 1976.

Anesthesia for elective termination of pregnancy [letter], by J. P. Annis. JAMA; JOURNAL OF THE AMERICAN MEDICAL ASSOCIATION 236(23):2942-2943, Decem- ber 27, 1976.

The association of multiple induced abortions with subse- quent prematurity and spontaneous abortion, by L. H. Roht, et al. ACTA OBSTETRICA ET GYNAECOLO- GICA JAPONIA 23(2):140-145, 1976.

Attempt at handling the new legal regulation to paragraph 218, by P. Stoll, et al. FORTSCHRITTE DU MEDIZIN 94(33):1893-1894, November 18, 1976.

Attitudes of rural Thai women towards induced abortion, by R. G. Burnight, et al. JOURNAL OF BIOSOCIAL SCIENCE 9(1):61-72, January, 1977.

Birth despite vasectomy and abortion held not a "wrong," by S. Gursky. JOURNAL OF LEGAL MEDICINE 5(7):29-31, July, 1977.

Caffeine and pregnancy. A retrospective survey, by P. S. Weathersbee, et al. POSTGRADUATE MEDICAL JOURNAL 62(3):64-69, September, 1977.

Can technology solve the abortion dilemma, by M. Maguire. CHRISTIAN CENTURY p. 918, October 27, 1976.

Case of convulsions with late onset after ketalar anesthesia, by A. Dimitrov, et al. AKUSHERSTVO I GINEKOLOGIIA (Sofia) 15(3):229-230, 1976.

Cervical dilatation with 16,16 dimethyl PGE2 p-benzaldehyde semicarbazone ester prior to vaccum aspiration in first trimester nulliparae, by S. M. Karim, et al. PROSTAGLANDINS 13(2):333-338, February, 1977.

Cervico-vaginal injuries in cases of second trimester termination of pregnancy, by V. N. Purandare, et al. PROSTAGLANDINS 13(2):349-354, February, 1977.

Changes in the concentration of cortisol in amniotic fluid after intra-amniotic prostaglandin for midtrimester abortion, by I. Z. MacKenzie, et al. BRITISH JOURNAL OF OBSTETRICS AND GYNAECOLOGY 84(8):608-612, August, 1977.

Changes in congenital oral cleft incidence in relation to induced abortions, by A. P. Polednak, et al. AMERICAN JOURNAL OF OBSTETRICS AND GYNECOLOGY 126(6):734-735, November 15, 1976.

Clinical and pathomorphological study on placentae during

abortions in the second trimester, by A. Sed'ova, et al. CESKOSLOVENSKA GYNEKOLOGIE 41(8):569-571, October, 1976.

Clinical and x-ray studies on the relationship between interruption of pregnancy and premature labor, by R. Voigt, et al. ZENTRALBLATT FUR GYNAEKOLOGIE 98(25):1589-1593, 1976.

Clinical applications of prostaglandins in obstetrics and gynecology, by F. J. Brunnberg. ACTA BIOLOGICA ET MEDICA GERMANICA 35(8-9):1243-1247, 1976.

Clinical comparison of abortifacient activity of vaginally administered prostaglandin E2 in two dosage forms, by T. J. Roseman, et al. AMERICAN JOURNAL OF OBSTETRICS AND GYNECOLOGY 129(2):225-227, September 15, 1977.

Clinical results of two-time abortion technics with special regard to ascending genital infections, by H. Kreibich, et al. ZENTRALBLATT FUR GYNAEKOLOGIE 99(12):755-762, 1977.

Coagulopathy with midtrimester induced abortion: association with hyperosmolar urea administration, by R. T. Burkman, et al. AMERICAN JOURNAL OF OBSTETRICS AND GYNECOLOGY 127(5):533-536, 1977. (Bio. Abstrs. August, 1977, 23526)

Comparative characteristics of the water-soluble afterbirth tissue proteins in normal and incomplete pregnancy, by T. S. Dluzhevskaia, et al. AKUSHERSTVO I GINEKOLOGIIA (Moscow) (3):37-41, March, 1977.

Comparative study of the causes of induced abortion and the knowledge of family planning, by M. D. Ramos Netto. REVISTA ENFERMAGEM EM NOVAS DIMENSOES 1(4):172, September-October, 1975.

A comparative study of plasma 17beta-oestradiol, progesterone, placental lactogen and chorionic gonadotrophin in abortion induced with intra-amniotic prostaglandin F2alpha, by R. H. Ward, et al. BRITISH JOURNAL OF OBSTETRICS AND GYNAECOLOGY 84(5):363-369, May, 1977.

Comparison between intra-amniotic administration of prostaglandin F2alpha and its 15-methyl derivative for induction of second trimester abortion, by O. Ylikorkala, et al. ANNALS OF CLINICAL RESEARCH 9(2):58-61, April, 1977. (Bio. Abstrs. November, 1977, 52789)

Complications following induced abortion by vacuum aspiration: patient characteristics and procedures, by M. Cheng, et al. STUDIES IN FAMILY PLANNING 8(5):125-129, May, 1977.

Complications in induced abortions, by H. Kirchhoff. WIENER MEDIZINISCHE WOCHENSCHRIFT 126(49-50): 696-699, December 3, 1976.

Conservative treatment of women in perforations of the uterus in legal abortions, by D. Mladenovic, et al. SRPSKI ARHIV ZA CELOJUPNO LEKARSTVO 104(2):119-127, February, 1976.

Cooperation of a gynecologist and pathologist in the study and evaluation of the chorion during early abortion, by P. Drac, et al. CESKOSLOVENSKA GYNEKOLOGIE 41(8):571-572, October, 1976.

Cortisol levels in amniotic fluid in prostaglandin F2alpha-induced midtrimester abortion, by Z. Koren, et al. AMERICAN JOURNAL OF OBSTETRICS AND GYNECOLOGY 127(6):639-642, March 15, 1977. (Bio. Abstrs. July, 1977, 10540)

Counselling for abortion, by M. Blair. MIDWIFE HEALTH VISITOR AND COMMUNITY NURSE 11(11):355-356,

November, 1975.

The court and a conflict of principles, by S. Callahan. HAST-INGS CENTER REPORT 7(4):7-8, August, 1977.

Court may OK government funding of abortions, by P. L. Geary. HOSPITAL PROGRESS 58(1):10+, January, 1977.

Culture and treatment results in endometritis following elective abortion, by R. T. Burkman, et al. AMERICAN JOURNAL OF OBSTETRICS AND GYNECOLOGY 128(5):556-559, 1977. (Bio. Abstrs. November, 1977, 57802)

Death after paracervical block [letter], by J. Slome. LANCET 1(8005):260, January 29, 1977.

Deaths from paracervical anesthesia used for first-trimester abortion, 1972-1975, by D. A. Grimes, et al. NEW ENGLAND JOURNAL OF MEDICINE 295(25):1397-1399, 1976. (Bio. Abstrs. May, 1977, 54151)

Declaration on procured abortion, by J. Hamer. C.I.C.I.A.M.S. NOUVELLES (2):7-18, 1975.

A developmental approach to post-abortion depression, by F. M. Burkle, Jr. PRACTITIONER 218(1304):217-225, February, 1977.

Dilatation and curettage for second-trimester abortions, by A. A. Hodari, et al. AMERICAN JOURNAL OF OBSTETRICS AND GYNECOLOGY 127(8):850-854, April 15, 1977. (Bio. Abstrs. September, 1977, 29734)

Effect of 15(s)15-methyl-PGF2alpha-methyl ester vaginal suppositories on circulating hormone levels in early pregnancy, by C. P. Puri, et al. PROSTAGLANDINS 13(2): 363-373, February, 1977.

Effect of induced (artificial) abortion on the secondary sex ratio in man, by G. D. Golovachev, et al. AKUSHER-STVO I GINEKOLOGIIA (Moscow) (12):40-43, December, 1976.

Effect of interruption on the prognosis of children from the following pregnancy, by J. Ringel, et al. CESKOSLO-VENSKA PEDIATRIE 31(8):442-445, August, 1976.

Elective abortion. Complications seen in a free-standing clinic, by G. J. Wulff, Jr., et al. OBSTETRICS AND GYNECOLOGY 49(3):351-357, March, 1977. (Bio. Abstrs. July, 1977, 5457)

Epidural analgesia in midtrimester abortion, by S. Grünstein, et al. INTERNATIONAL JOURNAL OF GYNAECOLO-GY AND OBSTETRICS 14(3):257-260, 1976. (Bio. Abstrs. August, 1977, 16420)

Estrogen content in the blood in the artificial interruption of a 1st pregnancy, by G. E. Kniga, et al. AKUSHERSTVO I GINEKOLOGIIA (Moscow) (6):62-63, June, 1976.

Eugenic indications in the current status of abortion, by G. Giocoli. MINERVA GINECOLOGIA 28(9):700-703, September, 1976.

Eugenic indications; problems provoked by present-day genetics, by G. Mollica. MINERVA GINECOLOGIA 28(9):714-716, September, 1976.

Evaluation of intramuscular 15(S)-15-methyl prostaglandin F2a tromethamine salt for induction of abortion, medications to attenuate side effects, and intracervical laminaria tents, by W. Gruber, et al. FERTILITY AND STERILITY 27(9):1009-1023, 1976. (Bio. Abstrs. March, 1977, 28807)

Extra-amniotic 15(S)-15 methyl PFG2a to induce abortion: a study of three administration schedules. PROSTA-

GLANDINS 12(3):443-453, 1976. (Bio. Abstrs. January, 1977, 10597)

Factors minimising mortality and morbidity from infection after intra-amniotic saline infusion for medical termination of pregnancy, by R. N. Ghosh, et al. JOURNAL OF THE INDIAN MEDICAL ASSOCIATION 66(11):283-285, June 1, 1976.

Failed prostaglandin F2alpha-induced abortion: a case report, by R. G. Cunanan, Jr., et al. OBSTETRICS AND GYNECOLOGY 49(4):495-496, April, 1977.

Failed termination of pregnancy due to uterus bicornis unicollis with bilateral pregnancy, by M. A. Pelosi, et al. AMERICAN JOURNAL OF OBSTETRICS AND GYNECOLOGY 128(8):919-920, August 15, 1977.

Failure to diagnose pregnancy as cause of late abortion [letter], by C. Brewer. LANCET 1(8001):46, January 1, 1977.

Fertility control—symposium on prostaglandins: comment, by W. E. Brenner. FERTILITY AND STERILITY 27(12):1380-1386, December, 1976.

Fetal loss, twinning and birth weight after oral-contraceptive use, by K. J. Rothman. NEW ENGLAND JOURNAL OF MEDICINE 297(9):468-471, September 1, 1977.

A further chromosome analysis in induced abortions, by M. Yamamoto, et al. HUMAN GENETICS 34(1):69-71, 1976. (Bio. Abstrs. March, 1977, 32690)

Hormone changes in relation to the time of fetal death after prostaglandin-induced abortion, by I. S. Fraser, et al. PROSTAGLANDINS 13(6):1161-1167, June, 1977. (Bio. Abstrs. November, 1977, 58981)

Human rights in relationship to induced abortion, by

C. Tietze. THE JOURNAL OF SEX RESEARCH 10(2): 97-109, 1974. (Socio. Abstrs. 1977, 77I4024)

Hypokalemia and cardiac arrhythmia associated with prostaglandin-induced abortion, by R. L. Burt, et al. OBSTETRICS AND GYNECOLOGY 50(1 Suppl):45S-46S, July, 1977.

Immunological characteristics of women with an interrupted pregnancy of unexplained etiology, by V. V. Kovalenko, et al. PEDIATRIIA AKUSHERSTVO I GINEKOLOGIIA (2):41-43, March-April, 1977.

Improvement of the surgical technic in induced abortions using a supplementary instrument (special handgrip with revolving support for interruption cannulas), by W. Anton, et al. ZENTRALBLATT FUR GYNAEKOLOGIE 98(22):1401-1403, 1976.

Increased reporting of menstrual symptoms among women who used induced abortion, by L. H. Roht, et al. AMERICAN JOURNAL OF OBSTETRICS AND GYNECOLOGY 127(4):356-362, February 15, 1977.

Induced abortion and brain damage, by A. Rett. WIENER MEDIZINISCHE WOCHENSCHRIFT 126(49-50):700-702, December 3, 1976.

Induced abortion and sterilization among women who became mothers as adolescents, by J. F. Jekel, et al. AMERICAN JOURNAL OF PUBLIC HEALTH 67:621-625, July, 1977.

Induced abortion in the 8-9th week of pregnancy with vaginally administered 15-methyl PFG2 methyl ester, by A. Leader, et al. PROSTAGLANDINS 12(4):631-637, 1976. (Bio. Abstrs. February, 1977, 22692)

Induced abortion with intramuscular administration of 15(S)-15methyl-prostaglandin F2 alpha, by H. Halle, et al.

ZENTRALBLATT FUR GYNAEKOLOGIE 99(9):537-540, 1977.

Induction of abortion and labor by extraamniotic isotonic saline, with or without addition of oxytocin, in cases of missed abortion, missed labor and antepartum fetal death, by M. Blum, et al. INTERNATIONAL SURGERY 62(2):95-96, February, 1977.

Induction of abortion in the 2d and 3d trimester with prostaglandins, PGE2 and PGF2 alpha. Indications for differences between the effect of PGE2 and PGF2 alpha on the pregnant uterus, by M. Cornely. MEDIZINISCHE MONATSSCHRIFT 31(2):73-79, February, 1977.

Induction of first and second trimester abortion by the vaginal administration of 15-methyl-PGF2alpha methyl ester, by M. Bygdeman, et al. ADVANCES IN PROSTAGLANDIN AND THROMBOXANE RESEARCH 2:693-704, 1976.

Induction of labor in patients with missed abortion and fetal death in utero with protaglandin E2 suppositories, by N. H. Lauersen, et al. AMERICAN JOURNAL OF OBSTETRICS AND GYNECOLOGY 127(6):609-611, March 15, 1977. (Bio. Abstrs. August, 1977, 16534)

Induction of midtrimester abortion by the combined method of continuous extravovular infusion of prostaglandin F2a and intracervical laminaria tents, by J. E. Hodgson, et al. FERTILITY AND STERILITY 27(12):1359-1365, 1976. (Bio. Abstrs. June, 1977, 70935)

Induction of mid-trimester abortion with intra-amniotic injection of prostaglandin F-2alpha, by A. J. Horowitz. MINNESOTA MEDICINE 60 (7 Pt 1):509-512, July, 1977.

Induction of midtrimester abortion with intra-amniotic urea and intravenous oxytocin, by W. G. Smith, et al. AMER-

ICAN JOURNAL OF OBSTETRICS AND GYNECOLOGY 127(3):228-231, February 1, 1977. (Bio. Abstrs. May, 1977, 59034)

Influence of the kind of anesthesia and length of hospitalization on the frequency of early complications of abortion, by L. Andolsek, et al. JUGOSLOVENSKA GINEKOLO-GIJA I OPSTETRICIJA 16(3):175-183, May-June, 1976.

The influence of physicians' attitudes on abortion performance, patient management and professional fees, by C. A. Nathanson, et al. FAMILY PLANNING PERSPECTIVES 9(4):158-163, July-August, 1977.

Interruption of early pregnancy by a new vacuum aspiration method, by S. Mihaly, et al. ORVOSI HETILAP 117(45): 2731-2734, November 6, 1976.

Intra-amniotic administration of 15(S)-15-methyl-prostaglandin F2a for the induction of midtrimester abortion, by J. R. Dingfelder, et al. AMERICAN JOURNAL OF OBSTETRICS AND GYNECOLOGY 125(6):821-826, 1976. (Bio. Abstrs. February, 1977, 17300)

Intra-amniotic prostaglandin F2alpha and urea for midtrimester abortion, by L. Wellman, et al. FERTILITY AND STERILITY 27(12):1374-1379, December, 1976. (Bio. Abstrs. June, 1977, 70933)

Intra-amniotic urea and prostaglandin F2a for midtrimester abortion: a modified regimen, by R. T. Burkman, et al. AMERICAN JOURNAL OF OBSTETRICS AND GYNECOLOGY 126(3):328-333, 1976. (Bio. Abstrs. February, 1977, 22702)

Intramuscular prostaglandin (15S)-15-methyl PFG2alpha (THAM) in midtrimester abortion, by E. S. Henriques, et al. PROSTAGLANDINS 13(1):183-191, January, 1977. (Bio. Abstrs. May, 1977, 59036)

Intrauterine extra-amnial administration of prostaglandin F2 alpha for the induction of abortion in primigravidae and problem cases, by G. Goretzlehner, et al. ZENTRAL-BLATT FUR GYNAEKOLOGIE 98(20):1252-1257, 1976.

Intrauterine extra-amniotic 15(S)-15-methyl prostaglandin F2a for induction of early midtrimester abortion, by A. G. Shapiro. FERTILITY AND STERILITY 27(9):1024-1028, 1976. (Bio. Abstrs. March, 1977, 28805)

Intrauterine prostaglandin E2 as an postconceptional aborti-facient, by I. Z. Mackenzie, et al. ADVANCES IN PRO-STAGLANDIN AND THROMBOXANE RESEARCH 2:687-691, 1976.

Introduction of second trimester abortions with 15-(S)-methyl prostaglandin F2alpha by intra-uterine and intra-muscular routes, by V. Hingorani, et al. JOURNAL OF THE INDIAN MEDICAL ASSOCIATION 66(11):279-283, June 1, 1976.

The Irish emigrant and the abortion crisis. WORLD OF IRISH NURSING 4(10):1-2, October, 1975.

The kinetics of extraamniotically injected prostaglandins to induce midtrimester abortion, by I. Z. MacKenzie, et al. PROSTAGLANDINS 13(5):975-986, 1977. (Bio. Abstrs. October, 1977, 40678)

Laparoscopic observation of the female pelvis following abor-tions by suction curettage, by P. K. Khan. INTERNA-TIONAL SURGERY 62(2):77-78, February, 1977.

Late sequelae of interrupted pregnancy, by G. Venzmer. KRANKENPFLEGE 30(10):290-291, October, 1976.

Let them eat cake, by G. J. Annas. HASTINGS CENTER REPORT 7(4):8-9, August, 1977.

The management of midtrimester abortion failures by vaginal evacuation, by R. T. Burkman, et al. OBSTETRICS AND GYNECOLOGY 49(2):233-236, February, 1977.

Markov chain model for events following induced abortion, by R. H. Shachtman, et al. OPERATIONS RESEARCH 24:916-932, September, 1976.

Maternal indications for abortion, by M. Mall-Haefeli. WIENER MEDIZINISCHE WOCHENSCHRIFT 127(1): 5-9, 1977.

Maternal serum alpha-fetoprotein in abnormal pregnancies and during induced abortion, by D. M. Hay, et al. JOURNAL OF REPRODUCTIVE MEDICINE 19(2):75-78, August, 1977.

Maternal serum and amniotic fluid alpha-fetoprotein as a marker of acute fetal distress in a midtrimester abortion model, by R. R. Weiss, et al. OBSTETRICS AND GYNECOLOGY 48(6):718-722, December, 1976.

The mechanism of midtrimester abortion induced by intra-amniotic instillation of hypertonic saline: a modification of Gustavii's lysosomal hypotehsis, by L. H. Honore. AMERICAN JOURNAL OF OBSTETRICS AND GYNECOLOGY 126(8):1011-1015, 1976. (Bio. Abstrs. April, 1977, 47767)

Medical and social aspects of pregnancy among adolescents. Part II. Comparative study of abortions and deliveries, by E. Rautanen, et al. ANNALES CHIRURGIAE ET GYNAECOLOGIAE FENNIAE 66(3):122-130, 1977.

Medical and surgical methods of early termination of pregnancy, by G. M. Filshie. PROCEEDINGS OF THE ROYAL SOCIETY OF LONDON; B: BIOLOGICAL SCIENCES 195(1118):115-127, December 10, 1976.

Menstrual regulation (M.R.) service (a preliminary report),

by A. R. Khan, et al. BANGLADESH MEDICAL RE-
SEARCH COUNCIL BULLETIN 1(2):90-96, October,
1975.

Method of payment—relation to abortion complications, by
R. G. Smith, et al. HEALTH AND SOCIAL WORK
1(2):5-28, May, 1976.

Methods of artificial termination of pregnancy with special
consideration of the use of prostaglandin, by R. Kepp.
GEBURTSHILFE UND FRAUENHEILKUNDE 36(9):
700-705, September, 1976.

Mid-trimester abortion and its complications [editorial].
MEDICAL JOURNAL OF AUSTRALIA 1(4):82-83,
January 22, 1977.

Mid-trimester abortion by dilatation and evacuation: a safe
and practical alternative, by D. A. Grimes, et al. NEW
ENGLAND JOURNAL OF MEDICINE 296(20):1141-
1145, May 19, 1977. (Bio. Abstrs. September, 1977,
35546)

Midtrimester abortion by intraamniotic prostaglandin F2alpha.
Safer than saline? by D. A. Grimes, et al. OBSTETRICS
AND GYNECOLOGY 49(5):612-616, May, 1977.

Midtrimester abortion: a comparison of intraamniotic prosta-
glandin F2a and hypertonic saline, by M. I. Ragab, et al.
INTERNATIONAL JOURNAL OF GYNAECOLOGY
AND OBSTETRICS 14(5):393-396, 1976. (Bio. Abstrs.
October, 1977, 40668)

Mid-trimester abortions [letter]. NEW ENGLAND JOUR-
NAL OF MEDICINE 297(9):511-512, September 1,
1977.

Midtrimester and missed abortion treated with intramuscular
15 (s)-15 methyl PGF2alpha, by A. P. Lange, et al. PRO-
STAGLANDINS 14(2):389-395, August, 1977.

Modification of the rate of complications in the inflammatory adnexa process and pregnancy interruption, by W.
Franz, et al. ZENTRALBLATT FUR GYNAEKOLOGIE
99(2):113-116, 1977.

Motivation for induced abortion and post-interruption sequelae, by V. Bebjakova. CESKOSLOVENSKA GYNEKOL-
OGIE 41(9):692-693, November, 1976.

Motives, process and consequences of abortion among the
population attending the Obstetrical Emergency Unit of
the Maternal Health Service, by E. B. Farina. REVISTA
DA ESCOLA DE ENFERMAGEN DA UNIVERSIDADE
DE SAO PAULO 9(2):323-346, August, 1975.

National survey of doctors, nurses and social workers on
liberalization of the Barbados abortion law, by M. D.
Hoyos, et al. WEST INDIAN MEDICAL JOURNAL
26(4):2-11, March, 1977.

Nursing decisions; experiences in clinical problem solving.
Series 2, number 8: Joyce H., an elective abortion patient,
by S. Kilby-Kelberg, et al. RN; NATIONAL MAGAZINE
FOR NURSES 40(6):55-61, June, 1977.

Pharmacokinetic studies on 15-methyl-PGF2alpha and its
methyl ester after administration to the human via various routes for induction of abortion, by K. Gréen, et al.
ADVANCES IN PROSTAGLANDIN AND THROMBO-
XANE RESEARCH 2:719-725, 1976.

Pituitary response to luteinizing hormone-releasing hormone
after induced abortion in the first and second trimesters,
by M. E. Domenzain, et al. FERTILITY AND STERILITY
28(5):531-534, May, 1977. (Bio. Abstrs. October, 1977,
37959)

Placental insufficiency; a Scylla and Charybdis situation, by
P. J. Boerrigter, et al. NEDERLANDS TIJDSCHRIFT
VOOR GENEESKUNDE 121(6):210-215, February 5,

1977.

Placental morphology in spontaneous human abortuses with normal and abnormal karyotypes, by L. H. Honoré, et al. TERATOLOGY 14(2):151-166, October, 1976.

Policlinical abortions using the Karman-catheter without anesthesia or cervix dilatation. LAKARTIDNINGEN 74(23):2281-2283, June 8, 1977.

Possible immunologic factors in natural selection of the sexes, by B. Seguy. JOURNAL DE GYNECOLOGIE, OBSTETRIQUE ET BIOLOGIE DE LA REPRODUCTION 5(5):617-620, July-August, 1976.

Postabortal amenorrhea due to cervical stenosis, by E. Hakim-Elahi. OBSTETRICS AND GYNECOLOGY 48(6):723-724, December, 1976. (Bio. Abstrs. March, 1977, 35625)

Postabortal laparoscopic tubal sterilization. Results in comparison to interval procedures, by I. M. Hernandez, et al. OBSTETRICS AND GYNECOLOGY 50(3):356-358, September, 1977.

Postcoital contraception [letter], by H. C. McLaren. BRITISH MEDICAL JOURNAL 1(6057):377, February 5, 1977.

Post-irradiation abortion: a slaughter of innocents? by G. V. Dalrymple, et al. JOURNAL OF THE ARKANSAS MEDICAL SOCIETY 73(11):474-476, April, 1977.

Postpartum and postabortion sterilization, by B. N. Purandare. INTERNATIONAL JOURNAL OF GYNAECOLOGY AND OBSTETRICS 14(1):65-70, 1976. (Bio. Abstrs. February, 1977, 23556)

The price of advice, by D. Mundy. NURSING TIMES 73(35):1344-1345, September 1, 1977.

A private practice management of mid-trimester abortion, by J. W. Tidwell, 2nd, et al. NORTH CAROLINA MEDI-CAL JOURNAL 38(3):148-150, March, 1977.

A probabilistic justification for abortion, by J. R. Greenwell. PHILOSOPHY RESEARCH ARCHIVES 2:1136, 1976.

Problem of family planning in women in the textile industry. An analysis of social indications for pregnancy interruption, by A. Zdziennicki. POLSKI TYGODNIK LEKAR-SKI 31(46):1993-1994, November 15, 1976.

Progesterone levels in amniotic fluid and maternal plasma in prostaglandin F2a-induced midtrimester abortion, by Z. Koren, et al. OBSTETRICS AND GYNECOLOGY 48(4): 473-474, 1976. (Bio. Abstrs. February, 1977, 22682)

Prostaglandin impact, by A. I. Csapo. ADVANCES IN PRO-STAGLANDIN AND THROMBOXANE RESEARCH 2:705-718, 1976.

Prostaglandin E2 in a diaphragm. A further note, by H. Schulman, et al. PROSTAGLANDINS 13(4):751-753, April, 1977.

Prostaglandin E2 induction of labor for fetal demise, by D. R. Kent, et al. OBSTETRICS AND GYNECOLOGY 48(4):475-478, 1976. (Bio. Abstrs. February, 1977, 22681)

Prostaglandin F2alpha, hypertonic saline, and oxytocin in midtrimester abortion, by A. Adachi, et al. NEW YORK STATE JOURNAL OF MEDICINE 77(1):46-49, January, 1977.

Prolactin and human placental lactogen changes in maternal serum and amniotic fluid in midtrimester induced abortions, by R. R. Weiss, et al. AMERICAN JOURNAL OF OBSTETRICS AND GYNECOLOGY 129(1):9-13, September 1, 1977.

Psychologic impact on nursing students of participation in
abortion, by A. Hurwitz, et al. NURSING RESEARCH
26:112-120, March-April, 1977.

Psychological effects of abortion (a study of 1739 cases), by
W. F. Tsoi, et al. SINGAPORE MEDICAL JOURNAL
17(2):68-73, June, 1976.

Psychoprophylaxis in midtrimester abortions, by C. Ander-
son, et al. JOGN; JOURNAL OF OBSTETRIC, GYN-
ECOLOGIC AND NEONATAL NURSING 5:29-33,
November-December, 1976.

A question of conscience [letter]. BRITISH MEDICAL
JOURNAL 2(6029):234-235, July 24, 1976.

Reasons for the artificial interruption of pregnancy, by I.
Dimitrov. AKUSHERSTVO I GINEKOLOGIIA (Sofia)
16(3):177-179, 1977.

Relative safety of midtrimester abortion methods. MEDI-
CAL LETTER ON DRUGS AND THERAPEUTICS
19(6):25-26, March 25, 1977.

Repeat abortion in Denmark: an analysis based on national
record linkage, by R. L. Somers. STUDIES IN FAMILY
PLANNING 8(6):142-147, June, 1977.

Repeated extra-amniotic administration of prostaglandin
F2a for midtrimester abortion, by M. Ragab, et al. IN-
TERNATIONAL JOURNAL OF GYNAECOLOGY AND
OBSTETRICS 14(4):337-340, 1976. (Bio. Abstrs.
September, 1977, 34567)

The report of the royal commission on contraception, sterilisation and abortion: a comparison with health professional policies, by D. Wills. NURSING FORUM (Auckland) 5:4-6, April-May, 1977.

Respect life, by K. Keron. SAIRAANHOITAJA (23-24):10-

11, December 7, 1976.

Review of induced-abortion technics in Czechoslovakia, by
F. Havranek. CESKOSLOVENSKA GYNEKOLOGIE
41(8):616-620, October, 1976.

Rh immunoglobulin utlization after spontaneous and induced abortion, by D. A. Grimes, et al. OBSTETRICS
AND GYNECOLOGY 50(3):261-263, September, 1977.

Risks and sequelae of induced abortion, by G. Giocoli-Nacci.
MINERVA GINECOLOGIA 28(9):721-725, September,
1976.

Role of the obstetrician in performing an abortion. Objections of conscience, by N. Damiani. MINERVA GINE-
COLOGIA 28(9):728-732, September, 1976.

The sacred rights of life, by J. Basile. C.I.C.I.A.M.S. NOU-
VELLES (3):25-37, 1976.

The safety of local anesthesia and outpatient treatment: a
controlled study of induced abortion by vacuum aspiration, by L. Andolsek, et al. STUDIES IN FAMILY
PLANNING 8(5):118-124, May, 1977.

Saline abortion: a retrospective study, by R. A. Kronstadt.
JOURNAL OF THE AMERICAN OSTEOPATHIC ASSO-
CIATION 76(4):276-281, December, 1976.

Saline induction of labor: a review with a report of a maternal
death, by F. W. Tysoe. TRANSACTIONS OF THE PA-
CIFIC COAST OBSTETRICAL AND GYNECOLOGICAL
SOCIETY 43:31-36, 1976.

Scope of the indications of abortion, by E. Martella. MINER-
VA GINECOLOGIA 28(9):694-697, September, 1976.

Second trimester abortion: single dose intraamniotic injection of prostaglandin F2a with intravenous oxytocin

augmentation, by G. Perry, et al. PROSTAGLANDINS 13(5):987-994, 1977. (Bio. Abstrs. October, 1977, 40677)

Second trimester abortion with intramuscular injections of 15-methyl prostaglandin F2a, by C. A. Ballard, et al. CONTRACEPTION 14(5):541-550, 1976. (Bio. Abstrs. March, 28800)

Sexology and abortion with respect to their psychological and socioeconomic repercussions, by A. De Leonardis. MINERVA GINECOLOGIA 28(9):737-739, September, 1976.

Social-hygienic characteristics of abortions in Leningrad, by I. V. Poliakov, et al. SOVETSKAE ZDRAVOOKHRANENIE (12):43-46, 1976.

Sociologic, ethical and psychological aspects of abortion, by R. De Vicienti. MINERVA GINECOLOGIA 28(9):739-741, September, 1976.

Somatic complications after induced abortion in hospitals in Telemark county, by P. Hoglend, et al. TIDSSKRIFT FOR DEN NORSKE LAEGEFORENING 97(3):134-136, January 30, 1977.

Statistics on maternal and child health: induced abortion, by T. Nakahara. JAPANESE JOURNAL FOR MIDWIVES 30(11):691, November, 1976.

Studies on the mechanisms of abortion induction by Trichosanthin. SCIENTIA SINICA 19(6):811-830, November-December, 1976.

A study of abortion in countries where abortions are legally restricted, by I. C. Chi, et al. JOURNAL OF REPRODUCTIVE MEDICINE 18(1):15-26, January, 1977.

A survey in a local urban area of induced abortion per-

formed in women and their marital status, by Y. J. Kim.
KOREAN NURSE 15(4):70-80, August 25, 1976.

Termination of pregnancy in the midtrimester using a new
technic. Preliminary report, by S. T. DeLee. INTERNA-
TIONAL SURGERY 61(20):545-546, October, 1976.

Termination of pregnancy with prostaglandin analogues, by
S. M. Karim, et al. ADVANCES IN PROSTAGLANDIN
AND THROMBOXANE RESEARCH 2:727-736, 1976.

Termination of pregnancy with vaginal administration of 16,
16 dimethyl prostaglandin E2 p-benzaldehyde semicarbazone ester, by S. M. Karim, et al. BRITISH JOURNAL
OF OBSTETRICS AND GYNAECOLOGY 84(2):135-
137, February, 1977.

To have or to have not—promotion and prevention of child-
birth in gynaecological work, by S. Macintyre. SOCIO-
LOGICAL REVIEW: MONOGRAPHS (22):176-193,
March, 1976.

Toxoplasmosis—its role in abortion, by R. C. Mahajan, et al.
INDIAN JOURNAL OF MEDICAL RESEARCH 64(6):
797-800, June, 1976. (Bio. Abstrs. February, 1977,
22293)

Unbiased consideration of applicants to medical schools, by
R. S. Schweiker. HOSPITAL PROGRESS 58(5):8, May,
1977.

Unsuccessful termination of pregnancy is an unrecognized
case of uterus bicornis/unicollis, by P. E. Andersen, Jr.
UGESKRIFT FOR LAEGER 139(12):713-714, March
21, 1977.

Untreated endocervical gonorrhea and endometritis following elective abortion, by R. T. Burkman, et al. AMERI-
CAN JOURNAL OF OBSTETRICS AND GYNECOLOGY
126(6):648-651, November 15, 1976. (Bio. Abstrs. April,

1977, 41724)

Use of combination prostaglandin F2a and hypertonic saline for midtrimester abortion, by M. Borten. PROSTA-GLANDINS 12(4):625-630, 1976. (Bio. Abstrs. February, 1977, 22694)

Uterine rupture following midtrimester abortion by laminaria, prostaglandin F2alpha, and oxytocin: report of two cases, by D. Propping, et al. AMERICAN JOURNAL OF OB-STETRICS AND GYNECOLOGY 128(6):689-690, July 15, 1977.

Uterine trauma associated with midtrimester abortion induced by intra-amniotic prostaglandin F2a with and without concomitant use of oxytocin, by G. Perry, et al. PROSTAGLANDINS 13(6):1147-1160, 1977. (Bio. Abstrs. December, 1977, 72336)

Vacuum extraction in interruption of pregnancy using a jagged cannula, by N. Gudac. JUGOSLOVENSKA GINEKOLOGIIA I OPSTETRICIJA 16(5-6):407-410, 1976.

Vaginal cytology after intra-amniotic injection of hypertonic urea for interruption of pregnancy during the second trimester, by B. Bercovici, et al. ARCHIVES D'ANA-TOMIE ET DE CYTOLOGIE PATHOLOGIQUE 25(2): 81-85, 1977.

The vaginal transverse low segment hysterotomy for second trimester therapeutic abortion, by G. Schariot, et al. GEBURTSHILFE UND FRAUENHEILKUNDE 36(8): 687-690, August, 1976.

Voluntary interruption of pregnancy, by A. Harlay. L'IN-FIRMIERE FRANCAIS (181):11, January, 1977.

WHO: excessive dilation may affect later pregnancy. FAMILY PLANNING PERSPECTIVES 9:134-135, May-June,

1977.

Work in progress. Menstrual induction with vaginal infusion
of the PFG2alpha analogue ICI 81008, by P. Mocsary.
PROSTAGLANDINS 13(4):807-808, April, 1977.

INFANTICIDE

INFECTION
see: Complications

ISOPTIN

ISOXSUPRINE

LAW ENFORCEMENT
see: Laws and Legislation

LAWS AND LEGISLATION
Abortion [letter]. LANCET 2(8031):247, July 30, 1977.

Abortion, abstract norms, and social control: the decision of
the West German federal constitutional court, by H.
Gerstein, et al. EMORY LAW JOURNAL 25:849-878,
Fall, 1976.

Abortion—action by nineteen year-old unmarried female
against the Arizona board of regents to determine the
constitutionality of a state statute prohibiting nontherapeutic abortions at the university hospital. JOURNAL
OF FAMILY LAW 15:113-118, 1976-1977.

Abortion aid barred by Bell in rape cases, by A. Clymer.
THE NEW YORK TIMES (M) August 2, 1:3, 1977.

Abortion aid gets a vote, by S. Cloud, Jr. THE NEW YORK
TIMES (M) August 7, XXIII, 20:5, 1977.

Abortion; almost legal. ECONOMIST 262:42+, January 29,
1977.

Abortion (amendment) bill [letter]. LANCET 1(8011):606, March 12, 1977.

Abortion and the autonomous womens movement, by S. Chelnov. SOCIALIST REVOLUTION 7(1):79-95, 1977. (Soc. Abstrs. 1977, 77I9912)

Abortion and child abuse; excerpt from Death before birth, by H. O. J. Brown. CHRISTIANITY TODAY 22:34, October 7, 1977.

Abortion and constitution: United States and West Germany, by D. P. Kommers. AMERICAN JOURNAL OF COMPARATIVE LAW 25:255-285, Spring, 1977.

Abortion and the court, by J. Kennedy. SIGN 57:22, September, 1977.

Abortion and democratic politics, by M. Simms. NEW HUMANIST 93:15-17, May-August, 1977.

Abortion and euthanasia: recent developments of the law, by D. J. Horan. FORUM 12:960-979, Summer, 1977.

Abortion and the husband's rights: a reply to Wesley Teo, by L. M. Purdy. ETHICS 86(3):247-251, 1976. (Soc. Abstrs. 1977, 77I9710)

Abortion and the law: the impact on hospital policy of the Roe and Doe decisions, by K. A. Kemp, et al. JOURNAL OF HEALTH POLITICS, POLICY AND LAW 1(3):319-337, Fall, 1976.

Abortion and maternal deaths [letter], by I. Chalmers. BRITISH MEDICAL JOURNAL 2(6037):698, September 18, 1976.

Abortion and the Supreme Court: some are more equal than others, by M. C. Segers. HASTINGS CENTER REPORT 7(4):5-6, August, 1977.

Abortion—the anti-life decision, by C. Read. CHRISTIAN READER p. 82, September-October, 1976.

Abortion cutoff causing hardship for poor women around country, by S. V. Roberts. THE NEW YORK TIMES (M) December 25, 20:1, 1977.

Abortion, fetal research, and the law, by J. M. Humber. SOCIAL THEORY AND PRACTICE 4:127-147, Spring, 1977.

Abortion foes gain support as they intensify campaign, by L. Johnston. THE NEW YORK TIMES (M) October 23, 1:1, 1977.

Abortion foes look to ultimate victory, by W. Robbins. THE NEW YORK TIMES (M) June 19, 24:1, 1977.

Abortion foes urged to join new causes. THE NEW YORK TIMES (M) March 28, 63:4, 1977.

Abortion for poor: legal confusion, by D. Henry. THE NEW YORK TIMES (M) July 24, XXIII, 1:1, 1977.

Abortion-fund fight expected in Albany, by R. J. Meislin. THE NEW YORK TIMES (M) December 9, 16:4, 1977.

Abortion hazards, by D. Lahiri, et al. JOURNAL OF THE INDIAN MEDICAL ASSOCIATION 66(11):288-294, June 1, 1976.

Abortion: the husband's constitutional rights, by W. D. H. Teo. ETHICS 85(4):337-342, 1975. (Socio. Abstrs. 1977, 7717168)

Abortion in Chinese law, by B. H.-k Luk. AMERICAN JOURNAL OF COMPARATIVE LAW 25:372-392, Spring, 1977.

Abortion in the law: an essay on absurdity, by L. H. Newton.

ETHICS 87:244-250, April, 1977.

Abortion in Mulago Hospital, Kampala, by C. Lwanga. EAST AFRICAN MEDICAL JOURNAL 54(3):142-148, March, 1977.

Abortion in South Carolina, by D. N. Bishop, et al. JOURNAL OF THE SOUTH CAROLINA MEDICAL ASSOCIATION 72(12):455-459, December, 1976.

Abortion is a hotly debated issue in many lands, by W. Safon. THE NEW YORK TIMES (M) January 22, 26:4, 1977.

The abortion issue and Secretary Califano [letter], by S. J. LaGumina. THE NEW YORK TIMES February 18, 26:6, 1977.

Abortion issue: a case against a constitutional amendment [letter], by R. L. Dujack. THE NEW YORK TIMES March 14, 28:4, 1977.

Abortion: an issue that won't go away, by P. Ferris. OBSERVER p. 13, January 30, 1977.

Abortion issues flares anew, by M. Waldron. THE NEW YORK TIMES (M) January 30, XI, 4:1, 1977.

Abortion: the last resort, by M. Segers. AMERICA p. 456, December 27, 1975.

Abortion law is approved in Israel, by W. Farrell. THE NEW YORK TIMES (M) February 1, 11:1, 1977.

Abortion law: a study of R. v. Morgentaler [(1975) 53 D L R (3d) 161]. SASKATCHEWAN LAW REVIEW 39:259-284, 1974-1975.

Abortion on demand [letter], by J. Bury. BRITISH MEDICAL JOURNAL 1(6066):975, April 9, 1977.

Abortion on request [letter], by M. Simms. LANCET
1(8008):423, February 19, 1977.

Abortion or contraception? by C. Giannice. MINERVA
GINECOLOGIA 28(7-8):671-675, July-August, 1976.

Abortion—Pennsylvania Medicaid regulations and procedures
denying non-therapeutic abortions to indigent women
held inconsistent with title XIX of the social security
act. JOURNAL OF FAMILY LAW 15:587-592, 1976-
1977.

Abortion—possible alternatives to unconstitutional spousal
and parental consent provisions of Missouri's abortion
law. MISSOURI LAW REVIEW 42:291-297, Spring,
1977.

Abortion—the question is whether the government should
pay, by S. Jacobs. NATIONAL JOURNAL 9:713-715,
May 7, 1977.

Abortion recordkeeping and right of privacy, by A. S. Kramer. JOURNAL OF CRIMINAL LAW AND CRIMINOLO-
GY 68:74-77, March, 1977.

Abortion statues after Danforth (Planned Parenthood of
Cent. Mo. v. Danforth, 96 Sup Ct 2831): an examination.
JOURNAL OF FAMILY LAW 15:537-567, 1976-1977.

Abortion utilization: does travel distance matter? by J. D.
Shelton, et al. FAMILY PLANNING PERSPECTIVES
8(6):260-262, November-December, 1976.

Abortion views and practices among Danish family physicians, by M. Gammeltoft, et al. JOURNAL OF BIO-
SOCIAL SCIENCE 8(3):287-292, (Socio. Abstrs. 1977,
77I3508)

Abortion vs. human rights, by J. Campbell. CHELSEA
JOURNAL p. 226, September-October, 1976.

Abortion: who pays; by S. Fraker, et al. NEWSWEEK 90: 12-13, July 4, 1977.

Abortions and public policy [editorial], by A. Yankauer. AMERICAN JOURNAL OF PUBLIC HEALTH 67(7): 604-605, July, 1977.

—, II. [editorial], by A. Yankauer. AMERICAN JOURNAL OF PUBLIC HEALTH 67(9):817-818, September, 1977.

Abortions: public and private facilities [Great Britain]. LABOUR RESEARCH 66:106-107, May, 1977.

Accord is emerging in congress on bar to medicaid abortion, by M. Tolchin. THE NEW YORK TIMES (M) September 28, 1:6, 1977.

Accord on abortion collapses again, by M. Tolchin. THE NEW YORK TIMES (M) November 2, 19:5, 1977.

Accord on abortion seems to be distant, by M. Tolchin. THE NEW YORK TIMES (M) October 6, 21:1, 1977.

Actions taken by the Supreme Court: abortion. THE NEW YORK TIMES (S) January 26, 14:1, 1977.

After Edeline: little guidance, by J. A. Robertson. HASTINGS CENTER REPORT 7:15-17, 45, June, 1977.

Again, back-alley and self-induced abortions, by Y. B. Burke. THE NEW YORK TIMES (M) August 22, 23:1, 1977.

Albany bars a halt in abortions study, by R. J. Meislin. THE NEW YORK TIMES (S) May 24, 39:6, 1977.

Albany senate passes court bill but its enactment is still distant: anti-abortion amendment, by R. J. Meislin. THE NEW YORK TIMES (S) May 25, II, 2:2, 1977.

Almost legal. ECONOMIST 262:42, 44, January 29, 1977.

And the poor get buried [letter], by W. Cates, Jr., et al.
FAMILY PLANNING PERSPECTIVES 9(1):2, January-
February, 1977.

Antiabortion bill stirs new debate, by M. Waldron. THE
NEW YORK TIMES (M) February 27, XI, 1:1, 1977.

Anti-abortion forces gain. THE NEW YORK TIMES (M)
June 26, IV, 1:1, 1977.

Anti-abortion petitions. THE NEW YORK TIMES (S) April
21, 18:6, 1977.

Assessment of the structure and function of the therapeutic
abortion committee, by M. E. Crass. CANADIAN MED-
ICAL ASSOCIATION JOURNAL 116(7):786+, April
9, 1977.

Attempt at handling the new legal regulation to paragraph
218, by P. Stoll, et al. FORTSCHRITTE DU MEDIZIN
94(33):1893-1894, November 18, 1976.

Attention may have shifted from it, but abortion remains a
major issue, by C. Hawkes. MACLEAN'S 90:80, November 14, 1977.

Badgley committee: abortion law retained, by E. Le Bourdais.
DIMENSIONS IN HEALTH SERVICE 54(4):34-35,
April, 1977.

The Badgley report on the abortion law [editorial], by W. D.
Thomas. CANADIAN MEDICAL ASSOCIATION JOUR-
NAL 116(9):966, May 7, 1977.

A ban on abortions paid for by medicaid criticized as unfair,
by M. Tolchin. THE NEW YORK TIMES (S) June 2, II,
5:1, 1977.

Benyon's progress [editorial]. LANCET 2(8029):120-121,
July 16, 1977.

Bill would restrict abortions on young, by L. Greenhouse. THE NEW YORK TIMES (M) June 10, IV, 15:4, 1977.

The birth of a bill restricting a women's rights, by J. Turner. GUARDIAN p. 11, February 17, 1977.

Califano declares dispute on abortion is unfair to poor. THE NEW YORK TIMES (M) October 12, 13:1, 1977.

Califano makes plans for abortion alternatives. OUR SUNDAY VISITOR 66:1, September 4, 1977.

Califano would bar U.S. aid to abortion, by N. Hicks. THE NEW YORK TIMES (M) January 14, 14:1, 1977.

Califano's appearance is picketed. THE NEW YORK TIMES (M) November 13, 42:1, 1977.

The Canadian abortion law [letter]. CANADIAN MEDICAL ASSOCIATION JOURNAL 116(3):238+, February 5, 1977.

Carey appoints panel on abortion consent. THE NEW YORK TIMES (S) January 9, 42:3, 1977.

Carter asks congress to disregard Ford proposals to cut funds for social programs, by D. E. Rosenbaum. THE NEW YORK TIMES (M) February 23, B, 5:5, 1977.

Carter staff prepares memo on abortion. THE NEW YORK TIMES (M) July 29, 16:1, 1977.

Case against abortion [review article], by R. Case. CHRISTIANITY TODAY 21:45-46, March 18, 1977.

Case study: the unwanted child: caring for a fetus born alive after an abortion, by Bok, et al. HASTINGS CENTER REPORT 6:10-15, October, 1976.

Catholic Hospital Association criticizes HEW's "cost-cutting"

proposals for abortion and living wills. HOSPITAL PRO-
GRESS 58:20-21, August, 1977.

Causes of late abortion [letter], by C. Brewer. LANCET
1(8008):422-423, February 19, 1977.

Child support: implications of abortion on the relative
parental duties. UNIVERSITY OF FLORIDA LAW
REVIEW 28:988-999, Summer, 1976.

A clinical comparison of prostaglandin F2alpha and intra-
amniotic saline for induction of midtrimester abortion,
by G. S. Berger, et al. ANNALES CHIRURGIAE ET
GYNAECOLOGIAE FENNIAE 66(1):55-58, 1977.

Compromise is voted by house and senate in abortion dispute, by M. Tolchin. THE NEW YORK TIMES (M)
December 8, 1:6, 1977; December 8, 14:4, 1977.

Compromise nearer on medicaid abortion, by M. Tolchin.
THE NEW YORK TIMES (M) September 30, 20:1,
1977.

Conferees ease the deadlock on medicaid abortions, by M.
Tolchin. THE NEW YORK TIMES (M) November 1,
29:1, 1977.

Conferees on medicaid abortions deadlocked after a futile
session, by M. Tolchin. THE NEW YORK TIMES (M)
September 13, 14:3, 1977.

Conferees still fail to agree on abortion, by M. Tolchin.
THE NEW YORK TIMES (M) November 28, 19:1,
1977.

Congress returning from recess faces vital issues at years end,
by M. Tolchin. THE NEW YORK TIMES (M) Novem-
ber 29, 18:1, 1977.

Congressmen offer new abortion plan, by M. Tolchin. THE

NEW YORK TIMES (M) October 1, 8:1, 1977.

Conspiracy of silence facilitates abortion in Brazil, by M.
Galanternick. THE NEW YORK TIMES (M) May 28,
46:1, 1977.

Contraceptive practice in the context of a nonrestrictive
abortion law: age-specific pregnancy rates in New York
City, 1971-1973, by C. Tietze. FAMILY PLANNING
PERSPECTIVES 7(5):192-202, 1975. (Socio. Abstrs.
1977, 7717046)

Contraceptive risk taking and abortion: results and implica-
tions of a San Francisco Bay Area study, by K. Luker.
STUDIES IN FAMILY PLANNING 8(8):190-196,
August, 1977.

A constitutional amendment to restrict abortion, by D.
Louisell. CATHOLIC MIND p. 25, December, 1976.

Constitutional law: abortion, parental and spousal consent
requirements, right to privacy. AKRON LAW REVIEW
10:367-382, Fall, 1976.

Constitutional law: abortion, parental consent, minors'
right to due process, equal protection and privacy.
AKRON LAW REVIEW 9(1):158-165, Summer, 1975.

Constitutional law—abortion—statute requiring spousal and
parental consent declared unconstitutional. CUMBER-
LAND LAW REVIEW 7:539-550, Winter, 1977.

Constitutional law—blanket parental consent requirement
for minor's abortion decision is unconstitutional. TEXAS
TECH LAW REVIEW 8:394-402, Fall, 1976.

Constitutional law: elimination of spousal and parental
consent requirements for abortion. WASHBURN LAW
JOURNAL 16:462-468, Winter, 1977.

Constitutional law—a state may constitutionally regulate the abortion decision during the first trimester of pregnancy if it can show that the regulation is necessary to protect a compelling state interest and the regulation, as applied, does not unnecessarily burden the woman's right to privacy. DRAKE LAW REVIEW 26:716-727, 1976-1977.

Constitutional law—substantive due process—abortion—reasonable statutory recordkeeping and reporting requirements upheld. BRIGHAM YOUNG UNIVERSITY LAW REVIEW 1976:977-999, 1976.

Constitutional protection for the unborn, by J. L. Bernardin. THE NEW YORK TIMES (M) February 26, 19:3, 1977.

Cooke, at reception on the east side, assails abortion, by G. Dugan. THE NEW YORK TIMES (M) January 22, 25:3, 1977.

The court and a conflict of principles, by S. Callahan. HASTINGS CENTER REPORT 7(4):7-8, August, 1977.

Court blocks abortion curb. THE NEW YORK TIMES (S) February 13, 36:1, 1977.

Court blocks on abortion for teen-aged student on male friend's plea. THE NEW YORK TIMES (S) April 22, 28:1, 1977.

The court, the congress and the president: turning back the clock on the pregnant [laws prohibiting use of federal funds to pay for abortions, and Supreme Court rulings], by R. Lincoln, et al. FAMILY PLANNING PERSPECTIVES 9:207-214, September-October, 1977.

Court hearing set on abortion funding, by M. Waldron. THE NEW YORK TIMES (M) July 10, XI, 1:5, 1977.

Court may OK government funding of abortions, by P. L. Geary. HOSPITAL PROGRESS 58(1):10+, January,

1977.

Court rules states may deny medicaid for some abortions, by
L. Oelsner. THE NEW YORK TIMES (M) June 21, 1:6,
1977.

Court to hear plea to bar abortions under medicaid, by W.
H. Waggoner. THE NEW YORK TIMES (S) June 25,
49:2, 1977.

Courts rule on constitutionality of hospital bans on elective
abortions. HOSPITAL LAW 10:3-4, January, 1977.

Criminologic considerations concerning criminal abortion, by
F. Carrieri. MINERVA GINECOLOGIA 28(9):725-728,
September, 1976.

Critical evaluation of legal abortion, by M. Harry. WORLD
MEDICAL JOURNAL 23:83-85, November-December,
1976.

Curb on medicaid funds for abortions defended. THE NEW
YORK TIMES (S) February 15, 49:4, 1977.

Curbs on medicaid abortions posing perils and problems for
the poor, by L. Oelsner. THE NEW YORK TIMES (M)
December 19, 35:3, 1977.

Cutoffs on medicaid prompt shift in thinking on abortion,
by L. Oelsner. THE NEW YORK TIMES (M) December
11, 82:3, 1977.

Death after legal abortion by catheter placement, by D. A.
Grimes, et al. AMERICAN JOURNAL OF OBSTETRICS
AND GYNECOLOGY 129(1):107-108, September 1,
1977.

Debating abortion, by J. Garn. NATIONAL REVIEW 29:
1299+, November 11, 1977.

Dilemmas and pressures. On patients and nurses—abortion legislation. Part 2, by E. Donachie. WORLD OF IRISH-NURSING 6:1+, June, 1977.

The Dutch on abortion: opinions on terminating life in the case of abortion, euthanasia, acts of war and punishment, by R. Veenhoven, et al. STIMEZO-RESEARCH 3:70, 1975. (Psycho. Abstrs. 1977, 10068)

Dutch tolerance of illegal abortions draws clients from all over Europe. THE NEW YORK TIMES (M) June 18, 48:4, 1977.

Ectopic pregnancy and first timester abortion, by L. A. Schonberg. OBSTETRICS AND GYNECOLOGY 49(1 Suppl):73-75, January, 1977.

Edelin case rekindles right-to-life hopes, by R. Adams. FAITH FOR THE FAMILY p. 9, November-December, 1975.

Edelin decision revisited: a survey of the reactions of Connecticut's OB/GYNs, by G. Affleck, et al. CONNECTICUT MEDICINE 41:637-640, October, 1977.

The effect of government policies on out-of-wedlock sex and pregnancy, by K. A. Moore, et al. FAMILY PLANNING PERSPECTIVES 9(4):164-169, July-August, 1977.

The effect of legalization of abortion on population growth and public health, by C. Tietze. FAMILY PLANNING PERSPECTIVES 7(3):123-127, 1975. (Socio. Abstrs. 1977, 7717047)

End to medicaid abortion funds, by R. Wilkins. THE NEW YORK TIMES (M) October 11, 24:3, 1977.

Equal rights plan and abortion are opposed by 15,000 at rally, by J. Klemesrud. THE NEW YORK TIMES (M) November 20, 32:5, 1977.

185

ERA, abortion attract uninvolved; women's meetings agenda items, by M. Papa. NATIONAL CATHOLIC REPORTER 13:1+, July 15, 1977.

Evolution of a women's clinic: an alternate system of medical care, by M. J. Gray, et al. AMERICAN JOURNAL OF OBSTETRICS AND GYNECOLOGY 126(7):760-768, December 1, 1976.

Experience with legal abortion, by H. Sjövall. LAKARTID-NINGEN 73(46):3991-3995, November 10, 1976.

Family planning measures—their merits and demerits, by D. Roy. JOURNAL OF THE INDIAN MEDICAL ASSO-CIATION 66(11):265-268, June 1, 1976.

Federal employees get aid for abortion, by L. K. Altman. THE NEW YORK TIMES (M) December 12, 27:1, 1977.

Federal judge again bids H.E.W. continue medicaid for abor-tions, by M. H. Siegel. THE NEW YORK TIMES (M) July 29, 1:1, 1977.

Federal judge lifts order requiring U.S. to pay for abortions, by E. J. Dionne, Jr. THE NEW YORK TIMES (M) August 5, 1:1, 1977.

Fetocide for convenience [letter], by J. J. van der Wat. SOUTH AFRICAN MEDICAL JOURNAL 52(5):165, July 23, 1977.

Gov. Grasso orders a halt to payments for elective abortions, by L. Fellows. THE NEW YORK TIMES (M) June 22, 17:4, 1977.

High court, congress act on abortion. NATIONAL CATHO-LIC REPORTER 13:8, July 1, 1977.

High court silence, by I. Silver. THE NEW YORK TIMES (M) August 6, 17:3, 1977.

High court's abortion rulings: what they mean. U. S. NEWS
AND WORLD REPORT 83:66, July 4, 1977.

House bars medicaid abortions and funds for enforcing
quotas, by M. Tolchin. THE NEW YORK TIMES (M)
June 18, 1:13, 1977.

House leaders seek to end standoff with senate over abortion
funds, by M. Tolchin. THE NEW YORK TIMES (M)
September 27, 24:3, 1977.

House liberals join conservatives in rejecting a new abortion
plan, by M. Tolchin. THE NEW YORK TIMES (M)
December 7, 19:3, 1977.

House rejects plan on medicaid abortion voted by the senate,
by M. Tolchin. THE NEW YORK TIMES (M) Novem-
ber 4, 1:6, 1977.

House votes change in stand on abortion, by M. Tolchin.
THE NEW YORK TIMES (M) October 13, 15:1, 1977.

House votes to bar abortion aid for victims of rape and incest. THE NEW YORK TIMES (M) August 3, 11:1,
1977.

How many illegal abortions? by C. Francome. BRITISH
JOURNAL OF CRIMINOLOGY 16:389-392, October,
1976. (Socio. Abstrs. 1977, 7718243)

How many trials will Morgentaler face? by E. Farkas. LAST
POST 5:13-14, December, 1976.

Husband's rights in abortion, by A. Etzioni. TRIAL 12:56-
58, November, 1976.

In search of conscience on abortion. THE NEW YORK
TIMES June 22, 22:1, 1977.

Incidence of abortive ova in abortion material, by P. Emmrich,

et al. ZENTRALBLATT FUR GYNAEKOLOGIE
99(9):541-546, 1977.

Incidence of post-abortion psychosis: a prospective study,
by C. Brewer. BRITISH MEDICAL JOURNAL 1(6059):
476-477, February 19, 1977.

Incidence of repeated legal abortion [letter], by C. Brewer,
et al. BRITISH MEDICAL JOURNAL 2(6048):1382,
December 4, 1976.

Inequities in abortion law found result of attitudes in people
and institutions, by J. S. Bennett. CANADIAN MEDI-
CALE ASSOCIATION JOURNAL 116(5):553-554,
March 5, 1977.

Interruption before and after March 9, 1972, by E. Heyer.
ZENTRALBLATT FUR GYNAEKOLOGIE 98(20):
1248-1251, 1976.

Israel selects middle-ground abortion law. THE NEW YORK
TIMES (M) February 6, IV, 7:1, 1977.

It will not go away. ECONOMIST 262:26, February 5,
1977.

Italy turns down an abortion bill. THE NEW YORK TIMES
(S) June 12, IV, 4:2, 1977.

Italy's abortion bill. THE NEW YORK TIMES (S) January
23, IV, 2:2, 1977.

Joseph Califano's "Alarming Words" [letter], by S. Raphael.
THE NEW YORK TIMES January 26, 22:6, 1977.

Kitchen-table justice, by T. Wilker. THE NEW YORK TIMES
June 28, 31:5, 1977.

Law for the nurse supervisor. Action for wrongful life, by H.
Creighton. SUPERVISOR NURSE 8:12-15, April, 1977.

Law of abortion with special reference to Commonwealth Caribbean, by P. K. Menon. THE ANGLO-AMERICAN LAW REVIEW 5:311-345, October-December, 1976.

LCWR thinks no effective anti-abortion law possible, by J. Kennedy. OUR SUNDAY VISITOR 66:2, August 21, 1977.

Legal abortion, by H. P. Tarnesby. MINERVA GINECOLO-GIA 28(5):458-473, May, 1976.

Legal abortion, by C. Tietze, et al. SCIENTIFIC AMERI-CAN 236(1):21-27, January, 1977.

Legal abortion: are American black women healthier because of it; [conference paper] by W. Cates, Jr. PHYLON 38:267-281, September, 1977.

Legal abortion during the first trimester of pregnancy at the University Hospital for women in Novi Sad (1960-1975), by B. M. Beric, et al. ZENTRALBLATT FUR GYNAE-KOLOGIE 99(6):371-376, 1977.

Legal abortion: a half-decade of experience, by J. Pakter, et al. FAMILY PLANNING PERSPECTIVES 7(6):248-257, 1975. (Socio. Abstrs. 1977, 7717028)

Legal abortion in Telemark, by P. Hoglend. TIDSSKRIFT FOR DEN NORSKE LAEGEFORENING 97(3):130-133, January 30, 1977.

Legal abortion in the United States, 1975-1976, by E. Sulli-van, et al. FAMILY PLANNING PERSPECTIVES 9(3):116-129, May-June, 1977.

Legal abortion mortality in the United States. Epidemiologic surveillance, 1972-1974, by W. Cates, Jr., et al. JAMA; JOURNAL OF THE AMERICAN MEDICAL ASSOCIA-TION 237(5):452-455, January 31, 1977. (Bio. Abstrs. May 1977, 59845)

Legal abortion: trends in various parts of the world, by C. Tietze, et al. SCIENTIFIC AMERICAN 236:21-27, January, 1977.

Legal abortions and trends in age-specific marriage rates, by K. E. Bauman, et al. AMERICAN JOURNAL OF PUB-LIC HEALTH 67(1):52-53, January, 1977.

Legal abortions in the United States: rates and ratios by race and age, 1972-1974, by C. Tietze. FAMILY PLANNING PERSPECTIVES 9(1):12-15, January-February, 1977.

Legal aspects of menstrual regulation: some preliminary observations, by L. T. Lee, et al. JOURNAL OF FAMI-LY LAW 14(2):181-221, 1975. (Socio. Abstrs. 1977, 7714360)

Legal considerations and prenatal genetic diagnosis, by L. F. Hifman, 3d. CLINICAL OBSTETRICS AND GYNE-COLOGY 19(4):965-972, December, 1976.

Legal enforcement, moral pluralism and abortion, by R. T. De George. PROCEEDINGS OF THE AMERICAN CATHOLIC PHILOSOPHICAL ASSOCIATION 49:171-180, 1975.

Legislators say abortion study invades privacy, by R. J. Meis-lin. THE NEW YORK TIMES (M) May 12, 1:4, 1977.

Lesson in judicial abdication: Roe v. Arizona Board of Re-gents [(Ariz) 549 P 2d 150] and the right of privacy. ARIZONA STATE LAW REVIEW 1976:499-524, 1976.

Lobbying on abortion issue intensifies as conferees remain deadlocked, by M. Tolchin. THE NEW YORK TIMES (M) September 15, II, 16:3, 1977.

Lobbyist on women's rights press congress for action. THE NEW YORK TIMES (M) August 13, 9:1, 1977.

The Lombardy Society of Obstetrics and Gynecology: oral ballot on the problem of abortion. ANNALI DI OSTE-TRICIA, GINECOLOGIA, MEDICINA PERINATALE 97(3):133-136, May-June, 1976.

Malpractice decisions you should know about. Is a husband's consent necessary for abortion; MEDICAL TIMES 104(10):160-162, October, 1976.

Management of the abortion problem in an English city, by J. B. Lawson, et al. LANCET 2(7998):1288-1291, December 11, 1976. (Bio. Abstrs. May, 1977, 59877)

Marches call for abortion ban. THE NEW YORK TIMES (S) January 24, 29:3, 1977.

Massachusetts Supreme Judicial Court reverses conviction of Dr. Kenneth Edelin, by L. H. Glantz. MEDICO-LEGAL BULLETIN 5:3-4, Winter, 1977.

Medicaid assistance for elective abortions: the statutory and constitutional issue. ST. JOHN'S LAW REVIEW 50: 751-770, Summer, 1976.

Medicaid-funded abortions not mandated by federal law: U.S. Supreme Court. HOSPITALS 51:17-18, August 1, 1977.

Medicaid is banned in some abortions, by W. H. Waggoner. THE NEW YORK TIMES (S) June 28, 67:4, 1977.

Medical opinion on abortion in Jamaica: a national Delphi survey of physicians, nurses, and midwives, by K. A. Smith, et al. STUDIES IN FAMILY PLANNING 7:334-339, December, 1976.

Medical termination of midtrimster pregnancy in a community hospital, by P. E. Stroup. JOURNAL OF THE MEDI-CAL SOCIETY OF NEW JERSEY 74(9):747-752, September, 1977.

Medical termination of pregnancy—its status, achievements and lacunae, by S. Grewal. JOURNAL OF THE INDIAN MEDICAL ASSOCIATION 66(11):269-275, June 1, 1976.

Medico-legal aspects of therapeutic abortion, by P. Zangani. MINERVA GINECOLOGIA 28(9):703-705, September, 1976.

Men's reactions to their partners' elective abortions, by A. A. Rothstein. AMERICAN JOURNAL OF OBSTETRICS AND GYNECOLOGY 128(8):831-837, August 15, 1977.

Mobilizing for abortion rights, by J. Benshoof. THE CIVIL LIBERTIES REVIEW 4:76-79, September-October, 1977.

The monstrous regiments battle for and against abortion. ECONOMIST 264:19-20, July 16, 1977.

Morbidity and mortality associated with legal abortion [letter], by M. Potts. MEDICAL JOURNAL OF AUSTRALIA 2(1):30-31, July 3, 1976.

Morgentaler [Morgentaler v. Regina (1975) 53 D L R (3d) 161] case: criminal process and abortion law, by B. M. Dickens. OSGOODE HALL LAW JOURNAL 14:229-274, October, 1976.

Mr. Carter's cruel abortion plan. THE NEW YORK TIMES June 13, 28:1, 1977.

Must we accept either the conservative or the liberal view on abortion? by H. V. McLachlan. ANALYSIS 37:197-204, June, 1977.

Never again! Never again? Can we lose our right to abortion? by R. B. Gratz. MS MAGAZINE 6:54-55, July, 1977.

The new abortion debate. COMMONWEAL 104:451-452, July 22, 1977.

A new ethical approach to abortion and its implications for the euthanasia dispute, by R. F. R. Gardner. JOURNAL OF MEDICAL ETHICS 1:127-131, September, 1975.

New Jersey briefs: timing of abortion. THE NEW YORK TIMES (S) April 25, 67:1, 1977.

New Jersey court rules hospitals cannot prohibit abortions. HOSPITALS 51:20-21, January 1, 1977.

New regulations on legal abortion, by A. Hollmann. DEUT-SCHE MEDIZINSCHE WOCHENSCHRIFT 102(7):252-254, February 18, 1977.

Newer fashions in illegitimacy, by R. H. Edmunds, et al. BRITISH MEDICAL JOURNAL 1(6062):701-703, March 12, 1977.

Of abortion, the law and Califano's views [letter], by K. P. Carroll. THE NEW YORK TIMES February 5, 18:6, 1977.

On abortion, the houses still remain miles apart, by M. Tolchin. THE NEW YORK TIMES (M) November 27, IV, 4:3, 1977.

On funding abortions, by F. S. Jaffe. THE NEW YORK TIMES July 29, 20:4, 1977.

One-third of Nassau pregnancies end in abortion, by R. R. Silver. THE NEW YORK TIMES (M) July 31, 21:1, 1977.

Operation of the abortion law [letter], by O. A. Schmidt. CANADIAN MEDICAL ASSOCIATION JOURNAL 117(3):214, August 6, 1977.

Opinion to the vibrodilatation of the cervix in induced abortions—report of 2 years of experiences with the Soviet vibrodilatator WG-I, by P. Landschek, et al. ZENTRALBLATT FUR GYNAEKOLOGIE 98(17):1049-1053, 1976.

Opponents on abortion issue gear for a new battle, by M. Tolchin. THE NEW YORK TIMES (M) December 9, 16:1, 1977.

Order barring woman's abortion arrives too late to halt surgery. THE NEW YORK TIMES (M) April 23, 51:5, 1977.

Parent and child—right of unwed minor to obtain abortion without parental consent. JOURNAL OF FAMILY LAW 14:637-643, 1975-1976.

The parliamentary scene, by T. Smith. JOURNAL OF MEDICAL ETHICS 3(2):100-101, June, 1977.

Patient's view of the role of the primary care physician in abortion, by R. H. Rosen. AMERICAN JOURNAL OF PUBLIC HEALTH 67:863-865, September, 1977.

Personal defeat, private hell [editorial]. THE NEW YORK TIMES January 31, 20:1, 1977.

Personality characteristics associated with contraceptive behavior in women seeking abortion under liberalized California law, by L. D. Noble. DISSERTATION ABSTRACTS INTERNATIONAL 35(7-B):3589-3590, 1975. (Psycho. Abstrs. 1977, 3141)

Physician acquitted of abortion conviction: Boston. HOSPITALS 51:20+, February 1, 1977.

Planned parenthood begins abortion aid drive, by J. Cummings. THE NEW YORK TIMES (M) July 10, 23:3, 1977.

Planned parenthood v. Danforth (96 Sup Ct 2831): resolving the antinomy. OHIO NORTHERN UNIVERSITY LAW REVIEW 4:425-440, 1977.

The politics of abortion, by J. Armstrong. CHRISTIAN CENTURY p. 215, March 10, 1976.

The politics of abortion: from the Supreme Court, Congress, and the Department of Health, Education, and Welfare, by P. Steinfels. COMMONWEAL 104:456, July 22, 1977.

The politics of pregnancy, by L. Edmunds. DAILY TELE-GRAPH p. 15, February 23, 1977.

Pregnancies of Irish residents terminated in England and Wales in 1974, by D. Walsh. IRISH MEDICAL JOUR-NAL 70(3):64, March 19, 1977.

President defends court's action curbing federal aid for abortion, by L. Foreman. THE NEW YORK TIMES (M) July 13, 1:4, 1977.

Principles of the current legal regulations on pregnancy inter-ruption. Results of the decision of the Federal constitu-tional court of 25 February, 1975, by G. Brenner. DEUT-SCHE KRANKENPFLEGEZITSCHRIFT 29(12):671-676, December, 1976.

Problems and risks of the legalization of abortion, by A. Andriani. MINERVA GINECOLOGIA 28(9):736-737, September, 1976.

Pro-"choice" groups lobby against abortion fund ban; lan-guage of senate amendment called crucial [concerning use of medicaid funds to pay for abortions for poor wo-men], by B. M. Hager. CONGRESSIONAL QUARTER-LY WEEKLY REPORT 35:1286-1287, June 25, 1977.

Proposed laws on abortion for the consideration of Parliament, by V. S. Pesce. MINERVA GINECOLOGIA 28(9):732-736, September, 1976.

Population growth and abortion legislation, by K. Sund-ström-Feigenberg. LAKARTIDNINGEN 73(44):3747-3752, October 27, 1976.

Quantitative interference with the right to life; abortion and Irish law, by M. Mathews. CATHOLIC LAWYER 22: 344-358, Fall, 1976.

Reasons for criminal abortion and complications of patients at Ramathibodi Hospital, 1975, by U. Kabusa. THAI JOURNAL OF NURSING 25(2):153-155, April, 1976.

Reimbursement for abortion. FEDERAL REGISTER 42: 40486, August 10, 1977.

Report of the committee on the operation of the abortion law, by V. Hunter. QUILL AND QUIRE 43(5):44, 1977.

Reported live births following induced abortion: two and one-half years' experience in upstate New York, by G. Stroh, et al. AMERICAN JOURNAL OF OBSTETRICS AND GYNECOLOGY 126(1):83-90, 1976. (Bio. Abstrs. March, 1977, 31315)

Reprise. THE NEW YORK TIMES July 14, 38:1, 1977.

Restricting medicaid funds for abortions: projections of excess mortality for women of childbearing age, by D. B. Petitti, et al. AMERICAN JOURNAL OF PUBLIC HEALTH 67:860-862, September, 1977.

Right to abortion: the end of parental and spousal consent requirements. ARKANSAS LAW REVIEW 31:122-126, Spring, 1977.

Right to an abortion—problems with parental and spousal

consent. NEW YORK LAW SCHOOL LAW REVIEW 22:65-86, 1976.

Right to life committee challenges health department: Rhode Island, by W. A. Regan. HOSPITAL PROGRESS 58:30+, February, 1977.

Right to life of potential persons, by E.-H. W. Kluge. DAL-HOUSIE LAW JOURNAL 3:837-848, January, 1977.

Right to medicaid payment for abortion, by P. A. Butler. HASTINGS LAW JOURNAL 28:931-977, March, 1977.

Roe vs. Ward: the rhetoric fetal life. CENTRAL STATES SPEECH JOURNAL 27(3):192-199, February, 1976.

Safety of abortion [letter], by W. V. Dolan. JAMA; JOUR-NAL OF THE AMERICAN MEDICAL ASSOCIATION 237(24):2601-2602, June 13, 1977.

Senate, in payroll plight, continues abortion curb, by M. Tol-chin. THE NEW YORK TIMES (M) November 5, 9:2, 1977.

Senate panel softens abortion provision: publicly funded abortions not required, high court says [the Supreme Court, June 20, ruled that states and cities did not have to spend public funds for abortions of an elective or nontherapeutic nature], by M. E. Eccles. CONGRES-SIONAL QUARTERLY WEEKLY REPORT 35:1284-1285+, June 25, 1977.

Senate vote forbids using Federal funds for most abortions, by A. Clymer. THE NEW YORK TIMES (M) June 30, 1:1, 1977.

Senate votes pregnancy benefits in disability plan for workers. THE NEW YORK TIMES (M) September 17, 8:1, 1977.

Senators elucidate shift on abortions, by M. Tolchin. THE

NEW YORK TIMES (M) July 1, 24:1, 1977.

Sex guilt in abortion patients, by M. Gerrard. JOURNAL OF CONSULTING AND CLINICAL PSYCHOLOGY 45(4):708, August, 1977.

Showdown seems near, by J. M. Naughton. THE NEW YORK TIMES (M) June 26, IV, 1:4, 1977.

Social hygiene aspects of criminal abortions among women of the city of Kalinin, by V. L. Krasnenkov. ZDRA-VOOKHRANENIE ROSSIISKOI FEDERATSII (5):19-22, 1977.

Some comments on the demographic and social effects of the 1967 Abortion Act, by R. Leete. JOURNAL OF BIOSOCIAL SCIENCE 8(3):229-251, July, 1976. (Socio. Abstrs. 1977, 7714000)

Some comments to the interruption statute novelized in 1973, by J. Presl. CESKOSLOVENSKA GYNEKOLOGIA 42(5):338-341, June, 1977.

Some laws relating to population growth; laws directly affecting fertility, by K. K. S. Wee. NURSING JOURNAL OF SINGAPORE 17:20-24, May, 1977.

State insists that bar on medicaid for abortion conforms to U.S. law, by W. H. Waggoner. THE NEW YORK TIMES (M) July 19, 75:1, 1977.

State limitations upon the availability and accessibility of abortions after Wade and Bolton. KANSAS LAW REVIEW 25:87-107, Fall, 1976.

State panel votes to restrict the use of medicaid funds for abortions, by A. Clymer. THE NEW YORK TIMES (M) June 22, 17:3, 1977.

State protection of the viable unborn child after Roe v.

Wade: how little, how late? LOUISIANA LAW REVIEW 37:270-282, Fall, 1976.

State senate passes bill allowing municipal courts to define obsenity and asks U.S. abortion action, by A. A. Narvaez. THE NEW YORK TIMES (M) January 25, 75:1, 1977.

Statistical analysis of first-trimester pregnancy terminations in an ambulatory surgical center, by N. Bozorgi. AMERICAN JOURNAL OF OBSTETRICS AND GYNECOLOGY 127(7):763-768, April 1, 1977.

A study of abortion and problems in decision-making, by M. Cotronco, et al. JOURNAL OF MARRIAGE AND FAMILY COUNSELING 3(1):69-76, 1977. (Socio. Abstrs. 1977, 7718557)

A study of abortion in countries where abortions are legally restricted, by I. C. Chi, et al. JOURNAL OF REPRODUCTIVE MEDICINE 18(1):15-26, January, 1977.

Study of therapeutic abortion committees in British Columbia, by W. J. Harris, et al. UNIVERSITY OF BRITISH COLUMBIA LAW REVIEW 11:81-118, 1977.

Substantive due process revisited: reflections on (and beyond) recent cases, by M. J. Perry. NORTHWESTERN UNIVERSITY LAW REVIEW 71:417-469, September-October, 1976.

Summary of Supreme Court actions: abortion. THE NEW YORK TIMES (S) May 24, 22:5, 1977.

Supreme Court abortion decisions—a challenge to use political process, by E. J. Schulte. HOSPITAL PROGRESS 58:22-23, August, 1977.

Supreme Court activities—abortion. THE NEW YORK TIMES (S) June 28, 15:1, 1977.

Supreme Court ignites a fiery abortion debate. TIME 110:6-8, July 4, 1977.

Supreme court June 20, 1977 abortion decisions, by M. Fisk. TRIAL 13:14-16+, August, 1977.

Supreme Court on medicare and abortion; medicaid-funding of nontherapeutic abortions. ORIGINS 7:86-90, June 30, 1977.

Supreme Court retreats from activist, public policy abortion stance, by E. J. Schulte. HOSPITAL PROGRESS 58:19, July, 1977.

Supreme Court ruling sparks moves to halt medicaid abortions, by G. Dullea. THE NEW YORK TIMES June 27, 32:1, 1977.

Supreme Court: states need not pay for "nontherapeutic" abortions via medicaid; public hospitals can deny service. FAMILY PLANNING PERSPECTIVES 9:177-179+, July-August, 1977.

The Supreme court's abortion decisions and public opinion in the United States, by J. Blake. POPULATION AND DEVELOPMENT REVIEW 3:45-62, March-June, 1977.

Supreme court's abortion rulings and social change, by D. W. Brady, et al. SOCIAL SCIENCE QUARTERLY 57:535-546, December, 1976.

The susceptibility of the postpartum and postabortal cervix and uterine cavity to infection with attenuated rubella virus, by R. J. Bolognese, et al. AMERICAN JOURNAL OF OBSTETRICS AND GYNECOLOGY 125(4):525-527, June 15, 1976.

Swiss voters asked to resolve abortion dispute, by V. Lusinchi. THE NEW YORK TIMES (M) May 6, 27:1, 1977.

Swiss voters to decide on allowing abortions. THE NEW YORK TIMES (S) June 28, 34:2, 1977.

Swiss voters uphold abortion ban. THE NEW YORK TIMES (M) September 26, 4:3, 1977.

Switzerland voting on abortion reform. THE NEW YORK TIMES (M) September 24, 45:1, 1977.

Talks aborted. ECONOMIST 264:48, September 3, 1977.

Ten-minute abortions, by W. O. Goldthorp. BRITISH MEDICAL JOURNAL 2:562-564, August 27, 1977.

There are some in media and congress who see abortion as money-saver for public, by J. Castelli. OUR SUNDAY VISITOR 66:3, July 24, 1977.

Third party consent to abortions before and after Danforth (Planned Parenthood of Cent. Mo. v. Danforth, 96 Sup Ct 2831): a theoretical analysis. JOURNAL OF FAMILY LAW 15:508-536, 1976-1977.

Third time unlucky: a study of women who have three or more legal abortions, by C. Brewer. JOURNAL OF BIO-SOCIAL SCIENCE 9(1):99-105, January, 1977. (Bio. Abstrs. December, 1977, 65346)

Though legal, abortions are not always available, by T. Schultz. THE NEW YORK TIMES (M) January 2, IV, 8:3, 1977.

Three states are likely to continue abortion funding for medicaid patient. MODERN HEALTHCARE, SHORT-TERM CARE EDITION 7(8):26, August, 1977.

Top women aides tell president why they oppose him on abortion, by B. Gamarekian. THE NEW YORK TIMES (M) August 27, 22:1, 1977.

Towards a practical implementation of the abortion decision: the interests of the physician, the woman and the fetus. DE PAUL LAW REVIEW 25:676-706, Spring, 1976.

Tying abortion to the death penalty; study by Paul Cameron, by J. Horn. PSYCHOLOGY TODAY 11:43+, November, 1977.

U.S. abortion panel disbanded by chief. THE NEW YORK TIMES (M) November 27, 1:1, 1977.

Vaginal administration of a single does of 16, 16 dimethyl prostaglandin E2 p-benzaldehyde semicarbazone ester for pre-operative cervical dilatation in first trimester nulliparae, by S. M. Karim, et al. BRITISH JOURNAL OF OBSTETRICS AND GYNAECOLOGY 84(4):269-271, April, 1977.

Validity of parental consent statutes after planned parenthood (Planned Parenthood of Cent. Mo. v. Danforth, 96 Sup Ct 2831). UNIVERSITY OF DETROIT JOURNAL OF URBAN LAW 54:127-164, Fall, 1976.

Vatican bids Italy's senate amend abortion bill. THE NEW YORK TIMES (S) January 23, 7:1, 1977.

Very young adolescent women in Georgia: has abortion or contraception lowered their fertility? by J. D. Shelton. AMERICAN JOURNAL OF PUBLIC HEALTH 67(7): 616-620, July, 1977.

Vexing abortion issue, by L. Fellows. THE NEW YORK TIMES (M) July 3, XXIII, 10:1, 1977.

Viability, values, and the vast cosmos, by D. J. Horan. CATHOLIC LAWYER 22:1-37, Winter, 1976.

The wages of sin? ECONOMIST 265:36, December 10, 1977.

We did it for the women. TIME 109:32, January 31, 1977.

White house backs subsidy for adopting unwanted children, by D. E. Rosenbaum. THE NEW YORK TIMES (M) July 9, 1:4, 1977.

Why a constitutional convention is needed; human life amendment, by E. J. McMahon. AMERICA 137:12-14, July 2, 1977.

Woman's meetings Friday in Albany will have a national focus, by N. Robertson. THE NEW YORK TIMES (M) July 5, 34:1, 1977.

Women at Albany meeting vote to support abortion, by J. Dunning. THE NEW YORK TIMES (M) July 11, 31:2, 1977.

Women end parley with plan for rights, by A. Quindlen. THE NEW YORK TIMES (M) November 22, 1:1, 1977.

Women hail attack on government over abortion, by R. Lindsey. THE NEW YORK TIMES (M) September 11, 27:1, 1977.

Women in administration protest Carter opposition to abortion aid. THE NEW YORK TIMES (M) July 16, 7:3, 1977.

Working together for Christ: facing the antilife challenge, by W. F. Sullivan. HOSPITAL PROGRESS 58(5):82-84+, May, 1977.

Wrongful birth in the abortion context—critique of existing case law and proposal for future actions. DENVER LAW JOURNAL 53:501-520, 1976.

The young must learn actions have results [letter], by G. M. Middlemiss. THE NEW YORK TIMES January 30, XXI, 19:5, 1977.

LISTERIOSIS

MALE ATTITUDES
see: Sociology and Behavior

MARCH OF DIMES

MEFENAMIC ACID

MENSTRUATION
see also: Complications
Induced Abortion

Increased reporting of menstrual symptoms among women who used induced abortion, by L. H. Roht, et al. AMERICAN JOURNAL OF OBSTETRICS AND GYNECOLOGY 127(4):356-362, 1977.

Legal aspects of menstrual regulation: some preliminary observations, by L. T. Lee, et al. JOURNAL OF FAMILY LAW 14(2):181-221, 1975. (Socio. Abstrs. 1977, 7714360)

Work in progress. Menstrual induction with vaginal infusion of the PGF2alpha analogue ICI 81008, by P. Mocsary. PROSTAGLANDINS 13(4):807-808, April, 1977.

MENTALLY RETARDED
Agonizing decisions in mental retardation, by R. C. Yeaworth. AMERICAN JOURNAL OF NURSING 77:864-867, May, 1977.

MICROBIOLOGY
see: Research

MISCARRIAGES
Amidation of proteins of different placental tissues in miscarriage, by T. S. Dluxhevskaia, et al. VOPROSY OKHRANY MATERINSTVA I DETSTVA 21(8):71-75, August, 1976.

Chromosome anomalies and miscarriage, by Iu. I. Novikov, et al. AKUSHERSTVO I GINEKOLOGIIA (Moscow) (12):32-35, December, 1976.

Cytogenetic studies in sterility and miscarriage, by V. I. Kucharenko, et al. AKUSHERSTVO I GINEKOLOGIIA (Moscow) (5):1-4, May, 1977.

Organization of specialized medical aid to women with habitual miscarriage in the Andizhan region, by N. T. Gudakova, et al. AKUSHERSTVO I GINEKOLOGIIA (Moscow) (5):54-55, May, 1977.

Risks of miscarriage after amniocentesis, by C. O. Carter. JOURNAL OF MEDICAL GENETICS 13(5):351, October, 1976.

Results of the overall treatment of patients suffering from miscarriages, by E. L. Maizel', et al. VOPROSY OKHRANY MATERINSTVA I DETSTVA 21(11):59-62, November, 1976.

Spina bifida and anencephaly: are miscarriages a possible cause? by K. M. Laurence, et al. BRITISH MEDICAL JOURNAL 2(6083):361-362, August 6, 1977.

MORBIDITY
see: Complications

MORTALITY
see also: Complications
Sepsis
Septic Abortion and Septic Shock

Abortion and maternal deaths [letter]. BRITISH MEDICAL JOURNAL 2(6029):232, July 24, 1976.

—, by A. Cartwright. BRITISH MEDICAL JOURNAL 2(6039):813, October 2, 1976.

—, by I. Chalmers. BRITISH MEDICAL JOURNAL 2(6037): 698, September 18, 1976.

Abortion deaths associated with the use of prostaglandin F2a, by W. Cates, Jr., et al. AMERICAN JOURNAL OF OB-STETRICS AND GYNECOLOGY 127(3):219-222, 1977. (Bio. Abstrs. June, 1977, 65533)

Deaths from paracervical anesthesia used for first-trimester abortion, 1972-1975, by D. A. Grimes, et al. NEW ENGLAND JOURNAL OF MEDICINE 295(25):1397-1399, December 16, 1976. (Bio. Abstrs. May, 1977, 54151)

Eisenmenger's syndrome in pregnancy: does heparin pro-phylaxis improve the maternal mortality rate? by J. A. Pitts, et al. AMERICAN HEART JOURNAL 93(3):321-326, 1977. (Bio. Abstrs. November, 1977, 58782)

Facts and artifacts in the study of intra-uterine mortality: a reconsideration from pregnancy histories, by H. Leri-don. POPULATION STUDIES 30(2):319-335, 1976. (Bio. Abstrs. January 1977, 5545 and Soc. Abstrs. 1977, 77I9623)

The intrauterine device and deaths from spontaneous abor-tion, by W. Cates, Jr., et al. NEW ENGLAND JOURNAL OF MEDICINE 295(21):1155-1159, November 18, 1976. (Bio. Abstrs. March, 1977, 35535)

Legal abortion mortality in the United States: epidemiologic surveillance, 1972-1974, by W. Cates, Jr., et al. JOUR-NAL OF THE AMERICAN MEDICAL ASSOCIATION 237:452-455, January 31, 1977. (Bio. Abstrs. May, 1977, 59845)

Maternal death and the I.U.D. [editorial]. LANCET 2(7997):1234, December 4, 1976.

—. [letter], by R. A. Sparks, et al. LANCET 1(8002):98,

January 8, 1977.

Morbidity and mortality associated with legal abortion [letter], by M. Potts. MEDICAL JOURNAL OF AUSTRALIA 2(1):30-31, July 3, 1976.

Publicity and the public health: the elimination of IUD-related abortion deaths, by W. Cates, Jr., et al. FAMILY PLANNING PERSPECTIVES 9(3):138-140, May-June, 1977.

Research of antibodies against toxoplasma gondii in subjects with repeated abortions, perinatal mortality and malformed newborns, by A. S. Castro, et al. ANNALI SCLAVO 18(1):75-81, 1976. (Bio. Abstrs. March, 1977, 29539)

Restricting medicaid funds for abortions: projections of excess mortality for women for childbearing age, by D. B. Petitti, et al. AMERICAN JOURNAL OF PUBLIC HEALTH 67(9):860-862, September, 1977.

Saline induction of labor: a review with a report of a maternal death, by F. W. Tysoe. TRANSACTIONS OF THE PACIFIC COAST OBSTETRICAL AND GYNECOLOGICAL SOCIETY 43:31-36, 1976.

MYCOPLASMA
Role of mycoplasma infections in repeat abortions [letter], by C. Alexandre, et al. NOUVELLE PRESSE MEDICALE 5(39):2631, November, 1976.

NAL
see: Laws and Legislation

NCCB

NAPTHALENE

NEONATAL

NEURAMINIDASE

NURSES

Abortion counselling: a new role for nurses, by B. Easterbrook, et al. CANADIAN NURSE 73:28-30, January,
1977.

Dilemmas and pressures. Part 2. On patients and nurses—
abortion legislation, by E. Donachie. WORLD OF
IRISH NURSING 6(6):1-2, June, 1977.

Ethics and nurses, by C. J. Rogan. NURSING MIRROR
AND MIDWIVES' JOURNAL 143:75-76, October 21,
1976.

Law for the nurse supervisor. Action for wrongful life, by
H. Creighton. SUPERVISOR NURSE 8:12-15, April,
1977.

A new role for nurses. . .abortion counselling. . .Toronto
General Hospital, by B. Easterbrook, et al. CANADIAN
NURSE 73:28-30, January, 1977.

Nurses and abortion, by M. J. Tobin. THE NEW YORK
TIMES January 30, XXI, 18:1, 1977.

Nurses and abortion: more viewpoints [letters]. THE NEW
YORK TIMES March 13, XXI, 27:1, 1977.

Nursing decisions. Experience in clinical problem solving.
Series 2, Part 8: H. Joyce, an elective abortion patient,
by R. De Tornyay, et al. RN; NATIONAL MAGAZINE
FOR NURSES 40:55-61, June, 1977.

Psychologic impact on nursing students of participation in
abortion, by A. Hurwitz, et al. NURSING RESEARCH
26:112-120, March-April, 1977.

Two measures of nurses' attitudes toward abortion as modified by experience, by D. V. Allen, et al. MEDICAL

CARE 15:849-857, October, 1977.

NURSING HOMES

OBSTETRICS

Clinical application of prostaglandins in obstetrics and gynecology, by F. J. Brunnberg. ACTA BIOLOGICA ET MEDICA GERMANICA 35(8-9):1243-1247, 1976.

Effect of abortion on obstetric patterns [letter], by A. F. Pentecost. BRITISH MEDICAL JOURNAL 2(6086): 578, August 27, 1977.

Ethical problems in obstetrics and gynaecology, by J. Bonnar. WORLD OF IRISH NURSING 6(4):1, April, 1977.

The Lombardy Society of Obstetrics and Gynecology: oral ballot on the problem of abortion. ANNALI DI OBSTETRICIA, GINECOLOGIA, MEDICINA PERINATALE 97(3):133-136, May-June, 1976.

Role and responsibility of the obstetrician in performing an abortion, by A. Coletta. MINERVA GINECOLOGIA 28(9):706-712, September, 1976.

Role of the obstetrician in performing an abortion. Objections of conscience, by N. Damiani. MINERVA GINECOLOGIA 28(9):728-732, September, 1976.

Tocolysis in obstetrics, by W. Grabensberger. OSTERREICHISCHE KRANKENPFLEGEZEITSEHRIFT 26(11):358-364, 1976.

Use of prostaglandins in obstetrics, by W. Wells, et al. REVISTA CHILENA DE OBSTETRICIA Y GINECOLOGIA 40(6):343-359, 1975.

ORCIPRENALINE

OUTPATIENT ABORTION
see: Hospitals

OXYTOCIN
Induction of abortion and labor by extraamniotic isotonic saline, with or without addition of oxytocin, in cases of missed abortion, missed labor and antepartum fetal death, by M. Blum, et al. INTERNATIONAL SURGERY 62(2):95-96, February, 1977.

Induction of midtrimester abortion with intra-amniotic urea and intravenous oxytocin, by W. G. Smith, et al. AMERICAN JOURNAL OF OBSTETRICS AND GYNECOLOGY 127(3):228-231, 1977. (Bio. Abstrs. May, 1977, 59034)

Prostaglandin F2alpha, hypertonic saline, and oxytocin in midtrimester abortion, by A. Adachi, et al. NEW YORK STATE JOURNAL OF MEDICINE 77(1):46-49, January, 1977.

Second trimester abortion: single dose intra-amniotic injection of prostaglandin F2a with intravenous oxytocin augmentation, by G. Perry, et al. PROSTAGLANDINS 13(5):987-994, 1977. (Bio. Abstrs. October, 1977, 40677)

Uterine rupture following midtrimester abortion by laminaria, prostaglandin F2alpha, and oxytocin: report of two cases, by D. Propping, et al. AMERICAN JOURNAL OF OBSTETRICS AND GYNECOLOGY 128(6):689-690, July 15, 1977.

Uterine trauma associated with midtrimester abortion induced by intra-amniotic prostaglandin F2a with and without concomitant use of oxytocin, by G. Perry, et al. PROSTAGLANDINS 13(6):1147-1160, 1977. (Bio. Abstrs. December, 1977, 72336)

PARAMEDICS

PARSLEY EXTRACT

PATIENT COUNSELING
see: Sociology and Behavior

PENTAZOCINE

PHARMACISTS

PHYSICIANS
see also: Psychology
Sociology and Behavior

Abortion on demand [letters] . THE NEW YORK TIMES
May 15, VI, 62, 1977.

Abortion views and practices among Danish family physicians, by M. Gammeltoft, et al. JOURNAL OF BIO-
SOCIAL SCIENCE 8(3):287-292, 1976. (Socio. Abstrs.
1977, 7713508)

Abortion: why the doctors are closing ranks against new
curbs, by P. Healy. TIMES p. 14, July 8, 1977.

Between guilt and gratification: abortion doctors reveal their
feelings, by N. Rosen. NEW YORK TIMES MAGAZINE
pp. 70+, April 17, 1977.

Doctors have varied reactions to abortion. OUR SUNDAY
VISITOR 66:3, May 29, 1977.

Dr. Mildred Jefferson speaks her mind; cond from the Boston
Sunday Globe, December 5, 1976, by O. McManus.
CATHOLIC DIGEST 41:63-67, June, 1977.

The influence of physicians' attitudes on abortion perfor-
mance, patient management and professional fees, by
C. A. Nathanson, et al. FAMILY PLANNING PERSPEC-
TIVES 9(4):158-163, July-August, 1977.

Towards a practical implementation of the abortion decision: the interests of the physician, the woman and the fetus. DE PAUL LAW REVIEW 25:676-706, Spring, 1976.

POLITICS
Abortion and democratic politics, by M. Simms. NEW HUMANIST 93:15-17, May-August, 1977.

The politics of abortion; from the Supreme Court, Congress, and the Department of Health, Education, and Welfare, by P. Steinfels. COMMONWEAL 104:456, July 22, 1977.

Prophecy and politics: abortion in the election of 1976, by J. Hitchcock. WORLDVIEW 20:25-26+, March, 1977.

Supreme Court abortion decisions—a challenge to use political process, by E. J. Schulte. HOSPITAL PROGRESS 58:22-23, August, 1977.

POPULATION
see also: Demography

The effect of legalization of abortion on population growth and public health, by C. Tietze. FAMILY PLANNING PERSPECTIVES 7(3):123-127, 1975. (Socio. Abstrs. 1977, 7717047)

Population growth and abortion legislation, by K. Sundström-Feigenberg. LAKARTIDNINGEN 73(44):3747-3752, October 27, 1976.

POTASSIUM AMPICILLIN

PREGNANCY INTERRUPTION
see: Induced Abortion

PROGESTERONE
A comparative study of plasma 17beta-oestradiol, proges-

terone, placental lactogen and chorionic gonadotrophin in abortion induced with intra-amniotic prostaglandin F2alpha, by R. H. Ward, et al. BRITISH JOURNAL OF OBSTETRICS AND GYNAECOLOGY 84(5):363-369, May, 1977.

Comparison of vaginal cytology with plasma progesterone levels in early human pregnancy, by I. Khanna, et al. INDIAN JOURNAL OF MEDICAL RESEARCH 64(9): 1267-1271, 1976. (Bio. Abstrs. May, 1977, 50500)

The gynecological and endocrinological sequelae after the use of MAP during the pregnancy, by E. Padovani, et al. FRACASTORO 68(1-2):101-117, 1975. (Bio. Abstrs. December, 1977, 66288)

Plasma progesterone in women with a history of recurrent early abortions, by S. K. Yip, et al. FERTILITY AND STERILITY 28(2):151-155, 1977. (Bio. Abstrs. June, 1977, 62721)

Prevention of the abortifacient action of antiprogesterone serum by progesterone, by A. I. Csapo, et al. AMERICAN JOURNAL OF OBSTETRICS AND GYNECOLOGY 128(2):212-214, May 15, 1977.

Progesterone levels in amniotic fluid and maternal plasma in prostaglandin F2a-induced midtrimester abortion, by Z. Koren, et al. OBSTETRICS AND GYNECOLOGY 48(4):473-474, 1976. (Bio. Abstrs. February, 1977, 22682)

Role of small doses of estrogens and progesterone in prevention of early abortions, by V. I. Bodiazhina, et al. AKUSHERSTVO I GINAKOLOGIIA (Moscow) (10):31-35, October, 1976.

PROSTAGLANDINS
The abortifacient and oxytocic effects of an intravaginal silicone rubber device containing a 0.5% concentration of

15(S)-15-methyl-prostaglandin F2alpha methyl ester, by N. H. Lauersen, et al. AMERICAN JOURNAL OF OB-STETRICS AND GYNECOLOGY 127(7):784-787, April 1, 1977.

The abortifacient effectiveness and plasma prostaglandin concentrations with 15(S)-15-methyl prostaglandin F2alpha methyl ester-containing vaginal silastic devices, by N. H. Lauersen, et al. FERTILITY AND STERILITY 27(12):1366-1373, December, 1976.

Abortion deaths associated with the use of prostaglandin F2a, by W. Cates, Jr., et al. AMERICAN JOURNAL OF OBSTETRICS AND GYNECOLOGY 127(3):219-222, 1977. (Bio. Abstrs. June, 1977, 65533)

Amniotic fluid adenosine 3' 5'—monophosphate in prosta-glandin-induced midtrimester abortions, by R. R. Weiss, et al. OBSTETRICS AND GYNECOLOGY 49(2):223-226, 1977. (Bio. Abstrs. July, 1977, 4344)

Changes in the concentration of cortisol in amniotic fluid after intra-amniotic prostaglandin for midtrimester abor-tion, by I. Z. MacKenzie, et al. BRITISH JOURNAL OF OBSTETRICS AND GYNECOLOGY 84(8):608-612, August, 1977.

Clinical application of prostaglandins in obstetrics and gynecology, by F. J. Brunnberg. ACTA BIOLOGICA ET MEDICA GERMANICA 35(8-9):1243-1247, 1976.

Clinical comparison of abortifacient activity of vaginally administered prostaglandin E2 in two dosage forms, by T. J. Roseman, et al. AMERICAN JOURNAL OF OB-STETRICS AND GYNECOLOGY 129(2):225-227, September 15, 1977.

A clinical comparison of prostaglandin F2alpha and intra-amniotic saline for induction of midtrimester abortion, by G. S. Berger. ANNALES CHIURGIAE ET GYNAE-

KOLOGIAE FENNIAE 66(1):55-58, 1977.

Clinical experiences with prostaglandin E2 and F2 alpha in the termination of pregnancy and labor induction in intrauterine fetal death, by J. Kunz, et al. SCHWEI-ZERISCHE MEDIZINISCHE WOCHENSCHRIFT 107(22):757-763, June 4, 1977.

A comparative study of plasma 17beta-oestradiol, progesterone, placental lactogen and chorionic gonadotrophin in abortion induced with intra-amniotic prostaglandin F2alpha, by R. H. Ward, et al. BRITISH JOURNAL OF OBSTETRICS AND GYNAECOLOGY 84(5):363-369, May, 1977.

Comparison between intra-amniotic administration of prostaglandin F2alpha and its 15-methyl derivative for induction of second trimester abortion, by O. Ylikorkala, et al. ANNALS OF CLINICAL RESEARCH 9(2):58-61, April, 1977. (Bio. Abstrs. November, 1977, 52789)

Cortisol levels in amniotic fluid in prostaglandin F2a-induced midtrimester abortion, by Z. Koren, et al. AMERICAN JOURNAL OF OBSTETRICS AND GYNECOLOGY 127(6):639-642, 1977. (Bio. Abstrs. July, 1977, 10540)

Effect of 15(s)15-methyl-PGF2alpha-methyl ester vaginal suppositories on circulating hormone levels in early pregnancy, by C. P. Puri, et al. PROSTAGLANDINS 13(2): 363-373, February, 1977.

The effect of prostaglandin F2a on endocrine parameters in early pregnancy, by M. Schmidt-Gollwitzer, et al. ARCHIV FUR GYNAEKOLOGIE 222(2):149-157, 1977. (Bio. Abstrs. September, 1977, 28936)

Effect of prostaglandin PGF2a on the synthesis on placental proteins and human placental lactogen (HPL), by O. Genbacev, et al. PROSTAGLANDINS 13(4):723-733, 1977. (Bio. Abstrs. September, 1977, 28782)

Evaluation of intramuscular 15(S)-15-methyl prostaglandin F2a tromethamine salt for induction of abortion, medications to attenuate side effects, and intracervical laminaria tents, by W. Gruber, et al. FERTILITY AND STERILITY 27(9):1009-1023, 1976. (Bio. Abstrs. March, 1977, 28807)

Evaluation of two dose schedules of 15(S)15 methyl PGF2a methyl ester vaginal suppositories for dilatation of cervix prior to vacuum aspiration for late first trimester abortions, by B. Zoremthangi, et al. CONTRACEPTION 15(3):285-294, 1977. (Bio. Abstrs. August, 1977, 16522)

Extra-amniotic 15(S)-15 methyl PGF2a to induce abortion: a study of three administration schedules. PROSTAGLANDINS 12(3):443-453, 1976. (Bio. Abstrs. January, 1977, 10597)

Failed prostaglandin F2alpha-induced abortion: a case report, by R. G. Cunanan, Jr., et al. OBSTETRICS AND GYNECOLOGY 49(4):495-496, April, 1977.

Fertility control—symposium on prostaglandins: comment, by W. E. Brenner. FERTILITY AND STERILITY 27(12):1380-1386, December, 1976.

Find D&E is safest method of midtrimester abortion, but saline is less risky than prostaglandins: JPSA. FAMILY PLANNING PERSPECTIVES 8:275, November-December, 1976.

Hormone changes in relation to the time of fetal death after prostaglandin-induced abortion, by I. S. Fraser, et al. PROSTAGLANDINS 13(6):1161-1178, 1977. (Bio. Abstrs. November, 1977, 58981)

Hypokalemia and cardiac arrhythmia associated with prostaglandin-induced abortion, by R. L. Burt, et al. OBSTETRICS AND GYNECOLOGY 50(1 Suppl):45S-46S,

July, 1977.

Induced abortion in the 8-9th week of pregnancy with vaginally administered 15-methyl PGF2 methyl ester, by A. Leader, et al. PROSTAGLANDINS 12(4):631-637, 1976. (Bio. Abstrs. February, 1977, 22692)

Induced abortion with intramuscular administration of 15(S)-15methyl-prostaglandin F2 alpha, by H. Halle, et al. ZENTRALBLATT FUR GYNAEKOLOGIE 99(9):537-540, 1977.

Induction of abortion in the 2d and 3d trimester with prostaglandins, PGE2 and PGF2 alpha. Indications for differences between the effect of PGE2 and PGF2 alpha on the pregnant uterus, by M. Cornely. MEDIZINISCHE MONATSSCHRIFT 31(2):73-79, February, 1977.

Induction of first and second trimester abortion by the vaginal administration of 15-methyl-PGF2alpha methyl ester, by M. Bygdeman, et al. ADVANCES IN PROSTAGLANDIN AND THROMBOXANE RESEARCH 2:693-704, 1976.

Induction of labor in patients with missed abortion and fetal death in utero with prostaglandin E2 suppositories, by N. H. Lauersen, et al. AMERICAN JOURNAL OF OBSTETRICS AND GYNECOLOGY 127(6):609-611, 1977. (Bio. Abstrs. August, 1977, 16534)

Induction of midtrimester abortion by the combined method of continuous extravovular infusion of prostaglandin F2alpha and intracervical laminaria tents, by J. E. Hodgson, et al. FERTILITY AND STERILITY 27(12):1359-1365, December, 1976. (Bio. Abstrs. June, 1977, 70935)

Induction of mid-trimester abortion with intra-amniotic injection of prostaglandin F-2alpha, by A. J. Horowitz. MINNESOTA MEDICINE 60(7 Pt 1):509-512, July, 1977.

Intra-amniotic administration of 15(S)-15-methyl prostaglandin F2a for the induction of mid-trimester abortion,
by J. R. Dingfelder, et al. AMERICAN JOURNAL OF
OBSTETRICS AND GYNECOLOGY 125(6):821-826,
1976. (Bio. Abstrs. February, 1977, 17300)

Intra-amniotic prostaglandin F2a and urea for midtrimester
abortion, by L. Wellman, et al. FERTILITY AND
STERILITY 27(12):1374-1379, 1976. (Bio. Abstrs.
June, 1977, 70933)

Intra-amniotic urea and prostaglandin F2a for midtrimester
abortion: a modified regimen, by R. T. Burkman, et al.
AMERICAN JOURNAL OF OBSTETRICS AND GYNE-
COLOGY 126(3):328-333, 1976. (Bio. Abstrs. February, 1977, 22702)

Intramuscular prostaglandin (15S)-15-methyl PGF2a (THAM)
in midtrimester abortion, by E. S. Henriques, et al.
PROSTAGLANDINS 13(1):183-191, 1977. (Bio.
Abstrs. May, 1977, 59036)

Intrauterine extra-amnial administration of prostaglandin F2
alpha for the induction of abortion in primigravidae and
problem cases, by G. Göretzlehner, et al. ZENTRAL-
BLATT FUR GYNAEKOLOGIE 98(20):1252-1257,
1976.

Intrauterine extra-amniotic 15(S)-15-methyl prostaglandin
F2a for induction of early mid-trimester abortion, by A.
G. Shapiro. FERTILITY AND STERILITY 27(9):1024-
1028, 1976. (Bio. Abstrs. March, 1977, 28805)

Intrauterine prostaglandin E2 as an postconceptional abortifacient, by I. Z. Mackenzie, et al. ADVANCES IN PRO-
STAGLANDIN AND THROMBOXANE RESEARCH
2:687-691, 1976.

Introduction of second trimester abortions with 15-(S)-
methyl prostaglandin F2alpha by intra-uterine and intra-

muscular routes, by V. Hingorani, et al. JOURNAL OF THE INDIAN MEDICAL ASSOCIATION 66(11):279-283, June 1, 1976.

The kinetics of extraamniotically injected prostaglandins to induce midtrimester abortion, by I. Z. MacKenzie, et al. PROSTAGLANDINS 13(5):975-986, 1977. (Bio. Abstrs. October, 1977, 40678)

Methods of artificial termination of pregnancy with special consideration of the use of prostaglandin, by R. Kepp. GEBURTSHILFE UND FRAUENHEILKUNDE 36(9): 700-705, September, 1976.

Midtrimester abortion by intraamniotic prostaglandin F2alpha. Safer than saline? by D. A. Grimes, et al. OBSTETRICS AND GYNECOLOGY 49(5):612-616, May, 1977.

Midtrimester abortion: a comparison of intra-amniotic prostaglandin F2a and hypertonic saline, by M. I. Ragab, et al. INTERNATIONAL JOURNAL OF GYNAECOLOGY AND OBSTETRICS 14(5):393-396, 1976. (Bio. Abstrs. October, 1977, 40668)

Midtrimester and missed abortion treated with intramuscular 15 (s)-15 methyl PGF2alpha, by A. P. Lange, et al. PRO-STAGLANDINS 14(2):389-395, August, 1977.

Pharmacokinetic studies on 15-methyl-PGF2alpha and its methyl ester after administration to the human via various routes for induction of abortion, by K. Gréen, et al. ADVANCES IN PROSTAGLANDIN AND THROM-BOXANE RESEARCH 2:719-725, 1976.

Preoperative cervical dilatation by oral PGE2, by A. S. Van Den Bergh. CONTRACEPTION 14(6):631-638, 1976. (Bio. Abstrs. April, 1977, 41035)

Progesterone levels in amniotic fluid and maternal plasma

in prostaglandin F2a-induced midtrimester abortion, by Z. Koren, et al. OBSTETRICS AND GYNECOLOGY 48(4):473-474, 1976. (Bio. Abstrs. February, 1977, 22682)

Prostaglandin E2 in a diaphragm. A further note, by H. Schulman, et al. PROSTAGLANDINS 13(4):751-753, April, 1977.

Prostaglandin E2 induction of labor for fetal demise, by D. R. Kent, et al. OBSTETRICS AND GYNECOLOGY 48(4):475-478, 1976. (Bio. Abstrs. February, 1977, 22681)

Prostaglandin F2alpha, hypertonic saline, and oxytocin in midtrimester abortion, by A. Adachi, et al. NEW YORK STATE JOURNAL OF MEDICINE 77(1):46-49, January, 1977.

Prostaglandin impact, by A. I. Csapo. ADVANCES IN PRO-STAGLANDIN AND THROMBOXANE RESEARCH 2:705-718, 1976.

The prostaglandins, by J. M. Beazley. NURSING TIMES 72:1800-1803, November 18, 1976.

Prostaglandins and post abortion luteolysis in early pregnancy, by A. Leader, et al. PROSTAGLANDINS 10(5): 889-897, 1976. (Bio. Abstrs. January, 1977, 4174)

Repeated extra-amniotic administration of prostaglandin F2a for midtrimester abortion, by M. Ragab, et al. INTER-NATIONAL JOURNAL OF GYNAECOLOGY AND OB-STETRICS 14(4):337-340, 1976. (Bio. Abstrs. September, 1977, 34567)

Second trimester abortion: single dose intra-amniotic injection of prostaglandin F2a with intravenous oxytocin augmentation, by G. Perry, et al. PROSTAGLANDINS 13(5):987-994, 1977. (Bio. Abstrs. October, 1977,

40677)

Second trimester abortion with intramuscular injections of 15-methyl prostaglandin F2a, by C. A. Ballard, et al. CONTRACEPTION 14(5):541-550, 1976. (Bio. Abstrs. March, 28800)

The synergistic effect of calcium and prostaglandin F2a in second trimester abortion: a pilot study, by L. Weinstein, et al. OBSTETRICS AND GYNECOLOGY 48(4):469-471, 1976. (Bio. Abstrs. February, 1977, 22683)

Termination of abnormal intrauterine pregnancies with intramuscular administration of dihomo 15 methyl prostaglandin F2alpha, by S. M. Karim, et al. BRITISH JOURNAL OF OBSTETRICS AND GYNAECOLOGY 83(11): 885-889, November, 1976.

Termination of pregnancy with prostaglandin analogues, by S. M. Karim, et al. ADVANCES IN PROSTAGLANDIN AND THROMBOXANE RESEARCH 2:727-736, 1976.

Termination of pregnancy with vaginal administration of 16, 16 dimethyl prostaglandin E2 p-benzaldehyde semicarbazone ester, by S. M. Karim, et al. BRITISH JOURNAL OF OBSTETRICS AND GYNAECOLOGY 84(2):135-137, February, 1977.

Therapeutic intra-amniotic, transabdominal induction of abortion in the 2nd trimenon using prostaglandin F2alpha, by E. Sacha, et al. GYNAEKOLOGISCHE RUNDSCHAU 16(4):261-263, 1976.

A tissue-selective prostaglandin E2 analog with potent antifertility effects, by H. J. Hess, et al. EXPERIENTIA 33(8):1076-1077, August 15, 1977.

Use of combination prostaglandin F2a and hypertonic saline for midtrimester abortion, by M. Borten. PROSTA-GLANDINS 12(4):625-630, 1976. (Bio. Abstrs. February, 1977, 22694)

Use of prostaglandins in obstetrics, by W. Wells, et al. RE-VISTA CHILENA DE OBSTETRICIA Y GINECOLOGIA 40(6):343-359, 1975.

Uterine rupture following midtrimester abortion by laminaria, prostaglandin F2alpha, and oxytocin: report of two cases, by D. Propping, et al. AMERICAN JOURNAL OF OB-STETRICS AND GYNECOLOGY 128(6):689-690, July 15, 1977.

Uterine trauma associated with midtrimester abortion in-duced by intra-amniotic prostaglandin F2a with and without concomitant use of oxytocin, by G. Perry, et al. PROSTAGLANDINS 13(6):1147-1160, 1977. (Bio. Abstrs. December, 1977, 72336)

Vaginal administration of a single dose of 16, 16 dimethyl prostaglandin E2 p-benzaldehyde semicarbazone ester for pre-operative cervical dilatation in first trimester nulliparae, by S. M. Karim, et al. BRITISH JOURNAL OF OBSTETRICS AND GYNECOLOGY 84(4):269-271, April, 1977.

Vaginal prostaglandin E2 for missed abortion and intrau-terine fetal death, by A. Rutland, et al. AMERICAN JOURNAL OBSTETRICS AND GYNECOLOGY 128(5): 503-506, 1977. (Bio. Abstrs. December, 1977, 64654)

Work in progress. Menstrual induction with vaginal infusion of the PGF2alpha analogue ICI 81008, by P. Mocsary. PROSTAGLANDINS 13(4):807-808, April, 1977.

PSYCHOLOGY
see also: Sociology and Behavior

Abortion applicants: characteristics distinguishing dropouts remaining pregnant and those having abortion, by M. E. Swigar, et al. AMERICAN JOURNAL OF PUBLIC

HEALTH 67:142-150, February, 1977.

Abortion counselling: a new role for nurses, by B. Easterbrook, et al. CANADIAN NURSE 73:28-30, January, 1977.

Are you sorry you had an abortion? Interviews, by M. Rockmore. GOOD HOUSEKEEPING 185:120-121+, July, 1977.

Attitudes of women who have had abortion, by I. Bogen. THE JOURNAL OF SEX RESEARCH 10(2):97-109, 1974. (Socio. Abstrs. 1977, 7714333)

Comments on Cameron and Tichenor's remarks on our 1966 paper, by H. Forssman, et al. PSYCHOLOGICAL REPORTS 39(2):400, 1976. (Psycho. Abstrs. 1977, 8100)

Comparative-obstetrical views and experimental investigations concerning psychosomatic disorders during pregnancy and parturition, by C. Naaktgeboren, et al. ZEITSCHRIFT FUER TIERZUECHTUNG UND ZUECHTUNGSBIOLOGIE 93(3-4):264-320, 1976. (Bio. Abstrs. October, 1977, 41331)

An epidemiological study of psychological correlates of delayed decisions to abort, by M. B. Bracken. DISSERTATION ABSTRACTS INTERNATIONAL 35(7-B):3425-3426, 1975. (Psycho. Abstrs. 1977, 3132)

Follow-up of 50 adolescent girls 2 years after abortion, by H. Cvejic, et al. CANADIAN MEDICAL ASSOCIATION JOURNAL 116(1):44-46, 1977. (Bio. Abstrs. November, 1977, 53455)

Grieving and unplanned pregnancy, by M. E. Swiger, et al. PSYCHIATRY 39(1):72-80, 1976. (Socio. Abstrs. 1977, 7715933)

How women feel about abortion: psychological, attitudinal

and physical effects of legal abortion, by L. M. Shalaby.
DISSERTATION ABSTRACTS INTERNATIONAL
36(4-A):2035, 1975. (Psycho. Abstrs. 1977, 10191)

Incidence of post-abortion psychosis: a prospective study, by
C. Brewer. BRITISH MEDICAL JOURNAL 1(6059):
476-477, February 19, 1977.

Influence of personality attributes on abortion experiences,
by E. W. Freeman. AMERICAN JOURNAL OF ORTHO-
PSYCHIATRY 47:503-513, July, 1977.

Interview follow-up of abortion applicant dropouts, by M. E.
Swiger, et al. SOCIAL PSYCHIATRY 11(3):135-143,
1976. (Psycho. Abstrs. 1977, 3120)

Obsessive-compulsive neurosis after viewing the fetus during
therapeutic abortion, by S. Lipper, et al. AMERICAN
JOURNAL OF PSYCHOTHERAPY 30(4):666-674,
1976. (Psycho. Abstrs. 1977, 8587)

The patient's view of the role of the primary care physician
in abortion, by R. H. Rosen. AMERICAN JOURNAL
OF PUBLIC HEALTH 67(9):863-865, September, 1977.

Predictive factors in emotional response to abortion: King's
termination study, by E. M. Belsey, et al. SOCIAL
SCIENCE AND MEDICINE 11:71-82, January, 1977.

Psychologic impact on nursing students of participation in
abortion, by A. Hurwitz, et al. NURSING RESEARCH
26(2):112-120, March-April, 1977.

Psychological aspects in medical termination of pregnancy,
by J. Joseph. CHRISTIAN NURSE pp. 20-22, June,
1976.

Psychological sequelae of abortion, by A. V. Gordon. NEW
ZEALAND PSYCHOLOGIST 5(1):37-47, 1976.
(Psycho. Abstrs. 1977, 6201)

The psychosocial factors of the abortion experience: a critical review. PSYCHOLOGY OF WOMEN QUARTERLY 1(1):79-103, February, 1976. (Soc. Abstrs. 1977, 77I5928)

Recent changes in the emotional reactions of therapeutic abortion applicants, by S. Meikle, et al. CANADIAN PSYCHIATRIC ASSOCIATION JOURNAL 22(2):67-70, March, 1977.

Requests for abortion: a psychiatrist's view, by R. Mester. ISRAEL ANNALS OF PSYCHIATRY AND RELATED DISCIPLINES 14(3):294-299, 1976. (Psycho. Abstrs. 1977, 13126)

Review of the progress of psychiatric opinion regarding emotional complications of therapeutic abortion, by G. W. Hubbard, II. SOUTHERN MEDICAL JOURNAL 70:588-590, May, 1977.

Role of psychotherapy in complex treatment of spontaneous abortions, by A. Z. Khasin, et al. AKUSHERSTVO I GINEKOLOGIIA (Moscow) (10):35-39, October, 1976.

Sex guilt in abortion patients, by M. Gerrard. JOURNAL OF CONSULTING AND CLINICAL PSYCHOLOGY 45:708, August, 1977.

Sexology and abortion with respect to their psychological and socioeconomic repercussions, by A. De Leonardis. MINERVA GINECOLOGIA 28(9):737-739, September, 1976.

Sexual experimentation and pregnancy in young black adolescents, by M. Gispert, et al. AMERICAN JOURNAL OF OBSTETRICS AND GYNECOLOGY 126(4):459-466, 1976. (Bio. Abstrs. February, 1977, 23255)

Sociologic, ethical and psychological aspects of abortion, by R. De Vicienti. MINERVA GINECOLOGIA 28(9):739-

741, September, 1976.

Submission to the Royal Commission on contraception, sterlization and abortion, by the New Zealand Psychological Society. NEW ZEALAND PSYCHOLOGIST 5(1):48-56, 1976. (Psycho. Abstrs. 1977, 6215)

The Swedish "Children born to women denied abortion" study: a radical criticism, by P. Cameron, et al. PSYCHOLOGICAL REPORTS 39(2):391-394, October, 1976.

Therapeutic abortion and psychiatric disturbance in Canadian women, by E. R. Greenglass. CANADIAN PSYCHIATRIC ASSOCIATION JOURNAL 21(7):453-460, November, 1976.

Therapeutic abortion, fertility plans, and psychological sequelae, by E. R. Greenglass. AMERICAN JOURNAL OF ORTHOPSYCHIATRY 47:119-126, January, 1977.

Third time unlucky: a study of women who have three or more legal abortions, by C. Brewer. JOURNAL OF BIOSOCIAL SCIENCE 9(1):99-195, 1977. (Bio. Abstrs. December, 1977, 65346)

PUBLIC HEALTH

Abortion as a public health argument, by G. Ciasca. MINERVA GINECOLOGIA 28(9):719-721, September, 1976.

The effect of legalization of abortion on population growth and public health, by C. Tietze. FAMILY PLANNING PERSPECTIVES 7(3):123-127, 1975. (Socio. Abstrs. 1977, 77I7047)

Publicity and the public health: the elimination of IUC-related abortion deaths, by W. Cates, Jr., et al. FAMILY PLANNING PERSPECTIVES 9:138-140, May-June, 1977.

RADIOLOGISTS

REFERRAL AGENCIES SERVICES
see: Sociology and Behavior

REGITINE

RELIGION AND ETHICS
Abortion, analogies and the emergence of value, by P. F. Camenisch. THE JOURNAL OF RELIGIOUS ETHICS 4:131-158, Spring, 1976.

Abortion and Catholic public officials: statement, by J. Marshall, et al. ORIGINS 7:136-138, August 11, 1977.

Abortion and the golden rule, by R. M. Hare. PHILOSOPHY AND PUBLIC AFFAIRS 4:201-222, Spring, 1975; Reply by G. Sher, 6:185-190, Winter, 1977.

Abortion and human rights, by N. C. Gillespie. ETHICS 87:237-243, April, 1977.

Abortion and the right to life, by L. S. Carrier. SOCIAL THEORY AND PRACTICE 3(4):381-401, 1975. (Socio. Abstrs. 1977, 7718239)

Abortion and the sanctity of life, by W. D. Cobb. ENCOUNTER (CHRISTIAN THEOLOGICAL SEMINARY) 38:273-287, Summer, 1977.

Abortion and simple consciousness, by W. S. Pluhar. THE JOURNAL OF PHILOSOPHY 74:159-172, March, 1977.

Abortion: a challenge to Halakhah, by B. Greenberg. JUDAISM p. 201, Spring, 1976.

Abortion: from the perspective of responsibility, by E. C. Gardner. PERKINS SCHOOL OF THEOLOGY JOURNAL 30:10-28, Spring, 1977.

Abortion in the law: an essay on absurdity, by L. H. Newton. ETHICS 87:244-250, April, 1977.

Abortion in the moral reflections of the Catholic physician, by N. Miccolis. MINERVA GINECOLOGIA 28(9):742-746, September, 1976.

Abortion, property rights, and the right to life, by L. H. O'Driscoll. PERSONALIST 58:99-114, April, 1977.

Abortion study with names. THE NEW YORK TIMES (M) May 15, IV, 1:5, 1977.

Abortion: waging war on the poor; reprint from Forum Letter, September 16, 1977, by R. Weuhaus. OUR SUN-DAY VISITOR MAGAZINE 66:11, November 13, 1977.

Agonizing decisions in mental retardation, by R. C. Yeaworth. AMERICAN JOURNAL OF NURSING 77:864-867, May, 1977.

The American way of death, by H. Brown. MOODY MONTH-LY p. 32, December, 1976.

An analysis of clergymen's attitudes toward abortion, by S. Price-Bonham, et al. REVIEW OF RELIGIOUS RE-SEARCH 17(1):15-27, 1975. (Socio. Abstrs. 1977, 7715263)

Another double standard; call to concern campaign. AMER-ICA 137:274, October 29, 1977.

Attitudes of women who have had abortion, by I. Bogen. THE JOURNAL OF SEX RESEARCH 10(2):97-109, 1974. (Socio. Abstrs. 1977, 7714333)

Bernardin finds gain in esteem for Catholics of U.S., by K. A. Briggs. THE NEW YORK TIMES (M) March 3, 16:2, 1977.

Born and the unborn alike; position of the Catholic Church, by A. Bernard. AMERICA 136:270-272, March 26, 1977.

C&C symposium, paying for abortion: is the court wrong? CHRISTIANITY AND CRISIS 37:202-207, September 19, 1977.

Catholic prelates organizing a drive against abortions, by K. A. Briggs. THE NEW YORK TIMES (M) August 17, 1:4, 1977.

Changing abortion debate, by R. N. Ostling. THEOLOGY TODAY 34:161-166, July, 1977.

Charges sisters' statement undermines bishops' stand, by T. Barbarie. OUR SUNDAY VISITOR 66:2, November 6, 1977.

Choose life: promoting the value and quality of life; LCWR Task Force report, August 28, 1977. ORIGINS 7:161+, September 1, 1977.

The Christian and abortion, by M. Leggett. CHRISTIAN STANDARD p. 7, December 5, 1976.

Civil law and Christian morality: abortion and the churches, by C. Curran. CLERGY REVIEW 62:227-242, June, 1977.

Danger: constitutional convention ahead, by E. Doerr. HUMANIST 37:50-51, March, 1977.

Demystification of life, by R. J. Henle. COMMONWEAL 104:457-460, July 22, 1977.

Do potential people have moral rights, by M. A. Warren. PHILOSOPHY AND PUBLIC AFFAIRS 7:275-289, June, 1977.

Ethical considerations of prenatal genetic diagnosis, by J. F. Tormey. CLINICAL OBSTETRICS AND GYNECOLOGY 19(4):957-963, December, 1976.

Ethical problems in obstetrics and gynaecology, by J. Bonnar. WORLD OF IRISH NURSING 6(4):1, April, 1977.

Ethics and nurses, by C. J. Rogan. NURSING MIRROR AND MIDWIVES' JOURNAL 143:75-76, October 21, 1976.

Grievous moral mischief, by J. A. Tetlow. AMERICA 137: 359, November 19, 1977.

Hare, abortion and the golden rule, by H. Sher. PHILOSO-PHY AND PUBLIC AFFAIRS 6:185-190, Winter, 1977.

Hare on abortion, by R. Werner. ANALYSIS 36:177-181, June, 1976.

Helping hand awaits unwed mothers, by A. A. Narvaez. THE NEW YORK TIMES (M) February 13, XI, 6:5, 1977.

Human rights; do we practice what we preach; address to Knights of Columbus, August 16, 1977, by J. Bernardin. ORIGINS 7:201-204, September 15, 1977.

The humanity of the unborn; reprint from The Washington Post July 25, 1977, by H. Hyde. L'OSSERVATORE ROMANO 37(494):15, September, 1977.

Humans and persons, by L. Newton. ETHICS p. 332, July, 1975.

In necessity and sorrow [book]. A review, by N. E. Zinberg. THE NEW YORK TIMES January 9, VII, p. 6, 1977.

Interview follow-up of abortion applicant dropouts, by M. E. Swiger, et al. SOCIAL PSYCHIATRY 11(3):135-143,

1976. (Psycho. Abstrs. 1977, 3120)

Jain and Judaeo-Christian respect for life, by J. A. Miles, Jr.
AMERICAN ACADEMY OF RELIGION JOURNAL
44:453-457, September, 1976.

Killing with kindness, by K. Marquart. CONCORDIA
THEOLOGY QUARTERLY 41:44-49, January, 1977.

Medical ethics: fact or fantasy? by A. Doyle. AORN JOUR-
NAL 23:827-831, April, 1976.

Methodist women to meet only where E.R.A. wins. THE
NEW YORK TIMES (S) April 27, 18:6, 1977.

Mormon turnout overwhelms women's conference in Utah,
by J. M. Crewdson. THE NEW YORK TIMES (M) July
25, 26:4, 1977.

Of abortion and the unfairness of life, by L. Morrow. TIME
110:49, August 1, 1977.

Of ballots and morality, by F. B. Donnelly. THE NEW
YORK TIMES March 21, 26:5, 1977.

Orthodoxy and attitudes of clergymen towards homosexuality
and abortion, by T. C. Wagenaar, et al. REVIEW OF RE-
LIGIOUS RESEARCH 18(2):114-125, 1977. (Socio.
Abstrs. 1977, 77I8158)

Performing abortions; excerpt from In necessity and sorrow:
life and death in an abortion hospital, by M. Denes.
COMMENTARY 62:4+, December, 1976; 63:18+, January; 22+, February, 1977.

Poll at synod finds liberal views on sex, by G. Dugan. THE
NEW YORK TIMES (M) July 3, 32:1, 1977.

Pope equates abortion with "murder" of young. THE NEW
YORK TIMES (S) January 2, 5:1, 1977.

Religious tension in Saint Cloud; refusal of United Way funds to agencies making abortion referrals, by J. M. Wall. CHRISTIAN CENTURY 94:1019-1020, November 9, 1977.

The right to life; two messages of the Italian Episcopal Conference. THE POPE SPEAKS 22:260-263, November 3, 1977.

The sacred rights of life, by J. Basile. C.I.C.I.A.M.S. NOU-VELLES (3):25-37, 1976.

Scholars call pro-abortion statement irresponsible; a call to concern, constitutes a cause for concern, according to an interfaith grouping. OUR SUNDAY VISITOR 66:2, November 13, 1977.

Semantics, future generations, and the abortion problem: comments on a fallacious case against the morality of abortion, by J. Narveson. SOCIAL THEORY AND PRACTICE 3(4):461-485, 1975. (Socio. Abstrs. 1977, 7718254)

Sociologic, ethical and psychological aspects of abortion, by R. De Vicienti. MINERVA GINECOLOGIA 28(9):739-741, September, 1976.

That controversial anti-abortion ad—Grey nuns were behind it, by J. Dunlop. MARKETING 82:2, January 10, 1977.

Theologian: we can't outlaw abortion, by M. Winiarski. NATIONAL CATHOLIC REPORTER 14:1-2, October 28, 1977.

Three levels of discussion about abortion, by J. Carlson. CATHOLIC MIND p. 22, November, 1976.

Toward a context for the ethics of abortion, by W. O. Cross. ANGLICAN THEOLOGICAL REVIEW 59:212-220, April, 1977.

Viability, values, and the vast cosmos, by D. J. Horan. CATHOLIC LAWYER 22:1-37, Winter, 1976.

Welcome prepared, by E. Schaeffer. CHRISTIANITY TODAY 21:28-29, April 1, 1977.

When does life begin? by S. Chandrasekhar. POPULATION REVIEW 15(1-2):50-59, 1971. (Socio. Abstrs. 1977, 7715952)

Why is abortion wrong, by J. Donceel. AMERICAN p. 65, August 16, 1975.

Working together for Christ: facing the antilife challenge, by W. F. Sullivan. HOSPITAL PROGRESS 58(5):82-84+, May, 1977.

RESEARCH

Abortion and other signs of disease in cows experimentally infected with sarcocystis fusiformis from dogs, by R. Fayer, et al. JOURNAL OF INFECTIOUS DISEASES 134(6):624-628, December, 1976.

Abortion and reproductive performance of cattle in northern Nigeria: a questionnaire survey, by S. Nuru, et al. TROPICAL ANIMAL HEALTH AND PRODUCTION 8(4): 213-219, November, 1976.

Abortion in a mare due to coccidioidomycosis, by R. F. Langham, et al. JOURNAL OF THE AMERICAN VETERINARY MEDICAL ASSOCIATION 170(2): 178-180, January 15, 1977.

Abortion in sheep and goats in Cyprus [letter], by P. Fiset. VETERINARY RECORD 99(16):323, October 16, 1976.

Abortions in sheep and goats in Cyprus [letter], by R. W. Crowther. VETERINARY RECORD 99(23):466, December 4, 1976.

Abortive infection of mice inoculated intraperitoneally with chlamydia ovis, by A. Rodolakis. ANNALES DE RE-CHERCHES VETERINARES 7(2):195-205, 1976.

Abruptio placentae in rhesus monkey causing brain damage to the fetus [letter] , by R. E. Myers, et al. AMERICAN JOURNAL OF OBSTETRICS AND GYNECOLOGY 126(8):1048-1049, December 15, 1976.

Action of prostaglandin F2 alpha on pregnancy in mice. Prevention of its abortive property by progesterone, by L. Mercier-Parot, et al. COMPTES RENDUS DES SEANCES DE LA SOCIETE DE BIOLOGIE ET DE SES FILIALES 170(3):529-532, October, 1976.

Advances in the diagnosis of bovine abortion, by H. W. Dunne, et al. PROCEEDINGS–ANNUAL MEETING OF THE UNITED STATES ANIMAL HEALTH ASSO-CIATION (77):515-523, 1974.

Analysis of the abortive action induced by prostaglandin F2 alpha in the mouse. Study of ova and their transplanta-tion, by L. Mercier-Parot. COMPTES RENDUS DES SEANCES DE LA SOCIETE DE BIOLOGIE ET DE SES FILIALES 170(3):532-536, October, 1976.

Bacterial infection in cows associated with abortion, en-dometritis and sterility, by I. Gelev. VETERINARNO-MEDITSINSKI NAUKI 13(6):15-23, 1976.

Bovine abortion [letter] , by J. G. Maddox. VETERINARY RECORD 99(25-26):517+, December 25, 1976.

Bovine leptospirosis: demonstration of leptospires of the Hebdomadis serogroup in aborted fetuses and a prema-ture calf, by W. A. Ellis, et al. VETERINARY RECORD 99(22):430-432, November 27, 1976.

Bovine leptospirosis: infection by the Hebdomadis serogroup and abortion–a herd study, by W. A. Ellis, et al. VET·

ERINARY RECORD 99(21):409-412, November 20, 1976.

Bovine mycotic abortion: some epidemiological aspects, by B. M. Williams, et al. VETERINARY RECORD 100(18): 382-385, April 30, 1977.

Brucella abortus in the bitch, by S. R. Bicknell, et al. VETERINARY RECORD 99(5):85-86, July 31, 1976.

The diagnosis of salmonella abortion in cattle with particular reference to salmonella dublin. A review, by M. Hinton. JOURNAL OF HYGIENE 79(1):25-38, August, 1977.

Effect of L-10503 (a novel antifertility compound) on the synthesis and metabolism of prostaglandins in vivo and in vitro in the pregnant rat placenta, ovary, kidney, and lung, and in rat deciduoma, by L. J. Lerner, et al. ADVANCES IN PROSTAGLANDIN AND THROMBOXANE RESEARCH 2:645-653, 1976.

The effect of prostaglandin F2alpha on pregnancy in rats and attempts to counteract its abortifacient action, by L. Mercier-Parot, et al. COMPTES RENDUS HERDOMADAIRES DES SEANCES DE L'ACADEMIE DES SCIENCES; D: SCIENCES NATURELLES 283(4): 353-355, September 13, 1976.

Equine herpesviruses: type 3 as an abortigenic agent, by L. J. Gleeson, et al. AUSTRALIAN VETERINARY JOURNAL 52(8):349-354, August, 1976.

Experimental and epizootiologic evidence associating ornithodoros coriaceus koch (Acari: Argasidae) with the exposure of cattle to epizootic bovine abortion in California, by E. T. Schmidtmann, et al. JOURNAL OF MEDICAL ENTOMOLOGY 13(3):292-299, December 8, 1976.

Experimentally induced pine needle abortion in range cattle,
by L. F. James, et al. CORNELL VETERINARIAN
67(2):294-299, April, 1977.

Failure to demonstrate equine rhinopneumonitis virus as a
cause of abortion in mares in New Zealand, by H. G.
Pearce, et al. NEW ZEALAND VETERINARY JOUR-
NAL 24(7):127-131, July, 1976.

The growth of the ewe abortion chlamydial agent in McCoy
cell cultures, by D. Hobson, et al. JOURNAL OF COM-
PARATIVE PATHOLOGY 87(1):155-159, January,
1977.

Habitual abortion in cats [letter], by G. M. Acland, et al.
AUSTRALIAN VETERINARY JOURNAL 50(4):179-
180, April, 1974.

The isolation of Actinobacillus equuli from equine abortion
[letter], by R. F. Webb, et al. AUSTRALIAN VETERI-
NARY JOURNAL 52(2):100-101, February, 1976.

The isolation of a leptospire from an aborted bovine fetus,
by W. A. Ellis, et al. VETERINARY RECORD 99(23):
458-459, December 4, 1976.

Isolation of mycoplasmas from an aborted equine foetus
[letter], by A. R. Moorthy, et al. AUSTRALIAN VET-
ERINARY JOURNAL 52(8):385, August, 1976.

Isolation of spirillum/vivbrio-like organisms from bovine
fetuses, by W. A. Ellis, et al. VETERINARY RECORD
100(21):451-452, May 21, 1977.

The isolation of a strain of leptospira serogroup ictero-
haemorrhagiae from an aborted bovine foetus, by W.
A. Ellis, et al. BRITISH VETERINARY JOURNAL
133(1):108-109, January-February, 1977.

A mucosal disease virus as a cause of abortion hairy birth

coat and unthriftiness in sheep. 1. Infiction of pregnant ewes and observations on aborted foetuses and lambs dying before one week of age, by J. W. Plant, et al. AUSTRALIAN VETERINARY JOURNAL 52(2):57-63, February, 1976.

New findings on the physiology of reproduction in the dog and cat: consequences for the control of estrus, contraception abortion and therapy, by W. Jöchle. DEUTSCHE TIERAERZTLICHE WOCHENSCHRIFT 83(12):564-569, December 5, 1976.

OH research at Northwick Park, by M. Hamilton. OCCUPATIONAL HEALTH (London) 29:108-112, March, 1977.

Organisms associated with abortion and reproductive problems in cattle, by I. H. Siddique, et al. MODERN VETERINARY PRACTICE 57(10):809-811, October, 1976.

Ovine enzootic abortion diagnosis [letter], by P. A. Bloxham, et al. VETERINARY RECORD 100(17):371-372, April 23, 1977.

Pathogenesis of mycotic abortion in cows, by E. P. Kremlev. VETERINARIIA (7):71-74, July, 1977.

Perinatal foal mortality. Causes of foal death in Switzerland, by J. Hösli. SCHWEIZER ARCHIV FUR TIERHEILKUNDE 119(3):103-110, March, 1977.

Possible role of feline T-strain mycoplasmas in cat abortion, by R. J. Tan, et al. AUSTRALIAN VETERINARY JOURNAL 50(4):142-145, April, 1974.

Preventing pregnancy after mismating in dogs. MODERN VETERINARY PRACTICE 57(12):1041-1042, December, 1976.

Prevention of abortion and premature labor in cattle and horses, by M. Vandeplassche, et al. DEUTSCHE TIER-

AERZLICHE WOCHENSCHRIFT 83(12):554-556, December 5, 1976.

Prevention of the pathology of fertility in cows, by E. P. Kremlev, et al. VETERINARIIA (9):60-62, 1976.

Prostaglandin F2alpha induced luteolysis, hypothermia, and abortions in beagle bitches, by P. W. Concannon, et al. PROSTAGLANDINS 13(3):533-542, March, 1977.

Recovery of uterine embryos in Rhesus monkeys, by P. R. Hurst, et al. BIOLOGY OF REPRODUCTION 15(4): 429-434, November, 1976.

Results of five-year survey on causes of bovine abortions, by K. Wohlgemuth, et al. PROCEEDINGS—ANNUAL MEETING OF THE UNITED STATES ANIMAL HEALTH ASSOCIATION (77):509-514, 1974.

Several years of diagnostic studies on the EHV 1 abortion in thoroughbred studs following the introduction of vaccination, by C. von Benten, et al. BERLINER UND MUNCHENER TIERARZTLICHE WOCHENSCHRIFT 90(9):176-180, May 1, 1977.

Stillbirth and abortion in hamsters by experimental infection with Japanese encephalitis virus. I. Occurrence of still-birth and abortion, by K. Takehara, et al. VIRUS 25(4): 253-260, 1975.

Studies on prostaglandin-induced abortion in guinea pigs, by W. Elger, et al. ADVANCES IN PROSTAGLANDIN AND THROMBOXANE RESEARCH 2:673-677, 1976.

A study of the pathogenesis of experimental salmonella dublin abortion in cattle, by G. A. Hall, et al. JOUR-NAL OF COMPARATIVE PATHOLOGY 87(1):53-65, January, 1977.

Subsequent fertility in heifers aborted using prostaglandins

at 45-60 days of pregnancy [letter], by R. I. Thain.
AUSTRALIAN VETERINARY JOURNAL 53(4):
198, April, 1977.

Summarizing data on bovine abortions with the aid of a
computer, by W. T. Hubbert, et al. PROCEEDINGS—
ANNUAL MEETING OF THE UNITED STATES ANI-
MAL HEALTH ASSOCIATION (77):500-508, 1974.

A summary of some of the pathogenetic mechanisms involved in bovine abortion, by R. B. Miller. CANADIAN
VETERINARY JOURNAL 18(4):87-95, April, 1977.

Surviving trophoblastic giant cells and ovarian function after
prostaglandin-induced abortion in the golden hamster,
by R. Pijnenborg. JOURNAL OF ENDOCRINOLOGY
71(2):271-272, November, 1976.

Suspected sarcocystis infections of the bovine placenta and
foetus, by B. L. Munday, et al. ZEITSCHRIFT FUR
PARASITENKUNDE 51(1):129-132, December 30,
1976.

Toxoplasmosis in sheep. The relative importance of the infection as a cause of reproductive loss in sheep in Norway, by H. Waldeland. ACTA VETERINARIA SCAN-
DINAVICA 17(4):412-425, 1976.

The use of cloprostenol for the termination of pregnancy
and the expulsion of mummified fetus in cattle, by P. S.
Jackson, et al. VETERINARY RECORD 100(17):361-
363, April 23, 1977.

RESPIRATORY SYSTEM

RIFAMPICIN

RIVANOL

RUBELLA
Epidemiology of rubella during 1971-1975. Comparison
with abortus cases and malformed newborn in Lombardia
(Italy), by V. Carreri, et al. ANNALI SCLAVO 18(5):
714-719, September-October, 1976.

SEPSIS

SEPTIC ABORTION AND SEPTIC SHOCK
see also: Complications
Sepsis

Amikacin for treatment of septic abortions: summary, by J.
Bravo-Scandoval, et al. JOURNAL OF INFECTIOUS
DISEASES 134(Suppl):S380, November, 1976.

Antibiotic therapy of septic puerperal and postabortion
diseases, by V. K. Prorokova, et al. PEDIATRIIA AKU-
SHERSTVO I GINEKOLOGIIA (3):33-36, May-June,
1977.

Biochemical indices in infectious diseases following labor and
abortion, by N. N. Kulikova, et al. AKUSHERSTVO I
GINEKOLOGIIA (4):35-39, April, 1976.

A case of toxoplasmosis detected by the Sabin-Feldman test,
by K. Altintas. MIKROBIYOLOJI BULTENI 11(1):
113-115, January, 1977.

A double-blind comparison of clindamycin with penicillin
plus chloramphenicol in treatment of septic abortion,
by A. W. Chow, et al. JOURNAL OF INFECTIOUS
DISEASES 135(Suppl):S35-39, March, 1977.

Efficacy of amikacin in septic abortion: serum and urine
antibiotic concentrations, by J. Bravo-Sandoval, et al.
JOURNAL OF INTERNATIONAL MEDICAL RE-
SEARCH 4(4):223-227, 1976.

Endotoxic shock in obstetrics, by R. Valle, et al. REVISTA

CHILENA DE OBSTETRICIA Y GINECOLOGIA
41(3):158-165, 1976.

Evaluation of hypercoagulability in septic abortion, by H.
Graeff, et al. HAEMOSTASIS 5(5):285-294, 1976.
(Bio. Abstrs. June, 1977, 63772)

Fever in a 22 years old woman. PRAXIS 65(38):1155-1156,
September 21, 1976.

Immunologic reacitivity in infectious diseases following labor
and abortion, by V. I. Kulakov, et al. AKUSHERSTVO I
GINEKOLOGIIA (Moscow) (4):32-35, April, 1976.

Management of the endotoxic shock in abortion, by G. Del
Rio, et al. REVISTA CHILENA DE OBSTETRICIA Y
GINECOLOGIA 41(3):166-173, 1976.

The management of septic abortion in an intensive care unit,
by R. D. Crane, et al. EUROPEAN JOURNAL OF IN-
TENSIVE CARE 2(3):135-138, November, 1976.

Maternal death and the I.U.D. [editorial]. LANCET 2(7997):
1234, December 4, 1976.

—. [letter], by R. A. Sparks, et al. LANCET 1(8002):98,
January 8, 1977.

Septic abortion due to invasive salmonella agona, by A. P.
Ball, et al. POSTGRADUATE MEDICAL JOURNAL
53(617):155-156, March, 1977.

Septic shock in obstetric-gynecologic practice, by I. T.
Riabtseva, et al. AKUSHERSTVO I GINEKOLOGIIA
(Moscow) (4):40-43, April, 1976.

Septicemia and abortion with the CU-7, by M. B. Viechnicki.
AMERICAN JOURNAL OF OBSTETRICS AND GYNE-
COLOGY 127(2):203, January 15, 1977.

Tactics in the management of patients with septic abortion, by S. A. Omarov, et al. AKUSHERSTVO I GINEKOLO-GIIA (Moscow) (4):46-48, April, 1976.

SOCIOLOGY AND BEHAVIOR
see also: Family Planning
Religion and Ethics

Abortion, abstract norms, and social control: the decision of the West German federal constitutional court, by H. Gerstein, et al. EMORY LAW JOURNAL 25:849-878, Fall, 1976.

Abortion applicants: characteristics distinguishing dropouts remaining pregnant and those having abortion, by M. E. Swigar, et al. AMERICAN JOURNAL OF PUBLIC HEALTH 67:142-146, February, 1977.

Abortion: back to square one [effect of anti-abortion movement], by L. Shapiro. MOTHER JONES 2:13-14, September-October, 1977.

Abortion: beyond rhetoric to access, by E. W. Freeman. SOCIAL WORK 21:483-487, November, 1976.

Abortion counselling: a new role for nurses, by B. Easterbrook, et al. CANADIAN NURSE 73:28-30, January, 1977.

Abortion: a dyadic perspective, by A. Rothstein. AMERICAN JOURNAL OF ORTHOPSYCHIATRY 47:111-118, January, 1977.

Abortion information: a guidance viewpoint, by P. L. Wolleat. SCHOOL COUNSELOR 22(5):338-341, 1975. (Psycho. Abstrs. 1977, 14033)

Abortion: let the silent majority prevail [editorial], by D. Anderson. CHATELAINE 50:2, January, 1977.

"Abortion on demand" [letter], by J. Bury. BRITISH MEDICAL JOURNAL 1(6066):975, April 9, 1977.

Abortion—one mother's view, by M. Duval. THE NEW YORK TIMES (M) October, 2, XI, 24:5, 1977.

Abortion or the unwanted child: a choice for a humanistic society. JOURNAL OF PEDIATRIC PSYCHOLOGY 1(2):62-67, Spring, 1976.

Abortion: a problem-solving approach. SOCIAL STUDIES 68(3):120-123, May-June, 1977.

Abortions and public policy, by A. Yankauer. AMERICAN JOURNAL OF PUBLIC HEALTH 67:817-818, September, 1977.

— [editorial], by A. Yankauer. AMERICAN JOURNAL OF PUBLIC HEALTH 67(7):604-605, July, 1977.

Anti-abortion myths. NEW HUMANIST 92:175-178, January-February, 1977.

Comments on Cameron and Tichnor's remarks on our 1966 paper, by H. Forssman, et al. PSYCHOLOGICAL REPORTS 39(2):400, October, 1976.

Consultation, when abortion is demanded, by W. Greve, et al. PSYCHOTHERAPY AND MEDICAL PSYCHOLOGY 27(2):58-63, March, 1977.

Contraception, abortion and veneral disease: teen-agers knowledge and the effect of education, by P. A. Reichelt, et al. FAMILY PLANNING PERSPECTIVE 7(2):83-88, 1975. (Socio. Abstrs. 1977, 7717089)

Contraceptive practice by women presenting to a free-standing abortion clinic, by S. Treloar, et al. MEDICAL JOURNAL OF AUSTRALIA 1(15):527-532, April 9, 1977.

Counselling for abortion, by M. Blair. MIDWIFE HEALTH
VISITOR AND COMMUNITY NURSE 11(11):355-356,
November, 1975.

Delivery or abortion in inner-city adolescents, by S. H. Fischman. AMERICAN JOURNAL OF ORTHOPSYCHIATRY
47:127-133, January, 1977.

The effect of attitude and statement favorability upon the
judgment of attitude statements. SOCIAL BEHAVIOR
AND PERSONALITY 4(2):249-255, 1976.

An empirical argument against abortion, by J. Newman.
NEW SCHOLASTICISM 60:384-395, Summer, 1977.

Facts about abortion for the teenager, by S. Greenhouse.
SCHOOL COUNSELOR 22(5):334-337, 1975. (Psycho.
Abstrs. 1977, 13407)

International trends. . .pregnancy and the unmarried girl, by
H. P. David. JOURNAL OF PSYCHIATRIC NURSING
AND MENTAL HEALTH SERVICES 15:40-42, Febru-
ary, 1977.

Just for the rich? ECONOMIST 263:44+, June 25, 1977.

Legal abortion among New York City residents: an analysis
according to socioeconomic and demographic characteristics, by M. J. Kramer. FAMILY PLANNING PERSPEC-
TIVES 7(3):128-137, 1975. (Socio. Abstrs. 1977,
7717343)

The logic of abortion, by B. Williams. LISTENER 98:258-
260, September 1, 1977.

Love, sex, permissiveness and abortion: a test of alternative
models, by A. M. Mirande, et al. ARCHIVES OF SEX-
UAL BEHAVIOR 5(6):553-566, 1976. (Bio. Abstrs.
May, 1977, 53780 and Soc. Abstrs. 1977, 7719674)

Men's reactions to their partners' elective abortions, by A. A. Rothstein. AMERICAN JOURNAL OF OBSTETRICS AND GYNECOLOGY 128(8):831-837, August 15, 1977.

More abortion patients are young, unmarried, nonwhite; procedures performed earlier, and by suction; 1/5 repeats. FAMILY PLANNING PERSPECTIVES 9(3):130-131, May-June, 1977.

National survey of doctors, nurses and social workers on liberalization of the Barbados abortion law, by M. D. Hoyos, et al. WEST INDIAN MEDICAL JOURNAL 26(4):2-11, March, 1977.

A new role for nurses: abortion counseling, by B. Easterbrook. CANADIAN NURSE 73(1):28-30, January, 1977.

On seeking abortion counseling [letter], by W. Cates, Jr., et al. AMERICAN JOURNAL OF PUBLIC HEALTH 67(8):780-781, August, 1977.

Outcome of pregnancy among women in anaesthetic practice, by P. O. D. Pharoah, et al. LANCET 1(8001):34-36, 1977. (Bio. Abstrs. June, 1977, 72223)

Personality characteristics associated with contraceptive behavior in women seeking abortion under liberalized California law, by L. D. Noble. DISSERTATION ABSTRACTS INTERNATIONAL 35(7-B):3589-3590, 1975. (Psycho. Abstrs. 1977, 3141)

Problem of family planning in women in the textile industry. An analysis of social indications for pregnancy interruption, by A. Zdziennicki. POLSKI TYGODNIK LEKARSKI 31(46):1993-1994, November 15, 1976.

Psychosocial characteristics of 13,365 women studied with regard to abortion, by A. G. de Wit Greene, et al. NEUROOGIA, NEUROCIRU, PSIQUIATRIA 16(2):109-

136, 1975. (Psycho. Abstrs. 1977, 3090)

Psychosocial correlates of delayed decisions to abort, by M. B. Bracken, et al. HEALTH EDUCATION MONO-GRAPHS 4(1):6-44, Spring, 1976.

The psychosocial factors of the abortion experience: a critical review. PSYCHOLOGY OF WOMEN QUARTERLY 1(1):79-103, February, 1976. (Soc. Abstrs. 1977, 7715928)

Reproductive counseling in patients who have had a spontaneous abortion, by B. J. Poland, et al. AMERICAN JOURNAL OF OBSTETRICS AND GYNECOLOGY 127(7):685-691, 1977. (Bio. Abstrs. August, 1977, 17466)

Request for abortion during the 2d pregnancy trimester, by P. E. Treffers, et al. NEDERLANDS TIJDSCHRIFT VOOR GENEESKUNDE 120(51):2255-2262, December 18, 1976.

Rural women resist old oppression, by S. Hassan. GUAR-DIAN p. 15, March 28, 1977.

Sexology and abortion with respect to their psychological and socioeconomic reprecussions, by A. De Leonardis. MINERVA GINECOLOGIA 28(9):737-739, September, 1976.

Smoking: a risk factor for spontaneous abortion, by J. Kline, et al. NEW ENGLAND JORNAL OF MEDICINE 297(15):793-796, October 13, 1977.

Social and demographic determinants of abortion in Poland, by D. P. Mazur. POPULATION STUDIES 29(1):21-35, 1975. (Socio. Abstrs. 1977, 7717345)

Social factors in the choice of contraceptive method: a comparison of first clinic attenders accepting oral contraceptives with those accepting intrauterine devices, by S. U. Kingsley, et al. JOURNAL OF BIOSOCIAL SCIENCE 9(2):153-162, 1977. (Bio. Abstrs. September, 1977, 29735)

Social policy and social psychology. "Social welfare inter-action" analysed from three theoritical perspectives, by A. Sellerberg. ACTA SOCIOLOGICA 19(3):263-272, 1976. (Socio. Abstrs. 1977, 7716255)

Sociologic, ethical and psychological aspects of abortion, by R. De Vicienti. MINERVA GINECOLOGIA 28(9): 739-741, September, 1976.

Submission to the Royal Commission on contraception, sterlization and abortion, by New Zeland Psychological Society. NEW ZEALAND PSYCHOLOGIST 5(1):48-56, 1976. (Psycho. Abstrs. 1977, 6215)

The Supreme court's abortion rulings and social change [im-pact on abortion policies of hospitals in Harris county (Houston), Tex.], by D. W. Brady, et al. SOCIAL SCI-ENCE QUARTERLY 57:535-546, December, 1976.

The Swedish "children born to women denied abortion" study: a radical criticism, by P. Cameron, et al. PSY-CHOLOGICAL REPORTS 39(2):391-394, October, 1976.

SODIUM CHLORIDE
see: Prostaglandins
Techniques of Abortion

SOMBREVIN
Sombrevin anesthesia in short-duration gynecological opera-tions, by A. R. Volchenkova, et al. AKUSHERSTVO I GINECOLOGIIA (Moscow) (2):56-57, 1977.

S.P.U.C.

SPONTANEOUS ABORTION
see also: Threatened Abortion

Aetiology of spontaneous abortion: a cytogenetic and epidemiological study of 288 abortuses and their parents, by J. G. Lauritsen. ACTA OBSTETRICIA ET GYNECOLOGICA SCANDINAVICA. SUPPLEMENT 52:1-29, 1976. (Bio. Abstrs. March, 1977, 26401)

The association of multiple induced abortions with subsequent prematurity and spontaneous abortion, by L. H. Roht, et al. ACTA OBSTETRICA ET GYNAECOLOGICA JAPONIA 23(2):140-145, April, 1976.

An attempt to evaluate the risk of death in utero, by C. Huraux-Rendu, et al. JOURNAL DE GYNECOLOGIE, OBSTETRIQUE ET BIOLOGIE DE REPRODUCTION 5(5):675-680, 1976. (Bio. Abstrs. April, 1977, 37255)

Basal body temperature recordings in spontaneous abortion, by J. Cohen. INTERNATIONAL JOURNAL OF GYNAECOLOGY AND OBSTETRICS 14(2):117-122, 1976. (Bio. Abstrs. June, 1977, 61966)

Causes of spontaneous abortions and their microscopic aspects, by Z. Szczurek, et al. GINEKOLOGIA POLASKA 48(5):451-458, May, 1977.

Cellular and humoral immune aspects in mixed wife-husband leukocyte cultures in spontaneous abortions, by I. Halbrecht, et al. ACTA EUROPAEA FERTILITATIS 7(3):249-255, September, 1976.

Chromosomal anomalies in early spontaneous abortion. (Their consequences on early embryogensis and in vitro growth of embryonic cells, by J. G. Boué, et al. CURRENT TOPICS IN PATHOLOGY 62:193-208, 1976.

Cytogenetic studies in spontaneous abortions, by S. Gilgenkrantz, et al. BULLETIN DE L'ASSOCIATION DES

ANATOMISTES (Nancy) 60(169):357-365, June, 1976. (Bio. Abstrs. September, 1977, 26622)

Developmental anomalies of the umbilical vessles (arteria umbilicalis singularis) and spontaneous abortion, by E. Horak, et al. ORVOSI HETILAP 118(29):1721-1726, July 17, 1977.

The effect of industrialization on spontaneous abortion in Iran, by N. Kavoussi. JOURNAL OF OCCUPATION-AL MEDICINE 19(6):419-423, 1977. (Bio. Abstrs. November, 1977, 59812)

Genetic counselling and prenatal diagnosis for chromosome anomalies. Use of study of spontaneous abortions, by J. Boué, et al. INTERNATIONAL JOURNAL OF GYNAECOLOGY AND OBSTETRICS 14(4):290-295, 1976. (Bio. Abstrs. September, 1977, 32528)

Genetically determined pathology of fertility in population of couples with spontaneous (habitual) abortions, by V. P. Kulazhenko, et al. GENETIKA 13(1):138-145, 1977. (Bio. Abstrs. October, 1977, 44940)

Identification by Q and G bands of chromosome anomalies in spontaneous abortion, by J. Boué, et al. ANNALES DE GENETIQUE 19(4):233-239, December, 1976.

Indications for amniocentesis for prenatal determination of fetal karyotype, by I. V. Lur'e. TSITOLOGIIA I GENE-TIKA 10(3):198-200, May-June, 1976. (Bio. Abstrs. January, 1977, 8195)

The intrauterine device and deaths from spontaneous abor-tion, by W. Cates, Jr., et al. NEW ENGLAND JOURNAL OF MEDICINE 295(21):1155-1159, 1976. (Bio. Abstrs. March, 1977, 35535)

Maternal serum alpha-fetoprotein and spontaneous abortion, by N. Wald, et al. BRITISH JOURNAL OF OBSTETRICS

AND GYNAECOLOGY 84(5):357-362, May, 1977.

Placental morphology in spontaneous human abortuses with normal and abnormal karyotypes, by L. H. Honoré, et al. TERATOLOGY 14(2):151-166, October, 1976.

Pregnancy during the hysterogram cycle, by R. L. Goldenberg, et al. FERTILITY AND STERILITY 27(11): 1274-1276, 1976. (Bio. Abstrs. March, 1977, 35650)

Prevention of spontaneous abortion by cervical suture of the malformed uterus, by M. Blum. INTERNATIONAL SURGERY 62(4):213-215, April, 1977.

Principles of medical genetic consultation in spontaneous abortions in women, by V. P. Kulazhenko, et al. AKUSHERSTVO I GINEKOLOGIIA (Moscow) (12):36-40, December, 1976.

Q and G banding techniques in the identification of chromosome anomalies in spontaneous abortions, by J. Bove, et al. ANNALES DE GENETIQUE 19(4):233-239, 1976. (Bio. Abstrs. July, 1977, 2248)

Reproductive counseling in patients who have had a spontaneous abortion, by B. J. Poland, et al. AMERICAN JOURNAL OF OBSTETRICS AND GYNECOLOGY 127(7):685-691, April 1, 1977.

Rh immunoglobulin utlization after spontaneous and induced abortion, by D. A. Grimes, et al. OBSTETRICS AND GYNECOLOGY 50(3):261-263, September, 1977.

Role of psychotherapy in complex treatment of spontaneous abortions, by A. Z. Khasin, et al. AKUSHERSTVO I GINECOLOGIIA (Moscow) (10):35-39, October, 1976.

Smoking: a risk factor for spontaneous abortion, by J. Kline, et al. NEW ENGLAND JOURNAL OF MEDICINE

297(15):793-796, October 13, 1977.

Subclinical spontaneous abortion, by G. D. Braunstein, et al. OBSTETRICS AND GYNECOLOGY 50 (1 Suppl):41S-44S, July, 1977.

Thymus-dependent lymphocyte activity during the normal course of pregnancy an in spontaneous premature interruption of pregnancy, by S. D. Bulienko, et al. AKU-SHERSTVO I GINEKOLOGIIA (Moscow) 5:50-53, May, 1976.

Tocolysis in prevention of spontaneous abortion, by V. Sulovic, et al. JUGOSLOVENSKA GINEKOLOGIJA I OPSTETRICIJA 16(5-6):411-419, 1976.

Vitamins C and E in spontaneous abortion, by J. S. Vobecky, et al. INTERNATIONAL JOURNAL FOR VITAMIN AND NUTRITION RESEARCH 46(3):291-296, 1976. (Bio. Abstrs. June, 1977, 61970)

STATISTICS

The abortion issue: past, present, and future, by K. W. Green, et al. CURRENT PROBLEMS IN PEDIATRICS 7:1-44, August, 1977.

Abortion statistics for the Federal Republic of Germany— notification requirements for the physician performing the abortion, by W. Christian. OEFFENTLICHE GE-SUNDHEITSWESEN 38(11):676-680, November, 1976.

Abortion study with names. THE NEW YORK TIMES (M) May 15, IV, 1:5, 1977.

Abortions in Singapore, by S. C. Chew. THE NURSING JOURNAL OF SINGAPORE 17:18-19, May, 1977.

Abortions on teenagers are estimated at 275,000. THE NEW YORK TIMES (S) March 9, 14:3, 1977.

Analysis of statistical data concerning artificial abortions in a number of foreign countries, by I. P. Katkova. SOVETSKAE ZDRAVOOKHRANENIE (7):30-34, 1976.

An attempt to evaluate the risk of death in utero, by C. Huraux-Rendu, et al. JOURNAL DE GYNECOLOGIE, OBSTETRIQUE ET BIOLOGIE DE REPRODUCTION 5(5):675-680, 1976. (Bio. Abstrs. April, 1977, 37255)

Attitudes related to the number of children wanted and expected by college students in three countries, by H. G. Gough, et al. JOURNAL OF CROSS-CULTURAL PSYCHOLOGY 7(4):413-424, 1976. (Psycho. Abstrs. 1977, 12581)

Attitudes toward abortion: a pilot crosscultural comparison, by V. L. Zammuner. GIORNALE ITALIANO DI PSICOLOGIA 3(1):75-116, 1976. (Psycho. Abstrs. 1977, 5750)

Children born to women denied abortion, by Z. Dytrych, et al. FAMILY PLANNING PESPECTIVES 7(4):165-171, 1975. (Socio. Abstrs. 1977, 7717333)

Contraceptive practice in the context of a non-restrictive abortion law: age-specific pregnancy rates in New York City, 1971-1973, by C. Tietze. FAMILY PLANNING PERSPECTIVES 7(5):192-202, 1975. (Socio. Abstrs. 1977, 7717046)

Effect of industrialization in spontaneous abortion in Iran, by N. Kavoussi. JOURNAL OF OCCUPATIONAL MEDICINE 19:419-423, June, 1977. (Bio. Abstrs. November, 1977, 59812)

The effect of legalization of abortion on population growth and public health, by C. Tietze. FAMILY PLANNING PERSPECTIVES 7(3):123-127, 1975. (Socio. Abstrs. 1977, 7717047)

Elective abortion. Complications seen in a free-standing clinic, by G. J. Wulff, Jr., et al. OBSTETRICS AND GYNECOLOGY 49(3):351-357, March, 1977. (Bio. Abstrs. July, 1977, 5451)

European experience with prenatal diagnosis of congenital disease: a survey of 6121 cases, by H. Galjaard. CYTO-GENETICS AND CELL GENETICS 16(6):453-467, 1976. (Bio. Abstrs. December, 1977, 65804)

Follow-up of 50 adolescent girls 2 years after abortion, by H. Cvejic, et al. CANADIAN MEDICAL ASSOCIA-TION JOURNAL 116(1):44-46, 1977. (Bio. Abstrs. November, 1977, 53455)

Induced abortion and sterilization among women who became mothers as adolescents, by J. F. Jekel, et al. AMERICAN JOURNAL OF PUBLIC HEALTH 67:621-625, July, 1977.

Legal abortion, by C. Tietze, et al. SCIENTIFIC AMERI-CAN 236:21-27, January, 1977.

Legal abortion mortality in the United States: epidemiologic surveillance 1972-1974, by W. Cates, Jr., et al. JAMA; JOURNAL OF THE AMERICAN MEDICAL ASSOCIA-TION 237(5):452-455, 1977. (Bio. Abstrs. May, 1977, 59845)

Legal abortions and trends in age-specific marriage rates, by K. E. Bauman, et al. AMERICAN JOURNAL OF PUB-LIC HEALTH 67:52-53, January, 1977.

Legal abortions in the United States: rates and ratios by race and age, 1972-1974, by C. Tietze. FAMILY PLANNING PERSPECTIVES 9:12-15, January-February, 1977.

Medical opinion on abortion in Jamaica: a national Delphi survey of physician, nurses, and midwives, by K. A. Smith, et al. STUDIES IN FAMILY PLANNING 7(12):

334-339, December, 1976.

Problems of abortion in Britain: Aberdeen, a case study [conference paper], by B. Thompson. POPULATION STUDIES 31:143-154, March, 1977. (Bio. Abstrs. October, 1977, 47974)

Psychosocial characteristics of 13,365 women studied with regard to abortion, by A. G. de Wit Greene, et al. NEUROOGIA, NEUROCIRU, PSIQUIATRIA 16(2):109-136, 1975. (Psycho. Abstrs. 1977, 3090)

Spring clip sterilization: one-year follow-up of 1079 cases, by J. F. Hulka, et al. AMERICAN JOURNAL OF OBSTETRICS AND GYNECOLOGY 125(8):1039-1043, 1976. (Bio. Abstrs. January, 1977, 5275)

Statistical analysis of first-trimester pregnancy terminations in an ambulatory surgical center, by N. Bozorgi. AMERICAN JOURNAL OF OBSTETRICS AND GYNECOLOGY 127(7):763-768, April 1, 1977.

Statistics on maternal and child health: induced abortion, by T. Nakahara. JAPANESE JOURNAL FOR MIDWIVES 30(11):691, November, 1976.

A study of the status of maternal health in Kwang-Ju area, by S. Park. KOREAN CENTRAL JOURNAL OF MEDICINE 31(3):297-302, 1976. (Bio. Abstrs. November, 1977, 52819)

A study on status of maternal and child health in urban and rural areas, by K. Cho. KOREAN CENTRAL JOURNAL OF MEDICINE 31(6):641-647, 1976. (Bio. Abstrs. November, 1977, 59835)

Suboptimal pregnancy outsome among women with prior abortions and premature births, by S. J. Funderburk, et al. AMERICAN JOURNAL OF OBSTETRICS AND GYNECOLOGY 126(1):55-60, 1976. (Bio. Abstrs.

January, 1977, 11577)

Very young adolescent women in Georgia: has abortion or contraception lowered their fertility? by J. D. Shelton. AMERICAN JOURNAL OF PUBLIC HEALTH 67:616-620, July, 1977.

STERILITY

Contraceptive use and subsequent fertility, by G. R. Huggins. FERTILITY AND STERILITY 28(6):603-612, 1977. (Bio. Abstrs. December, 1977, 71780)

Cytogenetic studies in sterility and miscarriage, by V. I. Kucharenko, et al. AKUSHERSTVO I GINEKOLOGIIA (Moscow) (5):1-4, May, 1977.

Fertility in women with gonadal dysgenesis, by F. I. Reyes, et al. AMERICAN JOURNAL OF OBSTETRICS AND GYNECOLOGY 126(6):668-670, 1976. (Bio. Abstrs. March, 1977, 32715)

Some laws relating to population growth: laws directly affecting fertility, by K. K. S. Wee. THE NURSING JOURNAL OF SINGAPORE 17:20-24, May, 1977.

Very young adolescent women in Georgia: has abortion or contraception lowered their fertility? by J. D. Shelton. AMERICAN JOURNAL OF PUBLIC HEALTH 67:616-620, July, 1977.

STERILIZATION

Birth control: contraception, abortion, sterilization, by Ferraris. MINERVA GINECOLOGIA 29(4):249-252, April, 1977.

Induced abortion and sterilization among women who became mothers as adolescents, by J. F. Jekel, et al. AMERICAN JOURNAL OF PUBLIC HEALTH 67:621-625, July, 1977.

Postpartum and postabortion sterilization, by B. N. Purandare. INTERNATIONAL JOURNAL OF GYNAECOLO-
GY 14(1):65-70, 1976. (Bio. Abstrs. February, 1977,
23556)

The report of the Royal Commission on Contraception,
Sterilisation and Abortion: a comparison with health
professional policies, by D. Wills. NURSING FORUM
(Auckland) 5(1-):4-6, April-May, 1977.

Spring clip sterilization: one-year follow-up of 1079 cases,
by J. F. Hulka, et al. AMERICAN JOURNAL OF OB-
STETRICS AND GYNECOLOGY 125(8):1039-1043,
1976. (Bio. Abstrs. January, 1977, 5275)

Submission to the Royal Commission on contraception,
sterilization and abortion, by New Zealand Psychological Society. NEW ZEALAND PSYCHOLOGIST 5(1):
48-56, 1976. (Psycho. Abstrs. 1977, 6215)

STILBESTROL

STUDENTS
see: Youth

SURGICAL TREATMENT AND MANAGEMENT
see also: Techniques of Abortion

Comparative evaluation of different methods of general
anesthesia during surgical termination of early pregnancy, by V. A. Glotova. VOPROSY OKHRANY
MATERINSTVA I DETSTVA 21(4):81-84, April,
1976.

Improvement of the surgical technic in induced abortions
using a supplementary instrument (special handgrip with
revolving support for interruption cannulas), by W.
Anton, et al. ZENTRALBLATT FUR GYNAEKOLO-
GIE 98(22):1401-1403, 1976.

Infant survival following uterine rupture and complete abruptio placentae, by S. Semchyshyn, et al. OBSTETRICS AND GYNECOLOGY 50(1 Suppl):74S-75S, July, 1977.

The management of septic abortion in an intensive care unit, by R. D. Cane, et al. EUROPEAN JOURNAL OF INTENSIVE CARE 2(3):135-138, November, 1976.

Policlinical abortions using the Karman-catheter without anesthesia or cervix dilatation. LAKARTIDNINGEN 74(23):2281-2283, June 8, 1977.

Prevention of spontaneous abortion by cervical suture of the malformed uterus, by M. Blum. INTERNATIONAL SURGERY 62(4):213-215, April, 1977.

The relationship of immediate post-abortal intrauterine device insertion to subsequent endometritis. A case-control study, by R. T. Burkman, et al. CONTRACEPTION 15(4):435-444, 1977. (Bio. Abstrs. August, 1977, 23522)

Statistical analysis of first-trimester pregnancy terminations in an ambulatory surgical center, by N. Bozorgi. AMERICAN JOURNAL OF OBSTETRICS AND GYNECOLOGY 127(7):763-768, April 1, 1977.

Surgical treatment of habitual abortion, by V. Krstajic, et al. SRPSKI ARCHIV ZA CELOKUPNO LEKARSTVO 104(7-8):527-529, July-August, 1976.

Tactics in the management of patients with septic abortion, by S. A. Omarov, et al. AKUSHERSTVO I GINEKOLOGIIA (Moscow) (4):46-48, April, 1976.

Treatment of cervix incompetence in pregnant women by means of Mayer's pessary. Discussion contribution on the paper of K. Jirátek, et al. "Directed therapy of threatened premature abortion—comparison of treatment results using cerclage and pessary," by E. Bechinie.

CESKOSLOVENSKA GYNEKOLOGIE 42(3):205-206, April, 1977.

SURVEYS
see: Sociology and Behavior

SYMPOSIA

SYNTOCINON

TECHNIQUES OF ABORTION
see also: Induced Abortion
Surgical Treatment and Management

The abortifacient and oxytocic effects of an intra-vaginal silicone rubber device containing a 0.5 per cent concentration of 15(S);15-methyl-prostaglandin F2alpha methyl ester, by N. W. Lauersen, et al. AMERICAN JOURNAL OF OBSTETRICS AND GYNECOLOGY 127(7):784-787, April 1, 1977.

The abortifacient effectiveness and plasma prostaglandin concentrations with 15(S)-15-methyl prostaglandin F2alpha methyl ester-containing vaginal silastic devices, by N. H. Lauersen, et al. FERTILITY AND STERILITY 27(12):1366-1373, December, 1976.

Abortion as a reality, by H. Schmidt-Matthiesen. THERAPEUTISCHE UMSCHAW 33(4):289-293, April, 1976.

Abortion induced through massage, by F. Havranek. CESKOSLOVENSKA GYNEKOLOGIE 42(7):532, August, 1977.

The abortion issue: past, present and future, by K. W. Green, et al. CURRENT PROBLEMS IN PEDIATRICS 7:1-44, August, 1977.

Another opinion on abortion. SYGEPLEJERSKEN 75(33): 13-14, August 20, 1975.

Avulsion of the ureter from both ends as a complication of interruption of pregnancy with vacuum aspirator, by C. Dimopoulos, et al. JOURNAL OF UROLOGY 118(1 Pt 1):108, July, 1977.

Case reports: unrecognized oviduct pregnancy and therapeutic abortion by uterine aspiration, by C. Villanueva. JOURNAL OF THE KANSAS MEDICAL SOCIETY 77(10):448-449, October, 1976.

Cervical dilatation with 16,16 dimethyl PGF2 p-benzaldehyde semicarbazone ester prior to vacuum aspiration in first trimester nulliparae, by S. M. Karim, et al. PROSTAGLANDINS 13(2):333-338, February, 1977.

Choice of analgesia or anesthesia for pain relief in suction curettage, by J. A. Rock, et al. OBSTETRICS AND GYNECOLOGY 49(6):721-723, June, 1977.

Clinical results of two-time abortion technics with special regard to ascending genital infections, by H. Kreibich, et al. ZENTRALBLATT FUR GYNAEKOLOGIE 99(12):755-762, 1977.

Combined outpatient laparoscopic sterilization with therapeutic abortion, by C. E. Powe, Jr., et al. AMERICAN JOURNAL OF OBSTETRICS AND GYNECOLOGY 126(5):565-567, November 1, 1976.

Comparison between intra-amniotic administration of prostaglandin F2a and its 15-methyl derivative for induction of second trimester abortion, by O. Ylikorkala. ANNALS OF CLINICAL RESEARCH 9(2):58-61, 1977. (Bio. Abstrs. November, 1977, 52789)

A comparison of flexible and nonflexible plastic cannulae for performing first trimester abortion, by L. Andolsek, et al. INTERNATIONAL JOURNAL OF GYNAECOLOGY AND OBSTETRICS 14(3):199-204, 1976.

Complications following induced abortion by vacuum aspiration: patient characteristics and procedures, by M. Cheng, et al. STUDIES IN FAMILY PLANNING 8(5):125-129, May, 1977.

Conservative treatment of women in perforations of the uterus in legal abortions, by D. Mladenovic, et al. SRPSKI ARHIV ZA CELOJUPNO LEKARSTVO 104(2):119-127, February, 1976.

Death after paracervical block [letter], by J. Slome. LANCET 1(8005):260, January 29, 1977.

Determination of Rh blood group of fetuses in abortions by suction curettage, by R. M. Greendyke, et al. TRANSFUSION (Phil) 16(3):267-269, 1976. (Bio. Abstrs. January, 1977, 1108)

Dilatation and curettage for second-trimester abortions, by A. A. Hodari, et al. AMERICAN JOURNAL OF OBSTETRICS AND GYNECOLOGY 127(8):850-854, 1977. (Bio. Abstrs. September, 1977, 29734)

Early termination of pregnancy by H. Karman's method, by D. Vasileva. AKUSHERSTVO I GINEKOLOGIIA (Sofia) 16(1):74-81, 1977.

Epidural analgesia in midtrimester abortion, by S. Grunstein, et al. INTERNATIONAL JOURNAL OF GYNAECOLOGY AND OBSTETRICS 14(3):257-260, 1976. (Bio. Abstrs. August, 1977, 16420)

Evaluation of intramuscular 15(S)-15-methyl prostaglandin F2a tromethamine salt for induction of abortion, medications to attenuate side effects, and intracervical laminaria tents, by W. Gruber, et al. FERTILITY AND STERILITY 27(9):1009-1023, 1976. (Bio. Abstrs. March, 1977, 28807)

Evaluation of two dose schedules of 15(S)15 methyl PGF2a

methyl ester vaginal suppositories for dilatation of cervix prior to vacuum aspiration for late first trimester abortions, by B. Zoremthangi, et al. CONTRACEPTION 15(3):285-294, 1977. (Bio. Abstrs. August, 1977, 16522)

Extrauterine contraceptive device and pregnancy. Spontaneous labor. Extraction of IUD by laparoscopy, by G. Galan, et al. REVISTA CHILENA DE OBSTETRICIA Y GINECOLOGIA 41(7):237-241, 1976.

Fertility control—symposium on prostaglandins: comment, by W. E. Brenner. FERTILITY AND STERILITY 27(12):1380-1386, December, 1976.

Find D&E is safest method of midtrimester abortion, but saline is less risky than prostaglandins: JPSA. FAMILY PLANNING PERSPECTIVES 8:275, November-December, 1976.

Induction of abortion and labor by extraamniotic isotonic saline, with or without addition of oxytocin, in cases of missed abortion, missed labor and antepartum fetal death, by M. Blum, et al. INTERNATIONAL SURGERY 62(2):95-96, February, 1977.

Induction of midtrimester abortion by the combined method of continuous extravovular infusion of prostaglandin F2alpha and intracervical laminaria tents, by J. E. Hodgson, et al. FERTILITY AND STERILITY 27(12):1359-1365, December, 1976.

Induction of mid-trimester aborton with intra-amniotic injection of prostaglandin F-2alpha, by A. J. Horowitz. MINNESOTA MEDICINE 60(7 Pt 1):509-512, July, 1977.

Influence of enflurance on blood loss from the pregnant uterus, by C. Van Damme, et al. ACTA ANESTHESIO-LOGICA BELIGCA 27(Suppl):259-261, 1976.

Interruption of early pregnancy by a new vacuum aspiration method, by S. Mihaly, et al. ORVOSI HETILAP 117(45):2731-2734, November 7, 1976.

Intrauterine extra-amnial administration of prostaglandin F2alpha for the induction of abortion in primigravidae and problem cases, by G. Göretzlehner, et al. ZENTRABLATT FUR GYNAEKOLOGIE 98(20):1252-1257, 1976.

Laparoscopic observation of the female pelvis following abortions by suction curettage, by P. K. Khan. INTERNATIONAL SURGERY 62(2):77-78, February, 1977.

The management of midtrimester abortion failures by vaginal evacuation, by R. T. Burkman, et al. OBSTETRICS AND GYNECOLOGY 49(2):233-236, February, 1977.

Medical and surgical methods of early termination of pregnancy, by G. M. Filshie. PROCEEDINGS OF THE ROYAL SOCIETY OF LONDON; B: BIOLOGICAL SCIENCES 195(1118):115-127, December 10, 1976.

Methods of artificial termination of pregnancy with special consideration of the use of prostaglandin, by R. Kepp. GEBURTSHILFE UND FRAUENHEILKUNDE 36(9): 700-705, September, 1976.

Mid-trimester abortion by dilatation and evacuation: a safe and practical alternative, by D. A. Grimes, et al. NEW ENGLAND JOURNAL OF MEDICINE 296(20):1141-1145, 1977. (Bio. Abstrs. September, 1977, 35546)

Midtrimester abortion: a comparison of intra-amniotic prostaglandin F2a and hypertonic saline, by M. I. Ragab, et al. INTERNATIONAL JOURNAL OF GYNAECOLOGY AND OBSTETRICS 14(5):393-396, 1976. (Bio. Abstrs. October, 1977, 40668)

Opinions to the vibrodilatation of the cervix in induced

abortions—report of 2 years of experiences with the
Soviet vibrodilatator WG-I, by P. Landschek, et al.
ZENTRALBLATT FUR GYNAEKOLOGIE 98(17):
1049-1053, 1976.

The relationship of immediate post-abortal intrauterine device insertion to subsequent endometritis. A case-control
study, by R. T. Burkman, et al. CONTRACEPTION
15(4):435-444, 1977. (Bio. Abstrs. August, 1977, 23522)

Relative safety of midtrimester abortion methods. MEDI-
CAL LETTER ON DRUGS AND THERAPEUTICS
19(6):25-26, March 25, 1977.

Repeated extra-amniotic administration of prostaglandin F2a
for midtrimester abortion, by M. Ragab, et al. INTER-
NATIONAL JOURNAL OF GYNAECOLOGY AND OB-
STETRICS 14(4):337-340, 1976. (Bio. Abstrs. September, 1977, 34567)

Review of induced-abortion technics in Czechoslovakia, by
F. Havranek. CESKOSLOVENSKA GYNEKOLOGIE
41(8):616-620, October, 1976.

The safety of local anesthesia and outpatient treatment: a
controlled study of induced abortion by vacuum aspiration, by L. Andolsek, et al. STUDIES IN FAMILY
PLANNING 8(5):118-124, May, 1977.

Saline abortion: a retrospective study, by R. A. Kronstadt.
JOURNAL OF THE AMERICAN OSTEOPATHIC
ASSOCIATION 76(4):276-281, December, 1976.

Ten-minute abortions, by W. O. Goldthorp. BRITISH
MEDICAL JOURNAL 2(6086):562-564, August 27,
1977.

Termination of pregnancy in the midtrimester using a new
technic. Preliminary report, by S. T. DeLee. INTER-
NATIONAL SURGERY 61(20):545-546, October, 1976.

Therapeutic abortion and its aftermath, by M. Stone. MID-WIFE, HEALTH VISITOR AND COMMUNITY NURSE 11(10):335-338, October, 1975.

Uterine perforation in connection with vacuum aspiration for legal abortion, by P. J. Moberg. INTERNATIONAL JOURNAL OF GYNAECOLOGY AND OBSTETRICS 14(1):77-80, 1976. (Bio. Abstrs. February, 1977, 53573)

Uterine rupture following midtrimester abortion by laminaria, prostaglandin F2alpha, and oxytocin: report of two cases, by D. Propping, et al. AMERICAN JOURNAL OF OB-STETRICS AND GYNECOLOGY 128(6):689-690, July 15, 1977.

Vacuum extraction in interruption of pregnancy using a jagged cannula, by N. Gudac. JUGOSLOVENSKA GINEKOLOGIJA I OPSTETRICIJA 16(5-6):407-410, 1976.

Vaginal administration of a single dose of 16, 16 dimethyl prostaglandin E2 p-benzaldehyde semicarbazone ester for pre-operative cervical dilatation in first trimester nulliparae, by S. M. Karim, et al. BRITISH JOURNAL OF OBSTETRICS AND GYNAECOLOGY 84(4):269-271, April, 1977.

The vaginal transverse low segment hysterotomy for second trimester therapeutic abortion, by G. Schariot, et al. GEBURSTSHILFE UND FRAUENHEILKUNDE 36(8): 687-690, August, 1976.

Whose interests? by J. Turner. NURSING TIMES 71(45): 1763, November 6, 1975.

TETRACYCLINE

TH 1165a

THERAPEUTIC ABORTION
Abortion—a positive experience [letter] ? by R. L. Matthews.
CANADIAN MEDICAL ASSOCIATION JOURNAL
116(8):836-837, April 23, 1977.

Abortion practice in NZ public hospitals. NURSING FORUM
(Auckland) 3(4):5-7, November-December, 1975.

Assessment of the structure and function of the therapeutic
abortion committee, by M. E. Krass. CANADIAN
MEDICAL ASSOCIATION JOURNAL 116:786+,
April 9, 1977.

Case reports: unrecognized oviduct pregnancy and therapeutic abortion by uterine aspiration, by C. Villanueva.
JOURNAL OF THE KANSAS MEDICAL SOCIETY
77(10):448-449, October, 1976.

Clinical experiences with prostaglandin E2 and F2 alpha
in the termination of pregnancy and labor induction in
intrauterine fetal death, by J. Kunz, et al. SCHWEI-
ZERISCHE MEDIZINISCHE WOCHENSCHRIFT
107(22):757-763, June 4, 1977.

Combined outpatient laparoscopic sterilization with therapeutic abortion, by C. E. Powe, Jr., et al. AMERICAN
JOURNAL OF OBSTETRICS AND GYNECOLOGY
126(5):565-567, November 1, 1976.

Comparative evaluation of different methods of general
anesthesia during surgical termination of early pregnancy, by V. A. Glotova. VOPROSY OKHRANY
MATERINSTVA I DETSTVA 21(4):81-84, April, 1976.

Concepts and limits of therapeutic abortion, by N. Ragucci.
MINERVA GINECOLOGIA 28(9):697-699, September,
1976.

Early termination of pregnancy by H. Karman's method, by
D. Vasileva. AKUSHERSTVO I GINEKOLOGIIA

(Sofia) 16(1):74-81, 1977.

Ethical considerations of prenatal genetic diagnosis, by J. F. Tormey. CLINICAL OBSTETRICS AND GYNECOLOGY 19(4):957-963, December, 1976.

Factors influencing the state of the fetus and the course of abortion after the intra-amniotic instillation of a saline solution, by A. Atanasov, et al. AKUSHERSTVO I GINEKOLOGIIA (Sofia) 16(1):62-66, 1977.

Follow-up of 50 adolescent girls 2 years after abortion, by H. Cvejic, et al. CANADIAN MEDICAL ASSOCIATION JOURNAL 116(1):44-46, 1977. (Bio. Abstrs. November, 1977, 53455)

Inconsistencies in therapeutic abortion report [letter], by T. B. MacLachian. CANADIAN MEDICAL ASSOCIATION JOURNAL 117(3):220-222, August 6, 1977.

Indication for pregnancy interruption in patients with heart diseases, by Y. Hatano. FORTSCHRITTE DU MEDIZIN 95(11):685-689, March 17, 1977.

Influence of enflurane on blood loss from the pregnant uterus, by C. Van Damme, et al. ACTA ANAESTHESIOLOGICA BELIGCA 27(Suppl):259-261, 1976.

Legal abortion during the first trimester of pregnancy at the University Hospital for Women in Novi Sad (1960-1975), by B. M. Beric, et al. ZENTRALBLATT FUR GYNAEKOLOGIE 99(6):371-376, 1977.

A life threatening pregnancy, by E. Moult. MATERNAL-CHILD NURSING JOURNAL 4(3):207-211, Fall, 1975.

Medico-legal aspects of therapeutic abortion, by P. Zangani. MINERVA GINECOLOGICA 28(9):703-705, September, 1976.

A new role for nurses: abortion counseling, by B. Easter-brook. CANADIAN NURSE 73(1):28-30, January, 1977.

Obsessive-compulsive neurosis after viewing the fetus during therapeutic abortion, by S. Lipper, et al. AMERICAN JOURNAL OF PSYCHOTHERAPY 30(4):666-674, October, 1976.

Pelvic abcess: a sequela of first trimester abortion, by C. B. Gassner, et al. OBSTETRICS AND GYNECOLOGY 48(6):716-717, 1976. (Bio. Abstrs. April, 1977, 39387)

Pregnancy in patients with heart diseases. Indications for interruption, control of pregnancy and condition of labor in the German Federal Republic, by P. Stoll. FORTSCHRITTE DU MEDIZIN 95(11):690, March 17, 1977.

Prenatal diagnosis and selective abortion, by T. Jenkins, et al. SOUTH AFRICAN MEDICAL JOURNAL 50(53):2091-2095, December 11, 1976.

Preoperative cervical dilatation by oral PGE2, by A. S. Van Den Bergh. CONTRACEPTION 14(6):631-638, 1976. (Bio. Abstrs. April, 1977, 41035)

The profilactic and therapeutic attitude in abortion, by C. Tatic, et al. VIATA MEDICALA; REVISTA DE IN-FORMORE PROFESIONALA SI STUNTIFICA A CODRELAR MEDII SANITARE 23(9):57-60, September, 1975.

Radiation-induced teratogen effects and therapeutic abortion, by F. E. Stieve. ROENTGENBLAETTER 29(10):465-482, October, 1976.

Recent changes in the emotional reactions of therapeutic abortion applicants, by S. Meikle, et al. CANADIAN PSYCHIATRIC ASSOCIATION JOURNAL 22(2):67-

70, March, 1977.

Requests for abortion: a psychiatrist's view, by R. Mester. ISRAEL ANNALS OF PSYCHIATRY AND RELATED DISCIPLINES 14(3):294-299, 1976. (Psycho. Abstrs. 1977, 13126)

A review of the progress of psychiatric opinion regarding emotional complications of therapeutic abortion, by G. W. Hubbard. SOUTHERN MEDICAL JOURNAL 70(5): 588-560, May, 1977.

Role and responsibility of the obstetrician in performing an abortion, by A. Coletta. MINERVA GINECOLOGICA 28(9):706-712, September, 1976.

Sombrevin anesthesia in short-duration gynecological operations, by A. R. Volchenkova, et al. AKUSHERSTVO I GINEKOLOGIIA (Moscow) (2):56-57, 1977.

Studies on the gonadotropin response after administration of LH/FSH-releasing hormone (LRH) during pregnancy and after therapeutic abortion in the second trimester, by S. Jeppsson, et al. AMERICAN JOURNAL OF OBSTE-TRICS AND GYNECOLOGY 125(4):484-490, June 15, 1976.

Study of therapeutic abortion committees in British Columbia, by W. J. Harris, et al. UNIVERSITY OF BRITISH COLUMBIA LAW REVIEW 11:81-118, 1977.

Termination of abnormal intrauterine pregnancies with intramuscular administration of dihomo 15 methyl prostaglandin F 2alpha, by S. M. Karim, et al. BRITISH JOURNAL OF OBSTETRICS AND GYNAECOLOGY 83(11): 885-889, November, 1976.

Therapeutic abortion and its aftermath, by M. Stone. MID-WIFE, HEALTH VISITOR AND COMMUNITY NURSE 11(10):335-338, October, 1975.

Therapeutic abortion and psychiatric disturbance in Canadian women, by E. R. Greenglass. CANADIAN PSYCHIA-TRIC ASSOCIATION JOURNAL 21(7):453-460, November, 1976.

Therapeutic abortion: extensions of restrictions of current indications, by T. Wierdis. MINERVA GINECOLOGIA 28(9):716-719, September, 1976.

Therapeutic abortion, fertility plans, and psychological sequelae, by E. R. Greenglass. AMERICAN JOURNAL OF ORTHOPSYCHIATRY 47(1):119-126, January, 1977.

Therapeutic intra-amniotic, transabdominal induction of abortion in the 2nd trimenon using prostaglandin F 2alpha, by E. Sacha, et al. GYNAEKOLOGISCHE RUNDSCHAU 16(4):261-263, 1976.

Treatment of endometritis after artificial abortion, by A. A. Vorontsov, et al. PEDIATRIIA AKUSHERSTVO I GINEKOLOGIIA (1):53-56, January-February, 1977.

Vaginal hysterectomy for therapeutic abortion and simultaneous sterilization, by K. A. Walz, et al. GEBURT-SHILFE UND FRAUENHEILKUNDE 36(10):868-871, October, 1976.

The vaginal transverse low segment hysterotomy for second trimester therapeutic abortion, by G. Schariot, et al. GEBURTSHILFE UND FRAUENHEILKUNDE 36(8): 687-690, August, 1976.

THREATENED ABORTION
Application of physiotherapy in threatened spontaneous abortion, by V. M. Strugatskif, et al. MEDITSINSKAIA SESTRA 35(11):27-32, November, 1976.

The characteristics of uterine contractile function in pregnant women in threatened abortion, by G. P. Kravets.

PEDIATRIIA AKUSHERSTVO I GINEKOLOGIIA (4): 39-41, July-August, 1976.

Clinical experiences with the gestagen turnial in treating threatened and habitual abortions, by A. Pociatek, et al. BRATISLAUSKE LEKARSKE LISTY 67(1):87-91, January, 1977.

Contribution to the treatment of threatened abortion, by J. Kunz, et al. SCHWEIZERISCHE MEDIZINISCHE WOCHENSCHRIFT 106(42):1429-1435, October 16, 1976.

The diagnosis and treatment of threatened miscarriage, by B. Faris. AUSTRALASIAN NURSES JOURNAL 4(4):7, October, 1975.

Diagnostic and prognostic importance of the chorionic gonadotropin test in threatened abortions, by D. Ia. Dimitrov. AKUSHERSTVO I GINEKOLOGIIA (Sofia) 16(3):220-221, 1977.

Glycosaminoglycans in the amniotic fluid in normal pregnancy and in cases of clinical signs of threatened fetus, by A. Bromboszcz, et al. GINEKOLOGIA POLASKA 47(11):1261-1267, November, 1976.

Hormone therapy in threatened abortion and premature labor, by G. Kikawa. JAPANESE JOURNAL FOR MIDWIVES 30(12):750-752, December, 1976.

Inflammation of the placenta in threatened abortion, by M. Iu. Makkaveeva, et al. AKUSHERSTVO I GINEKOLOGIIA (Moscow) (4):51-54, April, 1977.

Is there any evidence that the maternal HPL serum-concentration is of prognostic value in cases of threatened abortion? by P. Berle, et al. ZEITSCHRIFT FUR GEBURT-SCHILFE UND PERINATOLOGIE 181(3):211-217, June, 1977.

A new immunochemical tube test for pregnancy using the latex-agglutination inhibition reaction. II. Clinical results, by H. Hepp, et al. DEUTSCHE MEDIZINSCHE WO-CHENSCHRIFT 101(45):1639-1643, November 5, 1976.

Pattern of chorionic gonadotropins and placental lactogens during treatment of threatened and habitual abortion, by E. Samochowiec, et al. GINEKOLOGIA POLASKA 47(12):1363-1370, December, 1976.

Possibilities and limits of tocolytic treatment, by R. Brütigam, et al. WIENER MEDIZINISCHE WOCHENSCHRIFT 127(10):320-326, May 30, 1977.

The prognostic value of human placental lactogen levels in threatened abortion in general practice, by D. W. Gau, et al. JOURNAL OF THE ROYAL COLLEGE OF GENERAL PRACTITIONERS 27(175):91-92, February, 1977.

Rheography and rheometry of the internal genital organs in early normal pregnancy and in threatened abortion, by F. A. Syrovatko, et al. VOPROSY OKHRANY MA-TERINSTVA I DETSTVA 21(4):74-75, April, 1976.

Role of cerclage in the prevention of abortion and premature labor, by J. Kubinyi, et al. ZENTRALBLATT FUR GYNAEKOLOGIE 98(17):1043-1048, 1976.

Special aspects of blood circulation in the organs of the pelvis minor in threatening uterine abortion and disturbed tubal preganancy, by V. M. Zdanovskii, et al. VOPROSY OKHRANY MATERINSTVA I DETSTVA 22(5):59-62, May, 1977.

Tocolysis in obstetrics, by W. Grabensberger. OSTER-REICHISCHE KNANKENPFLEGE-ZEITSCHRIFT 26(11):358-364, 1976.

Treatment of cervix incompetence in pregnant women by

means of Mayer's pessary. Discussion contribution on the paper of K. Jiratek et al. "Directed thearapy of threatened premature abortion—comparison of treatment results using cerclage and pessary," by E. Bechinie. CESKOSLOVENSKA GYNEKOLOGIE 42(3):205-206, April, 1977.

Treatment of preclinical forms of threatened abortion in women with genital infantilism, by N. K. Moskvitina. AKUSHERSTVO I GINEKOLOGIIA (Moscow) 5:53-56, May, 1976.

The treatment of threatened abortion, by P. Berle, et al. GEBURTSHILFE UND FRAUENHEILKUNDE 37(2): 139-142, February, 1977.

Treatment of threatened abortion with gravibinan, by Z. Sternadel, et al. GINEKOLOGIA POLASKA 48(5): 509-512, May, 1977.

Treatment of threatened and habitual abortion with human chorionic gonadotrophin. The role of serum human placental lactogen determination, by C. Z. Vorster, et al. SOUTH AFRICAN MEDICAL JOURNAL 51(6):165-166, February 5, 1977.

Treatment of threatening abortion with diaphylline, by G. Illei, et al. ORVOSI HETILAP 118(21):1239-1240, May 22, 1977.

Urinary excretion of chorionic gonadotropin, estrogens and pregnanediol in threatened abortion, by O. N. Savchenko, et al. AKUSHERSTVO I GINEKOLOGIIA (Moscow) (8):52-56, August, 1976.

TOXOPLASMAS

A case of toxoplasmosis detected by the Sabin-Feldman test, by K. Altintas. MIKROBIYOLOJI BULTENI 11(1):113-115, January, 1977.

TOXOPLASMAS

Research of antibodies against toxoplasma gondii in subjects
with repeated abortions, perinatal mortality and malformed
newborns, by A. S. Castro, et al. ANNALI SCLAVO 18(1):
75-81, 1976. (Bio. Abstrs. March, 1977, 29539)

Toxoplasmosic endometritis, by A. Viglione, et al. MINERVA
GINECOLOGIA 29(4):253-260, April, 1977.

Toxoplasmosis: its role in abortion, by C. R. Mahajan, et al.
INDIAN JOURNAL OF MEDICAL RESEARCH 64(6):
797-800, 1976. (Bio. Abstrs. February, 1977, 22293)

Uterine toxoplasma infections and repeated abortions, by B.
Stray-Pedersen, et al. AMERICAN JOURNAL OF OB-
STETRICS AND GYNECOLOGY 128(7):716-721,
August, 1977.

TRANSPLACENTAL HEMORRHAGE
see: Complications

TRIPLOIDY
Clinical details, cytogenic studies, and cellular physiology of
a 69, XXX fetus, with comments on the biological effect
of triploidy in man, by C. M. Gosden, et al. JOURNAL
OF MEDICAL GENETICS 13(5):371-380, October, 1976.

Origin of triploidy and tetraploidy in man: 11 cases with
chromosomes markers, by T. Kajii, et al. CYTOGENE-
TICS AND CELL GENETICS 18(3):109-125, 1977.

TURINAL
Clinical experiences with the gestagen Turnial in treating
threatened and habitual abortions, by A. Pociatek, et al.
BRATISLAUSKE LEKARSKE LISTY 67(1):87-91,
January, 1977.

VETERINARY ABORTIONS
see: Research

YOUTH
see also: Laws and Legislation

Abortion—action by nineteen year-old unmarried female against the Arizona board of regents to determine the constitutionality of a state statute prohibiting nontherapeutic abortions at the university hospital. JOURNAL OF FAMILY LAW 15:113-118, 1976-1977.

Abortion rate is rising for girls aged 14 and under, 1975 data show. THE NEW YORK TIMES (M) October 26, 22:1, 1977.

Abortion on teenagers are estimated at 275,000. THE NEW YORK TIMES (S) March 9, 14:3, 1977.

Attitudes of American teenagers toward abortion, by M. Zelnik, et al. FAMILY PLANNING PERSPECTIVES 7(2): 89-91, 1975. (Socio. Abstrs. 1977, 7717096)

Contraception, abortion and veneral disease: teenagers knowledge and the effect of education, by P. A. Reichelt, et al. FAMILY PLANNING PERSPECTIVES 7(2):83-88, 1975. (Socio. Abstrs. 1977, 7717089)

Delivery or abortion in inner-city adolescents, by S. H. Fischman. AMERICAN JOURNAL OF ORTHOPSY-CHIATRY 47(1):127-133, January, 1977.

Facts about abortion for the teenagers, by S. Greenhouse. SCHOOL COUNSELOR 22(5):334-337, 1975. (Psycho. Abstrs. 1977, 13407)

Induced abortion and sterilization among women who became mothers as adolescents, by J. F. Jekel, et al. AMERICAN JOURNAL OF PUBLIC HEALTH 67(7): 621-625, July, 1977.

Medical and social aspects of pregnancy among adolescents. Part II. Comparative study of abortions and deliveries,

by E. Rautanen, et al. ANNALES CHIRURGIAE ET
GYNAECOLOGIAE FENNIAE 66(3):122-130, 1977.

Sexual experimentation and pregnancy in young black adolescents, by M. Gispert, et al. AMERICAN JOURNAL
OF OBSTETRICS AND GYNECOLOGY 126(4):459-
466, 1976. (Bio. Abstrs. February, 1977, 23255)

Very young adolescent women in Georgia: has abortion or
contraception lowered their fertility? by J. D. Shelton.
AMERICAN JOURNAL OF PUBLIC HEALTH 67:616-
620, July, 1977.

AUTHOR INDEX

Acland, G. M., 45
Adachi, A., 73
Adams, R., 36
Affleck, G., 36
Ait-Ouyahia, B., 56
Alexandre, C., 79
Allen, D. V., 92
Altintas, K., 23
Altman, L. K., 42
Andersen, P. E., Jr., 93
Anderson, C., 74
Anderson, D., 12
Andolsek, L., 27, 50, 79-80
Andriani, A., 72
Annas, G. J., 56
Annis, J. P., 17-18
Anton, W., 47
Archiprete, K., 1
Armstrong, J., 67
Ashford, T., 31
Atanasov, A., 41
Atkinson, 1
Azimi, P. H., 50

Ball, A. P., 81
Ballard, C. A., 80
Barbarie, T., 24
Bartsch-Sandhoff, M., 43
Basile, J., 79
Bauman, K. E., 55

Beazley, J. M., 73
Bebjakova, V., 62
Bechinie, E., 91
Belsey, F. M., 69
Bennett, J. S., 50
Benshoof, J., 61
Bercovici, B., 94
Berger, G. S., 26
Beric, B. M., 55
Berle, P., 52, 92
Bernard, A., 21
Bernardin, J. L., 30, 46
Bicknell, S. R., 22
Bishop, D. N., 10-11
Blair, M., 31
Blake, J., 87
Blandau, R. J., 1
Bloxham, P. A., 65
Blum, M., 49, 71
Bodiazhina, V. I., 79
Boerrigter, P. J., 67
Bogen, I., 19
Bok, 23
Bolognese, R. J., 88
Bonnar, J., 39
Borten, M., 93
Boué, J. G., 25, 43, 47, 74
Bove, A., 79
Bozorgi, N., 84
Bracken, M. B., 38, 74
Brady, D. W., 87

277

Gammeltoft, M., 14
Gandhi, G. M., 13
Garcia de Alba, J. E., 21
Gardner, E. C., 9-10
Gardner, R. F. R., 63
Garn, J., 34
Gassner, C. B., 66
Gau, D. W., 72
Geary, P. L., 32
Gelev, I., 20
Genbacev, O., 38
Gerrard, M., 81
Gerstein, H., 5
Ghosh, R. N., 41
Giannice, C., 12
Gilgenkrantz, S., 33
Gillespie, N. C., 6
Giocoli, G., 39, 78
Gispert, M., 81-82
Glantz, L. H., 57
Gleeson, L. J., 39
Glotova, V. A., 28
Godeau, P., 45
Gokal, R., 86
Goldenberg, R. L., 69-70
Goldstein, A. I., 61
Goldthrop, W. O., 88
Golovachev, G. D., 37
Gordon, A. V., 74
Gordon, S., 1
Göretzlehner, G., 52
Gosden, C. M., 26
Gough, H. G., 19
Gould, D., 62
Grabensberger, W., 90
Graeff, H., 40
Grant, A., 26
Gratz, R. B., 62
Gray, M. J., 40
Green, K. W., 11, 67
Greenberg, B., 9
Greendyke, R. M., 34

Greenglass, E. R., 89
Greenhouse, L., 21
Greenhouse, S., 41
Greenwell, J. R., 71
Greenwood, 2
Greve, W., 29
Grewal, S., 59-60
Grimes, D. A., 33, 34, 60, 78
Gruber, W., 40
Grunstein, S., 39
Gudac, N., 94
Gudakova, N. T., 65
Gursky, S., 21

Habib, Z. A., 58
Hager, B. M., 72
Haingorani, V., 52
Hakim-Elahi, E., 68-69
Halbrecht, I., 23
Hall, G. A., 85
Halle, H., 49
Hamer, J., 34
Hamilton, M., 64
Hare, R. M., 6
Harlay, A., 95
Harris, R. E., 19
Harris, W. J., 85
Harry, M., 32
Hassan, S., 79
Hatano, Y., 48
Havranek, F., 11, 77
Hawkes, C., 19
Hay, D. M., 58
Healy, P., 14
Henle, R. J., 34
Henriques, E. S., 51
Henry, D., 9
Hepp, H., 63
Hernandez, I. M., 69
Hess, H. J., 90
Heyer, E., 51
Heyes, H., 34

Hicks, N., 22
Hifman, L. F., III, 56
Hill, G., 18
Hinman, A. R., 15
Hinton, M., 35
Hitchcock, J., 72
Hobson, D., 44
Hodari, A. A., 35
Hodgson, J. E., 49
Hoglend, P., 55, 83
Hollmann, A., 63
Hong, S., 70
Honoré, L. H., 58-59, 67
Hook, E. G., 2
Horak, E., 34
Horan, D. J., 6, 95
Horn, J., 92
Horowitz, A. J., 49
Horta, J. L., 35
Hösli, J., 66
Hoyos, M. D., 62
Hubbard, G. W., 77-78
Hubbert, W. T., 86
Huggins, G. R., 31
Hulka, J. F., 83
Humber, J. M., 9
Hunter, V., 76
Huraux-Rendu, C., 19
Hurst, P. R., 75
Hurwitz, A., 73
Hyde, H., 46-47

Illei, G., 92

Jackson, P. S., 93
Jacobs, S., 13
Jaffe, F. S., 64
James, L. F., 40
Jekel, J. F., 48
Jenkins, T., 70

Jensson, O., 84
Jeppsson, S., 84
Jöchle, W., 63
Johnstoix, L., 9
Joseph, J., 73

Kabusa, U., 75
Kaedsawang, S., 10
Kajii, T., 65
Kalmar, R., 2
Karim, S. M., 2, 24, 88, 89, 94
Katkova, I. P., 17
Kavoussi, N., 37
Kemp, K. A., 7
Kennedy, J., 6, 54
Kenney, A. M., 69
Kent, D. R., 73
Kepp, R., 60
Keron, K., 77
Khan, A. R., 60
Khan, P. K., 54
Khanna, I., 27
Khasin, A. Z., 79
Khosravi, H., 24
Kikawa, G., 45
Kim, Y. J., 87
Kingsley, S. U., 82
Kirchhoff, H., 28
Kiriushchenkov, A. P., 53
Kivalo, I., 18
Klemesrud, J., 39
Kligerman, M. M., 43
Kline, J., 82
Kluge, E.-H. W., 78
Kniga, G. E., 39
Komlos, L., 27
Kommers, D. P., 6
Koop, C., 8
Koren, Z., 31, 72
Koval'chuk, L. S., 31